VICTORIA PENDLETON

WITH OSCAR MILLAR

The Fear Opportunity

How Feeling Your Fear Builds Strength and Confidence

BLUEBIRD

First published 2026 by Bluebird
an imprint of Pan Macmillan
The Smithson, 6 Briset Street, London EC1M 5NR
EU representative: Macmillan Publishers Ireland Ltd, 1st Floor,
The Liffey Trust Centre, 117–126 Sheriff Street Upper,
Dublin 1 D01 YC43
Associated companies throughout the world

ISBN 978-1-0350-6914-9

1 2 3 4 5 6 7 8 9

A CIP catalogue record for this book is available from the British Library.

Typeset by Palimpsest Book Production Limited, Falkirk, Stirlingshire
Printed and bound in the UK using 100% Renewable Electricity by CPI Group (UK) Ltd

Visit **www.panmacmillan.com/bluebird** to read more about all our books
and to buy them.

The Fear Opportunity

For my twinnie Alex

Contents

Introduction

When I tell people I've taken up extreme sports in my retirement from professional cycling, they generally respond to me in one of two ways. Both options approach my hobbies as pathologies to be diagnosed, but they offer up different *causes* for my *condition*. It's either nature or nurture, and the first group are certain that I must have simply been born this way. It's clear to them that the career I had was a result of an innate willingness to push myself to extremes, and skydiving, surfing or competing in the Cheltenham Festival is really just a continuation of that disposition. I'm sure there's some truth in this theory. My mum recently dug out a drawing I did as a ten-year-old, titled 'what I want to be when I grow up', and in it I'd painted myself as both a gold medallist and a professional jockey (as well as someone who would one day own not one, but *two* rabbits). This alone suggests that I've always had an appetite for risk and an openness to challenges (as well as some sort of clairvoyant ability to foresee the multiple medals and menagerie of animals that have been a feature of my life).

The second diagnosis – sorry, *response* – is that I was conditioned into this state by the pattern of my professional life as an Olympian. These analysts argue that the constant cycle of competition, elation and relief in which I lived somehow created an adrenaline-shaped hole that I simply had to fill afterwards with mountains and motorcycles. Again, this is plausible. There's no direct substitute for the feeling of working towards a gold medal for four years and performing under intense stress to win the race that matters. It's well documented that many sportspeople fall into patterns of addiction when their careers are over, and experts that work with them often point to a sort of dopamine dependency that develops through a lifetime in elite sport. Winning the Olympics or a World Championships offers a high that's hard to match outside of the sporting arena, and when our bodies are no longer capable of competition, many ex-professionals turn to addictive and self-destructive alternatives. You will see throughout this book that I do not see equivalence between the challenges I take on and harmful addictive behaviours. I'm not really a fan of the term 'adrenaline junkie'.

This is because I believe there is a third explanation for my desire to take on stressful challenges. Put simply, I think it is a *good idea*. I would argue that feeling, facing and *utilizing* fear is both rational and healthy. Yes, I understand how that sounds. Climbing Everest = rational. Racing at Cheltenham having hardly ridden a horse = healthy. It's counterintuitive, and even though racing thoroughbred horses is unlikely to be prescribed by your GP any time soon, I cannot shake the sense that these challenges enrich our lives. Like many people who do difficult things for pleasure, I believe that there are opportunities in the things that frighten us and deeper long-term benefits to stepping outside of our comfort zones. I suspect that my peaceful moments are more so for the shocks that I have endured, that my sense of what is possible is expanded, and my ordinary stresses are somehow transformed by the experience of extraordinary ones. We are stronger and more confident when we feel fear and act; it is our guide and our energy source, and if we follow it, we have an opportunity to replace the anxiety in our life which is nothing but a drain.

This might be the point at which you are wondering whether my suggestion that you climb Everest is actually that practical, given you have a school run in fifteen minutes. You may agree that racing in the next Grand National would really put stressful work presentations into perspective, but that substituting one for the other isn't really an option. So I should probably explain my view that comfort zones are relative. The challenges you pursue are entirely your own, defined by your circumstances, your stresses and your fear. Anything that gives you a sense of nervous energy, that you doubt you can overcome, and that fits within the possibilities of your schedule, will provide the benefits to your self-image, efficacy and wellbeing that I describe in this book.

We can each draw similar benefits from different challenges, because our comfort zones are as personal as our fears. You probably do things every day that I would find terrifying. Maybe you raise children. Maybe you work in an environment where you are regularly scrutinized. Perhaps you're a teacher and have to speak in front of crowds of fourteen-year-olds on a daily basis. These experiences would be my Everest, much more so than . . . well, Everest.

So when I give specifics, I hope I'm able to draw out the generalities. If I discuss the wellbeing impacts of white-water kayaking, understand that similar forces are at play when you convince yourself to perform at Wednesday Karaoke. When I talk about the mental health of mountain climbers, I want to make it clear that you can choose your own mountain (or poetry night, or parkrun). The challenges change but the opportunities are the same, and they exist in the relationship between facing our fear and feeling stronger for it. In a sense, this can be boiled down to:

- Feeling a stress response and putting it to use.

- Growing more self-aware and confident by doing things you doubted you were capable of.

- Learning to then see challenges as opportunities and adventures, and, by extension, experiencing your life more like the adventure that it is.

These features apply to the outer reaches of your comfort zone, so they could be anything from a surfing lesson to amateur dramatics or a conversation with an attractive barista. If something both scares and excites you, and if it in any way seems difficult, then there are good reasons to do it – and it need not require specialist equipment or a six-week trek to the Andes. What matters is the physical and mental impact of progressing from 'I couldn't do that', through 'I'm preparing to do that', and on towards 'I did that'.

You will see as we progress that there is a wealth of evidence regarding the benefits of doing difficult and frightening things. It won't just be a series of platitudes from this heavily tattooed ex-cyclist or from Southern Californian men who jump off cliff faces dressed like flying squirrels (this is a thing). We will speak with neuroscientists, adventure psychologists and child psychologists. We will deconstruct the gender norms around risk-taking (it's actually not a man's game) as well as the epidemic of chronic illness that has occurred because we process stress using hardware developed for avoiding lions rather than awkward interactions, and we will look at both big pictures and small ones. I will hopefully go some way to understanding whether challenges are good for us, or whether the people that think I was either born this way or conditioned into it by my career are in fact correct.

Certain aspects will seem quite personal to me. For example, in terms of the fear of change that we all must confront, I completed my 'life's work' (in other people's eyes) by the time I was thirty-two, when I retired as a professional cyclist. This may seem relatively unique, but in truth I went through the same processes that we all do when some period of our life ends and we must choose to move forward. Whether we're facing the end of a sporting career, an empty nest or the loss of a loved one, life continually requires us to feel our fear and step into the unknown. There are times when we all must fight or fly. These terrifying moments can be the most important of our lives. The times when we step into the unknown are often those we look back on most fondly and shine brightest in our memory. They have a certain energy and life force, and we have an opportunity to harness it, to reframe our fears and challenges into sources of momentum rather than the leaden, aimless weight of anxiety. Even better, we can do it every day, through small, surmountable challenges which prime us to see fear as the precursor to progress.

As we grow older, stepping into the unknown is something that needs practice. With age, our comfort zone can grow, and the distance to its edge can seem insurmountable as habit and routine settle us deeper within it. This is not always so much of an issue if we are entirely satisfied in our life. If you are perfectly happy, have great meaning in your life and have no issue with chronic (long-term) stress inside your comfort zone, then it should be obvious that you do not need to practise stepping out of it. If, like many others in developed nations, you still feel uncomfortably anxious amidst all this comfort, then there is an argument for making a change. This is the case for being afraid of *something* rather than worried about *everything*.

It's unfortunately common that while the certainty in our lives increases with age, the sense of joy and ease does not. This journey from a childhood where we live in a constant state of becoming and changing, to a youth of greater competence but no less risk and change, through to the years where most aspects of our life start to find their place, does not always bring us greater happiness or security. Many things become more stable and yet we grow more anxious. In light of this, I think it's worth considering whether calculated uncertainty (funny concept, I know) can be a useful antidote to the stresses of normality, and the normalization of stress, as well as a form of preparation for the seismic shifts that will at some point occur in our lives. If we give ourselves *real* things to be afraid of, we close out the space in which our anxiety and stress can fixate on hypothetical threats. I also believe that choosing to challenge ourselves offers us a chance to train for those moments when life really does challenge us. Controlling our stress response, planning effectively and believing in our ability to navigate hardship are all things we can, and should, practise.

For me to test these ideas, I will have to be quite open about my own life and my experiences. This feels like a risk to me. In fact, it's just the thing I've avoided for a number of years. While the demands of racing itself weren't a great issue for me, the attention and scrutiny that came with it was another matter, so in retirement I have mostly stepped back from public life. Now I am writing a book about facing fears which requires me to do just that. My hope is that I'll discover that I'm stronger than I thought, and that the risk is worth taking. It's often true that the stress of avoiding an imaginary threat is worse than the threat itself, and I believe that to be true today.

Which cuts to the root of the problem of how we deal with anxiety and stress in the twenty-first century. For all the time and money we've spent trying to control, limit and quash it, we don't seem to be getting any closer to stopping its spread. Making ourselves less stressed seems to be quite stressful, which suggests we should try something different. Maybe it's time we ask what happens when we pursue it, and try to own it. Maybe we have an opportunity to chase our fears, rather than let them chase us.

So let's go.

Yours intrepidly,
Victoria Pendleton

I. First Fears

How Children Challenge Themselves
and Learn Through Play

At five years old, and three foot five, a high wall was for climbing. Where adults would see a barrier, my brother Alex and I saw a springboard, a toy or a teacher that could show us just what was possible. We would start with questions like 'can we climb it?', advance to 'can we get across it?', and usually arrive at 'should we jump off it?' This simple thing, this mass of bricks, could be a playground or a testing ground. It offered us a chance to figure out our capabilities, and gain confidence in them, to see our limitations and learn by pushing them. While the rest saw a wall, and two children jumping off it, we were discovering the world and ourselves. This study of physics (children fall with a velocity proportional to their starting height) was our introduction to biology (cuts heal) and experienced through the almost magical chemistry of two twins exploring the world.

As tiny scientists, our twinship made us ideal research subjects. To us, any differences in our outcomes could only be the result of differences in action, of willing, approach or execution. We could learn from one another because, in our eyes, we were exactly the same. This may not have been entirely true, but our parents went to great lengths to instil a sense of equality between us. They chose not to raise us as a little boy and girl, but a pair of twins (or twinnies, to us), unencumbered by the limitations of gender that society might later choose to impose on us.

I know that some twins struggle with the shared nature of their experience; they feel their individuality is compromised by their partnership, the comparison is a thief of their joy and they receive halves where most children receive wholes. But this was not the case for Alex and me. We simply thought we were special, even if it was more our circumstances than our selves that were unique. Growing up alongside my brother gave me a freedom to pick traits, habits and hobbies from the (supposedly) masculine side of the aisle, and that gave me a fuller range of opportunities than many girls can access. Being like each other meant that we could be more like ourselves, and we could do so safely in the knowledge that our best friend would always be there beside us.

So we saw ourselves as blessed, not by God, but by the stars which fated us to be born into a team. We felt lucky, so we took that luck and ran with it, jumped with it and rode it along home-made slalom courses down Stofold. These car-door chicanes and alleyway bottlenecks were taken at high speeds on small bikes and roller skates; they were time trials, but also tests of our will. We challenged ourselves, and each other, for fun. I don't remember being scared, but I do remember being exhilarated at the possibility of scraped elbows or near misses. These were the sorts of challenges that we chose. There were risks, but they were a part of the course we designed, contributing to the joy we felt as much as the danger any adult might perceive. We felt in control, and when we were not, well, we had *chosen* not to be. Those slaloms were some of my first experiences of risk, and of the kind of proactive fear and challenge-seeking that this book advocates for.

I should be clear that I won't be encouraging you to jump off a wall or ride through an alleyway in the Home Counties any time soon. I will, however, ask you to consider doing something that fills you with a similar nervous excitement. Something that you *think* you could do, that you might *quite like* to be able to do, but wouldn't for reasons that you can seemingly justify. I hope that this book encourages you to challenge yourself, to do something a bit scary, that you might believe you could *someday* be capable of, if you can learn to think a bit more like a child.

I have no concern about encouraging you to do such things, whether it's speaking up with a colleague you find intimidating or joining a sports team, because there really is no harm in trying and, as we will see, so much to gain. A challenge is very different from a threat, just as an adventure is a world away from a worry, but as individuals and as a society we have lost a sense of these distinctions. Many of us feel anxious, or threatened by things that may not happen; we see risk where there is none and doubt our ability to cope in the face of hardships. I want to encourage you, like the twinnies you just met, to learn what you are capable of by testing yourself. I want to show you how seeking adventure can loosen worry's grip, how the pursuit of knowable fears can break our preoccupation with unknowable ones and demonstrate how strength, self-knowledge and confidence can be gained by putting your capabilities to the test. Simply put, I want to convince you that fear is an opportunity and worry a misuse of our imagination.

I want to do this, because I know life will test us all. The dependencies we create through love and connection leave us vulnerable, the things we gain can make us loss-averse and the passage of time can cause us to be preoccupied about possible pain rather than excited for life's opportunities. We should all practise resilience, both to develop it and to access the joy of the experiences that teach it. This can make us happier, stronger and more secure in our self-belief, but at its core and at the deeper end of life, it can even prepare us for those fears and hardships that underpin all others. We will all face a time when we confront our own mortality, or that of the people we love, and I believe that challenging ourselves and seeing just how strong we can be, can teach us skills that will empower us when those days inevitably come.

I have only recently come to understand how chosen challenges can give us greater strength to face unchosen ones. I learned much earlier how different controlled and uncontrollable fear can be. While Alex and I found joy in our frights of fancy as children, we experienced a very different form of fear close to our fifth birthday. It started with a game, much like everything did at that point. We were in a bramble patch, creating a hidden den surrounded by the thorns on wild rose bushes, but as we passed between the hedgerows Alex scratched his ear. I didn't notice and he thought nothing of it, so we continued playing until we heard 'dinner's ready!'.

My memory of what followed is not perfectly clear, but a few days later Alex became lethargic. Medical terms were discussed and doctors were consulted, my parents seemed worried and I vaguely sensed that I should be too. I didn't understand what was going on until I heard the words 'we could lose him' at the kitchen table. Somehow it seemed that his scratched ear had triggered septicaemia, which had indicated to the doctors that he might in fact have the early stages of leukaemia. The beauty of that wild rose bush had hidden the harsh truth of our mortality, and just as roses and thorns grew amidst one another, so it seemed sickness had hovered close beneath our laughter. As if in some dark fairy tale, our charmed story and inseparability diverged on the tip of a thorn. This was my introduction to the stark reality that fear is entirely dependent on our ability to understand its cause and our belief that we can overcome it. With a clear mind and self-belief, our fear can marshal our resources and provide our energy source. Without clarity and without self-belief, it only serves as a looming threat. I was afraid of Alex's illness, unable to understand it and aware on some level that I did not have the resources to help him overcome it. So I was powerless.

'We could lose him'. I understood that, even if I could not quite countenance it. The word 'could' seemed to me to be playing the role it did in phrases like 'we could win the lottery' or 'humans could colonize Mars'. It referred to a possibility so small as to be almost impossible, but still I felt afraid. It was a new fear, distinct from the nervous excitement of backyard games or dizzying heights, but one where control and hope had to be ceded. We could not be together, Alex had to go away, and I did too. We had to do our best and try to be good, but there was no second go at this. This was a new powerlessness, and the moment we first confronted death, after only a few short years of being alive.

Thanks to a remarkably swift diagnosis from our local GP, Alex went off to Great Ormond Street and I went to live with my grandparents while our older sister Nicola stayed with our father at home. I'm sure it hurt them to keep us apart, but my mother could not keep watch over all of us and my dad had to work, so they thought it was best to keep little Victoria at a safe distance. I know they were right, but with that distance my knowledge of the situation was reduced to the positive things I heard and clung to, 'he's getting the best care possible' or 'he *should* be fine'. I didn't have to see the fear in my parents' eyes or the pallor of Alex's skin. I didn't see him on his bad days and if my parents wept, I could not hear it. I was hidden and I was protected.

It is only now, when I look back at photos, that my heart breaks. My brother, my twin, my other half, is so small and so weak. His hair is gone and a bandage hides his canula, but he smiles with a hopefulness that only a child can muster in such circumstances. I see his suffering. I am not ashamed that I did not understand it at the time, only sad for my brother, who could be so small and yet be asked to endure so much. His bravery and the bravery of my parents saved me from sharing in the pain.

Amidst those thorns, the care of my grandparents was a rose. I loved them, and I loved living with them, so much so that after a time I declined to go back home on weekends. They were masters of play, somehow able to elevate basic household chores and errands to the status of games. They clearly knew me well, and saw how invested I could be in any activity that was designated as a challenge. To this day I will try to play at the hard things that I have to do, introducing boundaries, limits and challenges to activities that would otherwise be called hard work. In a 'turbo trainer sprint interval session' (they are as bad as they sound), I would not struggle to 'modulate output at thirty second intervals', but race against the chorus of my favourite songs. Similarly, I won't do a 10k run, but I will see how fast I can get from one tree to another in the distance. The playfulness I learned in childhood facilitated the professionalism of my adult life, and the new meaning I found in retirement.

I was lucky to live through such a difficult time with people who knew me in ways that I only understand now. I existed happily and optimistically at one step removed from Alex's life at Great Ormond Street. I perceived the whole situation through rose-coloured binoculars, and I was lucky that my distant optimism wasn't misplaced. After six months, my positive reading of the situation was proved to be correct. Alex was in remission; he *was* getting the best care possible; *he did* get better. He came home, and we became whole again.

How Children Learn About Risk Through Play

So the games began. Fortunately, we had not grown thorn-weary or cautious, and mortality did not cast its shadow over our risky play. We swung ropes over ditches, built improvised bike ramps and improved our times on the backyard slalom. We pushed our boundaries and we learned what we were capable of, well aware that scraped knees and lost teeth were a fair price to pay for freedom.

I spoke recently with an education researcher from Utrecht about these kinds of play. His name is Dr Martin van Rooijen, and in addition to his role as a government advisor and advocate, he has the quite wonderful title of 'play facilitator'. He watches children at play, and instead of trying to advise, simply learns from them and speaks up for their right to do so in the ways that they desire. To Martin, our improvised and somewhat ramshackle games were just the sort of thing he encourages. Martin pioneered something called 'loose parts' play, which is where children are offered objects rather than toys to play with as they choose. This has its origins in the experiences of children in the Second World War, when toys were limited and parental oversight was too, so urban children made their own games amidst the wreckage of their towns and cities. The landscape architect Carl Theodor Sørensen saw this and pioneered the idea of 'Adventure Playgrounds' in Denmark, which soon came to the UK in 1948. Unlike many modern adventure playgrounds, these were filled with what appears to the adult eye as, well, junk, and it was a visit to a British junkyard playground in the eighties that inspired Martin to take the idea back to the Netherlands.

Martin gives the children in his play sessions opportunities to play in the ways that they want to. He may give them barrels or office chairs and allow them to design their own games around them. What he finds is that while children engage in risky play, they consistently prove themselves to be very capable risk-assessors. They will spin an office chair as fast as they are comfortable to, or roll the barrel towards one another with a force that the recipient can tolerate. If they go too fast, or too hard, they may take a minor bump, but that is okay for them.[1] He has found that loose parts play also frees children from the gender- and age-coding they are confronted with by formal toys. These are not *products for girls* or '8+', they are wooden planks, and as such they can be anything children want them to be. The result is that children choose *who* they want to be more freely. Play across gender and age groups is more common, with smaller children often ending up at play with others a few years older than them because they are both drawn to the same object. This encourages creativity, and ingenuity, but it also means younger children are able to learn from the older ones and see what they may be capable of in the future. Through play, they can see what they can grow into and what they could experience.

When I described the makeshift ramps and rope swings of my youth, Martin was supportive. He believes that we underestimate children, much like how many of us underestimate our adult selves. He believes that risky, free play offers an opportunity for children to understand their capabilities and their boundaries and thus develop a sense of autonomy and capability – which is an important developmental experience, especially when we consider how many of us struggle with feedback and criticism. A lot of play now is evaluated and overseen by adults, judged even, and to Martin this denies children a crucial learning opportunity. If we teach that there is a right or wrong way to play, or suggest to children that they are incapable of developing safe (or dangerous) ways to move their bodies through the world, they are held back from developing their own ways of evaluating what feels right to them, and believing in that. When Alex and I built ramps over ditches, we were exploring some basic principles of engineering, but we were also learning about ourselves, what we enjoyed, what we could manage and how capable we were of bouncing back when we ended up in the mud. This may seem like child's play to most adults, but to someone like Martin, it is a pivotal moment in which children develop a sense of autonomy and resilience that will positively impact them across their entire lives.

The Relationship Between Challenge, Risk and Reward

There are, of course, still ample opportunities for children to develop such skills in the company of their caregivers, and we did that too. Soon after Alex returned home, we began cycling with our dad. We were desperate to join him on the bikes, as we could tell that cycling was his happy place, and we wanted to be in it with him and share in his adventures. My father had a hard childhood, and in many aspects he could seem distant or severe, but when we cycled with him we saw that this was the one place he had always felt he belonged, and we could see the joy that was within him. So our holidays took place on wheels, from a camper-van's four to our neat sets of two, travelling the country to ride up hills and race down passes. It was an adventure. On some trips I would spend my nights in shared dorms with women I had never met, and I see now how this too was a moment to learn genuine life skills. I would have to share many rooms, in many places, with other women throughout my life, and I was fortunate to practise it with these hikers, ramblers and cyclists before there were medals on the line.

We learned how to prepare for expeditions, how to pack small bags with only the essentials, to set up camps and clear them away. We saw how adventure takes thought and preparation, that flying down hills on mountain bikes is as much an exercise in planning as it is in carefree abandon. Certainly, some elements of our trip would seem like hard work, but I see now that, like all good work, there were rewards. We were learning to confront new situations, prepare for them and grow, and we got to do so with our parents in parts of the natural world that make people feel grounded and connected.

Just as I have come to see our adventurous holidays as formative experiences which taught me the mindsets and skills that I've relied on throughout my career and in retirement, so too do I now see other ways in which Alex and I learned lifelong lessons through play. Most of all, we developed a clear and healthy relationship between challenge and reward. I spoke to the brilliant Dr Eirini Flouri, a professor of development psychology at University College London, about why children engage in risky play, and the value of it, and she really helped me to understand just what we twins were learning from our games, as well as what we adults might learn from how children tackle risk and fear.

In her eyes, the way we played established an understandable connection between the difficulty of a task and the sense of reward we would feel, on an internal level, in completing it. This would prove invaluable to me as a competitor, but also as a woman who moves through a world that is sometimes challenging and unknowable. I was free to learn early that challenges and hardship are often a conduit to self-knowledge and joy, and she argues that childhood experiences of play can be formative for how we approach hardship through our adult lives. Her description of anxiety as loss-aversion, or a fear of unknown (and essentially unknowable) consequences, put this in clearer terms for me. She argues that an inability to engage with risk is consistent with fearfulness and anxiety. If we do not learn about the relationships between challenges and outcomes, we have a tendency to imagine the worst-case scenarios around any potential challenge, whether it is social, professional or physical. Even though the games Alex and I played were broadly physical, it seems they offered us an education that we could apply to social and professional situations too.

Eirini described a risk-tolerance spectrum on which the happy medium is a point where young people are capable of confronting, evaluating and even enjoying risk, but also understanding the point at which it presents harm. At one end she talked about a harmful relationship to risk, which we see in many young people who have experienced trauma in early life. This can often involve problematic relationships with drugs and alcohol, a tendency to engage in risky sexual behaviour and a disregard for their own wellbeing. This, naturally, constitutes a problematic relationship to risk, and a growing field of research is trying to understand the psychology and neurobiology that underpins it. One argument is that the experience of trauma is clearly painful, difficult and a source of sadness, so risk-taking behaviours become a strategy to overcome these negative feelings. Others point to the ways in which trauma can change our brains, limiting the function of our amygdala (the part that regulates our responses to threats) and resulting in an impaired ability to make decisions in risky situations.

At the other end of the spectrum, she described extreme risk-aversion, which she believes is prevalent across our society and which leads to timidity, anxiety and the potential to be crushed by any disappointing life event. A discussion of this society-wide shift could fill a book, and although she clarified it was beyond her professional expertise, Eirini offered potential suggestions for why it had come about.

> I think all kinds of risks – participating in sport, trying to find a romantic partner, starting a business – feel better when one invests in a society that applauds you for living according to the motivating values. But people no longer trust that there's any community or society that matters, or is invested in them – so all these risks now appear to be at higher cost.

She believes there has been an 'evaporation of a sense that my risks are valued socially. By my community.'

> When one looks at gender differences and similarities in these trends, then one frequently sees arguments that men have lost

the peer structures that rewarded failure, i.e. that would still recognize effort and offer consolation in failure. And then the kinds of risks we expect women to take were mostly based on risking abusive or oppressive family situations, and they've wised up to this.

By extension, we might argue that we have grown less tolerant of risky play for children because we lack the communities that guarantee their safety and support if they are hurt, and children themselves are denied access to the peer community which applauds them for taking on challenges and learning how to evaluate risk.

In the middle of our risk spectrum, we see people who have a willingness to engage with *evaluated* risk, based on both the riskiness of the action we are taking and the potential benefits that may come with taking it on. What we see here is that the extreme ends of the risk–tolerance spectrum involve an inability to appreciate risk, good or bad. In the case of someone who engages with harmful risk regularly, there is an inability to connect the damage they may do to their mind and body with the action they may want to complete, and as such they underestimate risk. Here, a greater understanding of the relationship between risk, harm and reward would be beneficial. In the opposite case, of our society-wide risk-aversion, we see that people tend to overestimate the problems that might arise from challenging situations. Here, too, a reappraisal of both risk, harm and reward would be beneficial.

If we take the example of being honest with a colleague we find intimidating, our risk-aversion may be based on an imagined outcome in which that colleague publicly shames us, our team inexplicably turns on us and we experience terrible career outcomes as a result of doing the thing that we want to do, but fear. We cannot properly connect the thing we need to do (speak up for ourselves) with the risk (which is an evaluation of the likely outcomes) and rewards. If we have not learned to connect challenge, risk and reward, we will tend to overstate the losses and understate the rewards, and as a result imagine worst-case outcomes and terrible disappointments from acting in support of our needs.

It was something of a surprise to be told that my experience building ramps in my garden could somehow prepare me for office politics, but it felt intuitively correct. As children, we were practising and testing the relationships between actions and outcomes. The only catastrophe we experienced (Alex's leukaemia) was nothing to do with risks we took (if anything, the rose, and the risk, only exposed the illness), but the rewards we gained were always to do with establishing a challenge for ourselves. Like scientists, we changed our inputs, from the level of challenge to the ways in which we took it on, and we learned from the consequences. Sometimes the jump was too great, but it was only from the pain that we experienced that we learned about our capabilities – and better still, we learned about discomfort and what we could tolerate.

I had to grow comfortable with discomfort in my life. As a professional athlete, there were simply no two ways about it. Any desirable outcome, at that level, requires a certain amount of hardship, be it physical training or mental, when preparing for a race or accepting a loss. I believe this to be true in ordinary life as well. The challenge of speaking to that difficult co-worker, for example, is heavily dependent on how much discomfort we think we can tolerate. The catastrophic outcomes of speaking up might be highly unlikely, but even they are potentially tolerable. If we have experienced the discomfort of a difficult conversation like that before, we may find that we do indeed have a certain tolerance for it, but it is only by experiencing it that we can know.

Furthermore, tolerance of discomfort is transferable between different experiences,[2] while intolerance of it can make us vulnerable to numerous psychological and behavioural challenges.[3] [4] This is best studied in terms of how experience of discomfort through exercise can lead to increased pain tolerance,[5] but it has also been shown that exposure to manageable stress increases our resistance to it in the future. It also feels true on a personal level. If we have done other hard things in our lives, no matter how big or small, we can lean on them as examples of our ability to tolerate discomfort in other settings. You may have experienced this in your own life, facing a difficult situation that seems too difficult or uncomfortable to bear, and you find some part of you turning to another hardship you have overcome. 'I've had two kids – I can definitely climb a hill', or 'I've climbed mountains – I can deal with a trip to the dentist'. We see that a tolerance for discomfort is transferable if we tell ourselves the right story, and just as the knees that I scraped trying to race through alleyways prepared me for monster pre-Olympic training camps, the hills (literal or figurative) you climb may prepare you for awkward office interactions. We tend to separate out the challenges in our lives and imagine that what powers us to one finish line cannot be relied upon in other times and places, but it can, and we can practise it.

Discomfort Tolerance and Stress Inoculation

As children, we play in part to discover what we are capable of, in part to understand the basic laws of cause and effect, and also to determine the discomfort we can tolerate. Eirini also mentioned another benefit of challenging play, close to all of these, which is 'stress inoculation'. This is a fantastic concept, and although we all understand on some level how inoculations work, it's worth returning to it.

The idea of inoculation is drawn from medical science, and as we will see throughout this book, concepts that apply to our bodies are often transferable to our minds. An inoculation exposes us to a small amount of a pathogen (say a virus or disease) that could harm us and teaches us how to process it. As such, when we are confronted with a large dose of it, we have some biological memory to rely on and knowledge of the antibodies required to fight it. Eirini suggested that this model could also be used to describe how we become tolerant to social or psychological stressors. We may inoculate ourselves to stress by committing to, for example, doing that first parkrun. We start out a bit worried about looking silly because we are not a runner, we feel a bit stressed because it could be hard, and may even catastrophize ourselves towards *'what if I can't breathe?'*

But we commit to it, and we do it. It turns out to be fine. We don't discover we have secretly been a cross-country athlete all along on a Saturday morning, but we get through it with a bit of walking, some friendly people and a decision to see it through. We leave feeling good about ourselves. But we have also exposed ourselves to a bit of stress, a bit of rumination about looking silly, some thoughts about whether we are up to a task, and some catastrophizing (we also know how to manage our breath on parkruns). This means that next time a stress is put upon us, we have a sort of psychological immune system to respond to it.

Say, for example, that it's announced we have to give a presentation. The audience will be far larger than we are used to and it's a last-minute addition to the diary. We have to do it tomorrow. Somehow our doubts and fears are similar to the parkrun and, as a result, our positive responses can be too.

- **We worry** about looking silly, because we are not someone who presents very often.

  - *Then again, we didn't run very often and the parkrun was fine. Fun even.*

- **We doubt** whether we are up to the task.
  - *I'm not sure, probably? I doubted I could make it around the park on Saturday and it turned out okay.*
- **We catastrophize.** What if I can't get the words out and I freeze and everyone starts laughing at me?
  - *Realize I might stumble over a word or two but that's human and I will just pick up and carry on.*
- **We act** by deciding to take a walk before, speak to some friendly people, and commit to seeing it through.

Much of what worked for the parkrun will work for the presentation, because what scares us about most situations, and what gets us through them, is generally the same. There's some doubt, there's some shame and there's some catastrophizing, and if we can practise engaging with these very normal tendencies in situations of our choosing, we can be inoculated for those that are not.

And so it seems, we can start that stress-inoculation process as children, which as we all know is the best time to get your jabs. The decision to jump the river on a rickety ramp provided an opportunity to become inoculated against the doubts that I was capable of it, the worry that people would laugh if I couldn't and the catastrophic possibility that I would break my arm (six weeks in a cast as a ten-year-old is equivalent to geological time).

Eirini reminds us that 'what will shake you will not break you' and hammering that point home, time and again, leaves you less inclined to either shaking or breaking. So, she recommends small amounts of stress inoculation, every day. The parkrun may actually be a bit further along on our stress-inoculation journey, a level three or four, after completing early levels which involve complimenting people's shoes, taking stairs two steps at a time (and possibly looking odd) or asking a question where once we would have been silent. It could be dancing, driving or diving. It doesn't matter; nothing is too small and if you feel like doing it but wouldn't have done it yesterday for reasons of fear, doubt, shame or catastrophe, then it's a potential opportunity for some stress inoculation.

Without that stress inoculation, if we let our doubts and fears hold us back, it becomes all too easy to underestimate ourselves. Just as Dr Martin van Rooijen noticed in his 'playwork' that adults tend to underestimate children's abilities, so too did Eirini mention that adults underestimate our own capacities. The two may be connected: we were taught as children to live within a very narrow conception of our abilities and so we don't trust our bodies to rise to challenges and we don't trust our minds to overcome the disappointment should they not. We grow cautious, and eventually we grow disappointed in ourselves. Just as children put themselves to the test to see how capable they are, and to learn new approaches to become more capable, we have to do it as adults or we will let the fear of failure become a fait accompli. The sad truth is that submission to the fear of failure (which we will discuss at length in Chapter 4) is the most guaranteed way to fail, because it means doing nothing. We tend to think of failure as an unsuccessful attempt, when this is clearly not true. An unsuccessful attempt is worlds away from an attempt not taken, and far better. A failure to try based on a fear of failing? Well, that's just a logical contradiction. We fail before we even start because we fear failing.

In Eirini's words, we need to fail – and fail often – to progress or to win. We are better off doing so as children (and allowing our children to do so), but if we need to do it as adults, then so be it. It may be easier to learn to accept failure as a child, and it may be hard in our maturity because we have piled on so many levels of imagined shame, but it is never too late to try. It might be uncomfortable, but, as we mentioned earlier, it's also *great* to learn to embrace discomfort.

Like a Russian Matryoshka doll, the skills that we practise in a proactive life are often hidden within one another. We may seek to become motivated, and find within that the need to gain an acceptance of failure. So too when we are adjusting our mindset to accept failure, we are encouraged to see the value in embracing discomfort. Just as the point of growth for a muscle comes through progressive overload (larger weights or numbers of repetitions), psychological growth may also require a similar process. We have to increase our chosen load, and accept that progress exists in the sweet spot after discomfort and before pain. My journey to the Olympics, mountaintops and races at Cheltenham is as much a story of discomfort as it is of joy. We accept physical discomfort as a necessary precursor to physical progress, and the same is true in our psychology – this is why no one speaks of the transformative power of staying in our comfort zone or *not* facing our fears.

I was glad when Eirini talked about parallels between physical and psychological growth through a tolerance for discomfort. She had already described a number of psychological processes through physical metaphors, but I don't think it was solely an attempt to make the complexities of developmental psychology intelligible to a sportsperson. The parallels are real. Just as children (and later athletes) can draw a connection between the discomfort of physical practice and the joy of progress and mastery, so too can we learn to appreciate some degree of psychological discomfort. She suggested that an appreciation of discomfort, be it physical or mental, was a crucial point of childhood development and one that we are less accepting of as carers and educators in the contemporary world. We believe that to allow children an experience of discomfort is to fail them, when, in fact, in manageable and understandable forms, it is positively impactful. The ability to *choose* discomfort, and to see its role in progress, is a vital component of resilience, a subject we will discuss at length later on, but one that underpins our ability to do those hard things that make us feel satisfied.

EXERCISE: HOW TO PLAY AS AN ADULT [6] [7] [8] [9]

I. Try a New Physical Activity with an Element of Risk

Prompt:

Choose a physical activity that feels slightly outside your comfort zone – such as rock climbing, wild swimming or even a challenging hike. The goal is not recklessness, but to safely test your limits and experience uncertainty.

Why:

Research shows that risky play builds physical confidence, self-belief and better judgement, as well as resilience and motivation. These benefits, well documented in childhood, are likely to extend into adulthood. Researchers also argue that risky play allows us to attach 'exhilarating positive emotion' to things that might otherwise create negative emotions, so the inclusion of 'play' turns risk from a word that means *danger* to one that spells *fun*.

2. Engage in Outdoor Exploration

Prompt:

Spend time in natural environments where you can encounter manageable risks – such as navigating uneven terrain, crossing streams or exploring new trails. Go alone or with friends, but allow for spontaneous decision-making and minor uncertainty.

Why:

Most of the research on risky play hones in on *outdoor* play. This is partly because natural environments promote health,[10] but also because nature contributes to healthy uncertainty. Outdoor play provides unpredictability in terms of landscape, location and plants or animals we may find. It encourages different ways of thinking and behaving, offering both a chance to get lost and opportunities to find ourselves.

3. Participate in Social or Competitive Play

Prompt:

Join a team sport or group activity where outcomes are uncertain and mistakes are part of the experience (e.g., netball, ultimate frisbee or improv theatre). Allow yourself to take risks, make errors and learn from them.

Why:

Although we may call these activities 'sports' or 'theatre', we could just as well call them organized adult play. The National Institute for Play points to the importance of such activities for our emotional and social wellbeing as adults, but also the opportunities they afford us to practise acceptance ('we lost, we'll play differently next time') and reframing ('my improv group is fun, maybe public speaking isn't so bad').

4. Pursue a Creative or Professional Risk

Prompt:

Take on a creative project or professional challenge where success is not guaranteed – such as public speaking or submitting a creative project to a public forum (e.g., creative writing group/

poetry night/open mic). Focus on the learning and growth that comes from embracing uncertainty.

Why:
Adults who experienced and managed risk in play as children are better equipped to assess risk, show resilience and maintain positive dispositions in adulthood. Taking on new challenges continues to build these capacities, whatever individuals should choose. One very interesting study[11] honed in on how 'interactions with animals' helped healthcare professionals improve their tolerance of uncertainty to reduce stress and burnout risk.

5. Reflect on Your Experience with Risk

Prompt:
After engaging in any risky play activity, journal about your feelings before, during and after. Did you feel nervous, excited or accomplished? What did you learn about your limits or your ability to handle uncertainty?

Why:
Research suggests that stimulating, risky experiences can help us build better self-efficacy, resilience and stress-tolerance,[12] but that it is through self-reflection afterwards that we can really enhance these impacts.[13]

Safety Note: While embracing risk is beneficial, always assess the environment and your own abilities to ensure risks are reasonable and do not pose serious harm.

Hardship and Satisfaction

If you were to list the greatest satisfactions of your life, be they achievements, crucial relationships or ongoing projects, would you be able to find some discomfort that you chose to tolerate? Your professional successes may have required the discomfort of examinations and trials; your relationships probably opened you up to vulnerability and doubt; your great projects and life-time's works probably presented some moments that you just had to stick out. We can find comfort and satisfaction in simple things, undoubtedly, but those simple things so often require some discomfort and hardship to build. Eirini suggests that a tolerance for discomfort is something we learn in childhood, but, thankfully, can cultivate in adulthood. We can seek out meaningful, but uncomfortable avenues to growth, and in the process grow not only because we have practised them but because the practice itself is teaching us to be comfortable in an uncomfortable situation.

In fact, so many of the fears and opportunities that we will describe in this book follow similar patterns. They can be learned as children, but renewed at any age. They require a willingness to engage with something difficult. They offer the option of doing something hard now as an alternative to the eventual discomfort, anxiety and powerlessness that comes with choosing what seems like the easier path. Hardship becomes easier, but trying to avoid it through a lifetime grows hard.

The chapters of this book describe the fears, and opportunities, of a lifetime. We first practise them as children, but there is no point at which we stop learning or relying on the skills they teach us. As a child at play, we learned how to deal with the unknown (Chapter 6) through exploration. We confronted failure (Chapter 4) by unsuccessfully pushing our boundaries. We learned the self-belief and risk-evaluation that protects against anxiety (Chapter 7). We began to accept our bodies and our minds for what they are, and developed our own internal sense of what we were capable of and what mattered. Through this we became resilient against the fear of standing out, of our difference (Chapter 8). It may be hard to believe now, but even at that most early stage of our lives, we were working on the sense of presence, self-awareness and control that can support us when confronted with our most fundamental fear of death (Chapter 9). Just as our childhood primes us for what follows, I hope this introduction to my childhood has prepared you for the path we will take throughout this book.

Just as many people see a wall but children see an opportunity, so too can we learn to see hardships as a route to a life more comfortably lived. Our fears can be our opportunities if we take the approach of children, of learners and testers, and find room to play in ways that at first seem challenging but that teach us lifelong lessons. While we may have more to lose than we did as children, we have just as much to gain, and given that our adult challenges are greater, we have more reason than ever to learn how to take them on.

- -

KEY TAKEAWAYS

1. Testing ourselves, for the sake of it (aka playfully), can help us learn what we are capable of and ways in which we can grow.

2. Choosing our own forms of challenge and play will allow us to be creative in our approaches, motivated through autonomy and more aware than ever that we can choose both the games we play and the sort of player or person we want to be.

3. We can focus our mind's eye on challenge and reward, rather than risk and punishment.

4. What we learn from one hard thing we choose will help us confront something harder we do not.

5. We can inoculate against stress, and grow comfortable with discomfort, but only by seeking those things out. So start small, and raise the bar.

Look at a wall. See a playground.

2. Fear, Reframed

Why the Stories We Tell Ourselves Matter

It may surprise you to discover that the traits which make an Olympic champion often do not make for a popular teenage girl. When your tendency is to prioritize toughness over lightness, victory over friendship and sport over games, you're not so much a social butterfly as some sort of irritating hornet in the eyes of your classmates. That was my experience, and one which I grudgingly accepted. Maybe I would never be popular, but I could feel capable when I played sports, and if that meant from time to time other girls would simply move out of the way rather than compete for a ball in a game of hockey, then I knew what my choice would be.

I was quiet, I was driven, and I was understood to be a tomboy. We will discuss this idea more in our next chapter on the gender lenses we apply to challenge and fear, but for now I'll simply say that in Bedfordshire in the 1980s and '90s, being a tomboy was the opposite of being popular. I didn't understand why, and I desperately wanted things to be different, to be *both* myself and at least slightly popular, but that seemed to be out of my control. The social life I wanted was out of reach, and as my secondary education progressed it appeared that my academic situation would be similarly disappointing. I wasn't a naturally gifted student, but I was a keen one. I wanted to listen, study and learn, but just as forces beyond my control conspired to leave me socially unfulfilled, so too did they leave me academically unsatisfied. It would have been one thing to be unpopular and academically successful, but my learning environment, like my friendships, was not one I felt I could control.

My school was not great. Classrooms were chaotic and many teachers struggled to maintain order amidst a riot of deodorant flamethrowers and seemingly feral – in my fifteen-year-old eyes – boys. I had little hope of learning in the classroom and so I began to ask teachers for copies of the syllabus so that I could study on my own time at home. I'm quite proud of fifteen-year-old Vic on that count. It showed a certain amount of self-belief to decide to take matters into my own hands, but it was far from ideal. I wasn't learning, and I didn't make many friends, and there's not much to be said for school if those things are not possible.

These were two pillars of my self-esteem that remained unsatisfied, but I think I could have navigated through those challenges if I had at least been able to play sports freely. While I had never felt great social or academic self-efficacy (the belief that you can learn and progress in something), I had always felt capable in my body and at games, but I had to compromise in terms of the sport I was allowed to play. There was very little provision for girls my age to play in serious sports teams and a tacit agreement that the playground was for 'boys' sports'. This meant that the one place in which I felt truly competent, truly in control after those years spent playing with Alex, was also denied to me. So, instead of games in the playground, I resorted to running laps around it. I was, quite literally, marginalized.

This is another sign of some resilience in young Vic. I lacked the confidence to step in and demand my place at the school's sporting table, but I at least decided to run rather than hide. It did not make my life feel meaningful, though. I still felt a complete absence of control over my social, academic and physical life and no sense of progress. I grew unhappy and anxious and this led me to develop a number of compulsive control-seeking behaviours. I began to wash my hands obsessively, rubbing them until they were red-raw, desperate for certainty that I could make myself clean. I sought control over my food, and ran those playground laps with an intensity, a *necessity*, that bordered on compulsion.

I lacked control over both my present and my future, and so turned to these alternative ways of adding structure to my life. They clearly didn't work. I could not substitute hygiene for friendship, academic success or sporting challenges. As people often do, I acted on a symptom (feeling a lack of control) rather than a cause (lacking opportunities to control my outcomes) and it was only later that I found other, more proactive ways of feeling in control. It turned out that what I needed were more positive, satisfying challenges – controllable fears, in fact – to make my life feel meaningful. I needed agency (the ability to intentionally influence our life circumstances), autonomy, and experiences of stressors (demanding, challenging environments and experiences) and stress (the response to them) that felt manageable, rather than the chaotic and ongoing feeling that I couldn't make my life what I wanted it to be.

Spoiler alert, I did find those challenges. It was not long before I regained a sense of control over my life through challenge, and in doing so I moved past the feeling of impotence and chaos that marked my teenage anxiety. In this chapter, we're going to look at how the stories we tell ourselves about fear, about the way we face challenges and our ability to overcome those challenges, are so important. You'll see that these are mindset changes that anyone can make. But first, I want to return to the subject of chronic (constant) stress and look at how it differs from the discrete (momentary and tied to an event) stress of a fear or challenge. It's clear to me now that, back then, I was trying to manage chronic stress through control-seeking behaviour – and this is very common – but it was being able to experience *discrete* stress that actually helped me. It is only by understanding how the two differ that we can appreciate how discrete stress can help us to avoid its chronic counterpart.

Zebra Thinking

Chronic stress, which is often consistent with anxiety, is different from a fear response. They both involve the same physical processes and act on the same hardware in our bodies and our minds, but the key differences are in narrative – the story we tell ourselves about what is happening – and the timelines. To explain this, to understand this key aspect of our humanity, it is useful to do as the great Harvard neuroscientist Robert Sapolsky did in his fascinating book of the same name and ask 'Why Zebras Don't Get Ulcers'. We share a great deal of neurological hardware with zebras, and although our brains may operate at a higher level of complexity and our bodies take different shapes, at the funda-mental level we function in similar ways. Therefore, even if it might sound strange, we *can* better understand human anxiety by looking at a zebra's fears.

Zebras, like most mammals, engage their stress responses when they face an *acute physical* crisis, such as being attacked by a lion. This is useful, because the stress response is a signal to deprioritize all the processes which don't contribute to avoiding a lion (cell repair, sexual arousal, remembering sources of water) and prioritize those that do (getting oxygenated blood to the muscles, scanning for escape routes, noticing other lions). This is healthy and logical, but unfortunately we humans use the same stress responses for very different threats, which operate at very different timescales and complexity than the short-term threat of a lion. While a zebra can be stressed for a few minutes, and live or die because of it, our stress responses can be activated by *hypothetical* things which remain a potential threat for months, years or lifetimes. We activate physical responses which are designed for temporarily avoiding lions to help us navigate seemingly perennial challenges, like office politics, mortgages and the climate crisis.

When we turn on these stress responses, our bodies stop resting and repairing (*there's no time for repair, there's a ~~lion~~ mortgage on the horizon!*), which means we face more health conditions, and a great deal of psychological distress. We spend our lives preparing for unknown, ongoing threats as if they were visible lions, and as such the world feels out of our control, dangerous and unpredictable. As a teenager, I felt a vague sense that my world was not as it should be, that it was unpredictable and uncontrollable, and as a result my stress responses switched on in anticipation of a constant threat. My response was to try to create order, control and predictability, but hand-washing and overly structured eating did nothing to help me gain a sense of autonomy or growth. Those control-seeking behaviours controlled me, and as such did nothing to develop the sense of agency I needed. My brain was activated in the same way a zebra's would at the sight of a lion, but there was no response or action available to bring an end to the sense of threat.

So I, like many of us, applied potent stress responses designed for known, immediate threats, to unknown or even hypothetical ones. Living beneath these for months or years can make us sick. This is a problem of framing or narrative, but fortunately there are narrative responses to it. The first is to understand the difference between what we in the modern world call stress and what we call fear. While scientists talk about those zebras acting on a 'stress response', we do not think of them as being 'stressed'. They are confronted with a threat and a challenge and they must act on it. This is what we call 'fear' throughout this book. A fear is something you can face. Stress, worry or anxiety are exactly the things that a zebra does not experience, and as much as possible we should try to turn the things that make us stressed (worried and powerless) into fear opportunities (clearly demarcated challenges that require a response). If we can make our stresses understandable, and appreciate our ability to confront them as challenges rather than life-or-death threats, we unravel the narrative error that stems from our brain's hardware telling us the wrong story. So let's look at how.

Making Stress Coherent

After the Second World War, the pioneering sociologist and academic Aaron Antonovsky was motivated to understand the ways in which certain people managed to experience its horrors without significant damage to their mental health. In his eyes there had to be some character traits, mindsets or approaches which united those who were able to survive the war and be happy. In his seminal 1979 work *Health, Stress and Coping*,[1] he presented the concept of 'Salutogenesis', which argued that we should focus as much on how we promote health as avoid illness when it comes to understanding resilience.

His work led him to conclude that our ability to remain resilient in the face of stress depends on the extent to which we can see stress and hardship of any kind in a 'coherent' way, which is 'structured', 'manageable' and 'meaningful'. His argument was that stress is not *inherently* harmful, if people can find a way to understand it. If we have a 'sense of coherence' or structure about our hardships, then we will be much more likely to maintain good health (physical and mental) even in difficult circumstances. If you look at the example in the box below, you will see how an ordinary stressful situation can be transformed by reshaping it with structure, manageability and meaning.

EXAMPLE: MAKING STRESS STRUCTURED, MANAGEABLE AND MEANINGFUL

The window of time between work and dinner is too short. There are family responsibilities (pick-ups and drop-offs) and unforeseen events. So when it comes to dinner time, there is a sense that creating a healthy dinner is impossible.

Structured: We know this is a stressor that will occur between certain times on certain days of the week – between five and seven on a weeknight. Telling ourselves it's not an *always* or a *forever* problem is the first step towards structuring it.

Manageable: This will disappoint some of the parenting influencers out there, but what you provide does not need to be perfect; what you *can* do is enough. If it's salad or soup and sandwiches, that's good enough. It's not perfect, but it's better than making yourself ill with stress, so determining what's manageable should be a priority.

Meaningful: Remind yourself that whatever you do, it is a meaningful act. You are providing for people, in difficult circumstances. It's not always going to be easy, but it is a profound thing you are doing. You are nourishing (yes, tomato pasta is nourishment) and it's part of the imperfect but meaningful project of raising a family. Hold on to that sense of meaning.

The sense of chaos I experienced as a teenager was not something I felt I could structure or manage, and it felt meaningless. In Antonovsky's eyes, this would explain why my stress turned to distress. We all need to understand *why* we feel stressed or afraid, *how* we can process it, and *where* we are headed with it, towards learning or growth. If you can introduce these three stages to your stresses, you will have made them coherent through cause, response and effect.

While, on occasion, especially in times of war, persecution or disaster, the world *is* unpredictable, most of us who feel stress in the day-to-day are not facing hardship on that scale. If we take the example of time pressure, which can be a constant source of stress in our lives, as shown in the box above, we can see how a structured response could help turn this often disorientating experience from something which impacts our health into something harmless, even if it is imperfect.

Antonovsky concluded that developing a structured response to stress is key whatever its origin, and to do so, we should look to develop the sense that the world is predictable and understandable. To this end, we can observe the things that stress us and try to make sense of them. But he also found that the people who experienced stress and came out happier and stronger were those who believed that they had the resources to cope with life's demands. Finally, he saw that those who viewed life's challenges as a meaningful part of a purposeful life had a more coherent and less distressing experience of stress, even in extreme circumstances. This is another story we tell that turns our fears and our stressors from problems to milestones.

What's great is that these are mindsets and approaches that we can practise, and it's clear to me that they are an important antidote to the sense of threats and stressors as random, unpredictable and unmanageable. Antonovsky takes stressors, fears and threats and asks us to think about them, to actively appreciate our ability to deal with them and to see hardships as important milestones in the journey of a lifetime – to reframe them as challenges, not lions. This approach is more considered, controlled and surmountable than the mindset involved in chronic stress, which is about *unknowns* and a voice inside that shouts some version of 'Run!'

The best advice for a zebra facing a lion is to run, but a better and healthier approach when confronted with contemporary human challenges is to stop and comprehend the threat or fear, appreciate it, and have faith in our ability to manage it and find meaning by reframing it as a challenge or part of our meaningful journey.

The Challenge Mindset

When it comes to cultivating the ability to see the difficult things in our lives as challenges (which are understandable, manageable and meaningful) as opposed to threats (which are not), Antonovsky was a pioneer. I spoke to Dr Rachel Arnold, who runs the Stress, Anxiety, Resilience, and Thriving (StART) programme at Bath University, which focuses on understanding how individuals in highly pressured domains thrive. Alongside her colleague Lee Moore, a sports psychologist, she explained their cutting-edge research with individuals who work in seemingly different, but undeniably stressful, environments. Unsurprisingly, Dr Arnold and Moore seemed very cool, calm and collected as they told me about their studies with midwives,[2] athletes[3] and military professionals. They began by telling me that they have repeatedly found that a 'challenge' mindset, rather than a 'threat' one, improves both performance and health (both physical and mental). One central difference between these two outlooks is that the former frames difficult situations as opportunities for development or success, while the latter only sees the problems that may arise.

For instance, a midwife may apply a 'challenge mindset' to a difficult patient and see an opportunity to work on their communication skills, or a soldier might reframe inclement weather from a threat to a chance to broaden the space in which they apply their skills. What there is to gain from a challenge is clear, and we can think about our approach towards it. On the other hand, threats can be infinite and overwhelming because of the sheer number of hypothetical catastrophes that we must try to avoid. We can broadly think of a threat mindset as consistent with anxiety, but a challenge mindset as one we use when we feel fear and act upon it.

The extent to which we are able to see a difficulty as a challenge or a threat – as a source of disorientating anxiety or energizing fear – will depend on a number of factors. Some of these relate to our preparation – if we feel like we have a set of skills that can be applied in new situations or if we have memories of how our challenging experiences have helped us progress in the past (think back to the parkrun or the public speaking). Others are the result of training and support to adopt a challenge mindset in stressful situations. Dr Arnold and Dr Moore's studies with midwives led them to recommend dedicated training on how to adopt a challenge mindset by noting and recalling all of the ways in which they have grown *because* of the hard situations they have previously been confronted with. This primes them to see the opportunity for growth the next time a hard situation should arise. Alongside this, they also recommended increased organizational support and individual programmes of mindfulness, which makes sense, as feeling supported and aware of our emotions can be the difference between feeling alone and confused (threatened) and challenged in difficult times.

It was the introduction of challenges into my life that jump-started me out of a threat mindset as a teenager, when I joined the Adventure Scouts. While I was not aware that my anxiety and

control-seeking behaviours were tied to a lack of comprehensi-
bility, manageability or meaningfulness that Antonovsky would
recognize, I experienced it through the *desperate* desire to challenge myself and my body. I had always felt proud of my ability
to do hard things, to learn and to grow, and I needed an outlet
for that. I found it through the Adventure Scouts.

I had already worked my way through the Scouts and the
Brownies and the Guides (for non-UK readers, these are all
youth groups); you name it – if they had badges, I'd been there.
I had travelled up through the ranks, collecting whatever
sewable affirmation I could acquire, until I was told I could now
join the Rangers. That sounded good to me – there was a seriousness to the name, an implication that we would cover some
sort of geographical or practical range. I wanted to know where
we'd be ranging, what kind of responsibilities we would have
and whether I would need to sign some sort of waiver in anticipation of the high-risk, high-reward activities we would take
on.

Instead, we were given a pencil skirt and an air-hostess hat.
We were offered the chance to work towards our International
Cookery Badge and I was told in no uncertain terms that we
would not be jumping off anything. It was not what I had in
mind. I am not trying to devalue cooking, domestic or international, but if offered the choice between eating cold beans on
a mountaintop and getting into a kitchen, I would always take
the beans. I'm glad there were international cookery badges for
people who wanted to cook, but I was deeply disappointed there
wasn't an alternative for those of us who wanted to walk a
different path.

A few months later, a friend of mine told me she had joined
the Adventure Scouts and insisted I would love it. I was wary,
careful not to let my hopes get the better of me. For all I knew
they may have been offering adventures in dusting or scouting

for newer, more restrictive pencil skirts, but my friend assured me that this was different. The Adventure Scouts were genuinely interested in adventure, and while, like most good things (it seemed), they had never previously allowed girls to join, they had recently changed their policy.

I was glad they did. The couple who ran the group were genuinely committed to helping young people experience adventure and learn new skills. Their own children were already signed up, two older boys and a daughter around my age, and together we went rock climbing, kayaking and potholing. Most weekends we took on activities that many teenagers would not be accustomed to, and they trusted us to find safe ways to navigate them while offering the care and support we needed. Some aspects might seem a bit risky to the uninitiated. We once went canyoning, effectively careering down a ravine along a natural water slide, and my guide's only advice was to 'aim for the dark bit of the water'. In truth, there was not much more they could say. The beauty of adventurous activities is that they can be made up of incredibly simple moments, but amount to grand adventures when you stitch them together.

My memories of that time are incredibly happy, and there was a noticeable change in my wellbeing. My compulsion towards control-seeking behaviours diminished and I gained a certain sense of self-efficacy and control. While my tendency to seek a challenge had only been a source of frustration in a school environment where I could not find it, and my desire to put my body to the test created the same outcome in a playground where I was denied access to play, now I saw these things as assets. I needed challenges, and places where I could feel in control.

I should be careful to say that I am not offering clinical advice to people who are struggling with symptoms of obsessive compulsive disorders. As far as I am aware, while there are numerous examples of adventure therapy, I don't have grounds to argue that adventure is something we should prescribe to anyone struggling with this mental-health condition. I can only outline my experience, and at a time when I sought order compulsively in the face of chaos, the ability to experience challenges which felt structured, manageable and meaningful – unlike the other stressors I faced, which felt like unmanageable threats – seemed to reorient my experiences of the stresses I faced elsewhere.

Arousal Reappraisal

My experiences with the Adventure Scouts helped me to become focused on actively seeking out challenges and overcoming them, rather than running from the threat of chaos and disorder, and it made a huge difference. I was no longer a human zebra, constantly alert to myriad threats, but a young woman focused on challenging herself, understanding the stresses that came with those challenges, and overcoming them. I gained self-esteem and self-belief, while also experiencing something called 'arousal reappraisal' first-hand. This is an interesting concept, and offers another insight into how narrative and framing can positively impact the way we experience hard things in our lives, and our lives overall.

Arousal reappraisal, as Rachel Arnold explained in our conversation, is quite simply the way we think about our stress responses. These are the usual physical signifiers: sweaty palms, a racing heart and changes in our respiration. These will be familiar to all of us as the signs that we are growing stressed, anxious or overwhelmed. If you have ever approached a presentation or a difficult conversation and felt that if you could only be free from these *symptoms* of your stress, you would be fine – or that, actually, you are not terrified on a conscious level, but your breath, skin and heart are making you appear and feel so – then you will recognize how frustrating this form of arousal can be. Some people take beta-blockers in anticipation of such a situation, and the fact that these primarily act on our stress responses (heart rate, circulation), rather than our mind, suggests we may sometimes *act* more stressed (physically) than we *feel* (mentally).

The message from Rachel, however, was that we don't need to medicate away our stress responses, but reframe them. This is the essence of arousal reappraisal. You may notice that in my definition of stress responses in the previous paragraph I described them as signifiers that we are 'stressed, anxious or overwhelmed'. In fact, we could just as easily describe these responses as the things our body does when it needs to perform a difficult task. An increased heart rate and breathing faster are the measures your body must take to oxygenate your blood, and whether it is a physical or intellectual challenge you are taking on, this is essential. In fact, learning to see our fear responses as a positive form of preparation for challenges, rather than a negative reaction to threats, is a central argument of this book. It is one way in which the problem of fear becomes the fear opportunity: appreciating our fear responses and reappraising our stress responses as signifiers of physical readiness rather than psychological turmoil actually *changes how we feel and perform*. 'Arousal reappraisal' involves recognizing our stress responses as the healthy functioning of our bodies rather than markers of distress, and that very understanding makes us more capable of dealing with the stressor causing them. Just as we can learn to see challenges rather than threats, to see hardships as structured, manageable and meaningful, so too can we see our physical responses to them in a positive way that makes us not only feel, but actually *be*, more capable.

Stress as Fuel

Arousal reappraisal is only one of the ways by which we can learn to appreciate our fear responses. While a change in narrative can allow us to rethink our sweaty palms, and transform them from experiences of discomfort to positive reflections of our body's function, the pioneering Austrian endocrinologist Hans Selye went further. Known by some as 'The Father of Stress', Selye was the first person, in 1976, to make the argument that we could experience stress and stress responses as *positive* and *empowering*.[4] He argued, as Antonovsky did, that stress need not make us unhappy or unhealthy. He found that when we believe ourselves capable of meeting the challenges of a stressor, we become capable of using our stress responses for *good*. He argued that the hormones adrenaline and cortisol, which we often blame for our discomfort or anxiety around threats, are in fact the fuel which provide us with the energy and heightened focus we need to confront challenges. To Selye, stress responses and the hormones associated with them are the drivers that allow us to move beyond our comfort zone and face our fears.

There is a beautiful cycle at play here. If we reframe our fear responses as a fuel for acting outside of our comfort zone, then we grow more capable of going there. By leaving our comfort zone, we experience growth that we otherwise would not, not least in our self-belief and self-efficacy. To complete the circle, it is this self-belief and self-efficacy that Selye argues underpins our ability to take stress and make it useful. The input of stress, through a process of reframing, becomes fuel for a growth in our self-belief. Our growing sense of confidence and strength allows us to engage with even greater challenges and we tap into a sort of renewable energy. All it takes is some reframing.

If this seems too good to be true, like snake oil or some appeal to magic in which words affect transformative changes in the world, then I would like to reassure you. These phenomena have been well researched over a long period of time. Dr Alia Crum, an American psychologist who is the principal investigator of the Stanford Mind and Body Lab, focuses on how mindsets affect human behaviour as well as physical and mental-health outcomes. In particular, she is a world authority on the subject of belief and how it can change reality, and she has conducted numerous studies on the power of the 'stress-as-enhancing' mindset.[5] Her research has consistently found that subjects who are taught to view stress as a useful thing outperform those who do not. *Seeing* stress as enhancing *makes* it enhance. Participants who view stress as enhancing repeatedly show fewer negative physiological responses to stressors, fewer symptoms of anxiety or depression and higher levels of energy. They also have lower levels of cortisol (which we can broadly say contributes to negative experiences of stress) and higher levels of DHEA hormones. These hormones are anabolic; they are drivers of growth in the body. So while we can say that seeing stress as enhancing primes our minds to grow from challenges, it quite literally encourages our bodies to grow too.

Dr Crum's research on narrative isn't limited to stress though. She led a fantastic study[6] that showed how the perception of exercise, for example, can enhance the effectiveness of it. The trial involved eighty-four chambermaids, working in seven different hotels, who were split into two groups. The first group was told that the work they do is good exercise, which satisfies the surgeon general's recommendation for an active lifestyle, and given clear examples as to how their work was, in fact, a workout. The second group were not. After four weeks, the first group not only perceived themselves to be fitter, but actually showed a decrease in weight, blood pressure, body fat, waist-to-hip ratio and body mass index. By *believing* that their movement was exercise, it *made* the movement into exercise. Equally, she has shown that our body will metabolize the same food differently depending on whether or not we consider it indulgent or healthy.[7] Dr Crum's research demonstrates that the frames we use and the stories we tell change our minds and our bodies.

Words, narratives and frameworks are keys that have unlocked some of the most powerful forces in the world. Our materialist worldview might lead us to accept that energy cannot be created through words, or ideas, but it would be a mistake to think it cannot be unlocked through them. Revolutions begin with words, lifelong love affairs do too, and even science, which we may (mistakenly) think of as the opposite of storytelling, begins with ideas too. Our minds and bodies also have the opportunity to be transformed by words. The power in my legs was transformed through words, narratives and frameworks. I would hardly have won a race, let alone multiple golds, without the intervention of the Team GB psychiatrist Steve Peters, who we will meet in Chapter 4. He didn't change my force output, training programme or technique, but through words he changed my narratives about fear and failure, reward and victory. With those narratives, I went from almost giving up to the success I later achieved.

We Can *All* Be Heroes

Our narrative, or the stories we tell ourselves, can transform fears into challenges, panic into fuel, and stress into progress, but what happens when we develop a narrative about a whole lifetime? What happens when we view our entire life as heroic, and the challenges within it as the necessary components for making the story work? You may think I have gone too far now. That you could accept me in my 'words change the world' moment, but that treating the school run as if it were battling Voldemort is just too much. You may think that it is a stretch to call you a hero, or your life heroic. But why? Why are you not deserving of that credit? You *have* been heroic! You've chosen at some point to do the hard thing for reasons other than self-interest. You will have dedicated some parts of your life to someone other than yourself, or battled against something bigger than you. Heroism isn't about magic, and it isn't about fighting beasts, it's about choosing to do something new, something hard or something right. Heroism can take place in an office or on the school run because the narrative of 'the Hero's Journey' is relative and true to all of us, and the act of placing ourselves within it can be transformative, when it comes to reducing anxiety, improving mental health and building self-belief.

So forgive me for what seems like a digression into heroism, and trust me that this will remain relevant to our discussion of fear and narrative. The literary theorist Joseph Campbell outlined the concept of 'the Hero's Journey',[8] but like many things that were formalized by Western men in the twentieth century, he didn't discover it. In fact, 'the Hero's Journey' is a narrative structure that is common in cultures around the world. It underlies stories and myths across millennia and continents, with this basic structure used by communities who we have no reason to believe shared a culture. It is a simple structure, and you will know it well because you have seen it, read it or heard it in one form or another tens or hundreds of times. A hero is called to adventure, they travel out from the safety of their home, cross a threshold, and with the help of others learn something powerful about themselves. When they return to their starting place, they have changed for the better.

If that is familiar, it is because it is the structure of both *The Lord of the Rings* and *The Epic of Gilgamesh*. It is the dramatic arc of *Moana*, *The Wizard of Oz*, *Star Wars* and the *New Testament*. It is a structure so common that some argue it is primeval, almost sacred – a story that humans use time and again to remind ourselves, and motivate ourselves, to broaden our horizons. It has remained in place for thousands of years, because humans have always had to motivate ourselves to face the fears beyond our comfort zones, and it is this narrative that offers us a reminder that doing so will lead to growth. The universality of the story is not just geographical or temporal, it is in the scope and variety of challenges it makes space for. The decision of our early ancestors to move down from the trees was an early heroic narrative. The moon landings were too. But that same structure can just as easily be applied to your decision to start doing Zumba. Small changes in our lives, be they new approaches, habits or locations, fit into the hero narrative regardless of their size, as long as they follow the following structure:

- A choice to do something new

- Some struggle to adapt to the outcomes of that decision

- Some growth as a result of sticking to it

When we place our experiences within a heroic narrative, it focuses us towards even greater growth, motivation and attention to the benefits we might access. Taken together, these small heroic journeys constitute a life lived more proactively, but they also fit rather seamlessly into the adoption of a heroic narrative about our *whole life*. As we will see, this can have powerful impacts on how we approach the good and bad that comes with it.

Creation of a narrative about our life is a central pillar of numerous self-help and therapeutic approaches. A narrative can create structure and meaning, and we have seen in the work described across this chapter how powerful those things can be. Some therapists use Guided Life Autobiography as a means to help individuals feel more in control of their lives, although it is more common in group settings. This is a practice by which ordinary people set out to write their own biographies (which we often reserve for the 'famous' or 'heroic') and, in the process of evaluating, sharing and shaping their stories, learn new ways to think about their experiences and themselves. Group members often report feeling *accomplished*, because self-knowledge is in itself an accomplishment, but also because we are more capable of seeing our life journey as a series of accomplishments when we take this narrative approach. Here we see that taking the time to treat our lives as worthy of discussion makes us feel more worthy of our own respect.

The Heroic Imagination Project,[9] a nonprofit research group who use findings in psychology to equip ordinary people with the knowledge to help them act heroically during hard times, goes further and encourages the specific shift towards a heroic account of our lives. In their view, individuals only have the power to make positive changes at a local or global level when they believe in their ability to make those changes. The best way to cultivate that self-belief is to learn to see ourselves as heroes and then act.

Finally, we can point to the Positive Psychology movement as another that encourages people to foster resilience and purpose through a reinterpretation of their lives as a transformative journey.

These varied researchers and therapeutic practitioners in different schools and fields all seem to agree on a central idea, which has been borne out across numerous studies. Individuals who frame their challenges as part of a meaningful narrative report higher levels of wellbeing[10] [11] and the adoption of a Hero's Journey Framework fosters a sense of agency which encourages individuals to take proactive steps towards personal growth. We all benefit from a good story, quite literally in the case of how we narrate our lives.

And we can *all* benefit from treating our lives as heroic journeys. Should you think your life is too mundane to qualify as one, then I would argue that the problem is not your life, but the lack of value you place on it. Being born, growing from childhood to adulthood and building a life is an incredible thing, regardless. We do not need to fight monsters or run into burning buildings to see heroism in it; we simply have to have chosen change and growth. The hero's journey has been re-written in a thousand ways, because it is the structure, not the hero or the scale of their challenges, that matters. The universality of it is in its simplicity: when we challenge ourselves, we grow, and we want to tell stories about ourselves and others who have.

EXERCISE: DEVELOPING A HERO'S JOURNEY NARRATIVE ABOUT OUR LIVES

- Where were you born?
- When did you choose to leave the safety of your parents' care, or had to by way of circumstances?
- Where did you go?
- What was hard about adapting to that new place?
- What did you learn about yourself?
- What did you learn to do that you could not before?
- What was your hardest moment?
- How did you overcome it?
- What are you proud of?
- Where did you return to and start building a new place from which new change could begin?

That is a hero's arc.

Now let's start again, from right now.

○ Where are you?

○ What is the next thing in your life that will be a departure from your usual way of life?

○ How might you have to adapt?

○ What could you learn about yourself?

○ What could you learn to do?

○ What might be hard?

○ How might you overcome it?

○ What might make you feel proud?

○ When you return to this place from where you started, how could you have grown?

Our lifetime is a hero's journey, full of smaller ones, of calls to adventure and growth, and if you do not see your life in that way, then your first journey will be towards greater appreciation of yourself and what you have achieved. This, too, is an adventure.

What we see in this new framing is a structure. Just as Antonovsky suggested, the more structure we can create around our challenges and our fears, the better we will feel about them. We learn that because a new challenge often bears some similarities to those we have overcome before, we *can manage* it. Finally, we see the third aspect of Antonovsky's framework: meaningfulness. A journey is never aimless, because the idea of ourselves as heroes gives it direction and purpose, wherever it may lead. Compare a wandering person with a hero on a journey, and weigh up how much more meaning is implied by that second formulation. They may be doing the same thing, but one is imbued with and empowered by meaning. The fears and stresses that befall a hero are very different from the surprises that could interrupt a walk, so frame your walks as heroic journeys, and your surprises as stressors that are priming your heroic mind and body to act. You face challenges, not threats, your fears are stress responses that enhance your ability to respond, and you succeed or fail to overcome them and grow in the process. At the very least, you have practised a 'stress-as-enhancing mindset', and, as we have seen, that is a powerful mechanism for growth.

The Placebo Effect

Narrative should never be underestimated. I learned that as a sportsperson who experienced vastly different levels of perform-ance as a result of the stories I told myself, but my small-case (N of 1) studies are borne out by one of the best researched phenomena in neuroscience. That phenomenon is the placebo: the measurable, physiological or psychological effect a human experiences simply by believing something to be true. The placebo is so widely researched because it is used as part of almost *every* good-quality research study, across pharmacology, neuroscience and medicine, in order to compare the effects of the chemical or drug that is being tested.

The power of the placebo should never be underestimated either. Thousands of studies have shown that simply taking a sugar pill can reduce our anxiety, lower our blood pressure and boost our immune system. As Dr Crum argues, they work because 'our mindsets activate our body's natural healing abilities' and as such they are 'the psychological and social foundation on which the total effect of any drug or therapy is placed'. In short, our narrative is often doing much of the legwork when it comes to our health.

Empowering narrative frameworks about the fears and challenges that appear in our lives are also powerful placebos, transformative tools that impact our subconscious through our conscious minds. When we apply a narrative framework and prime our body to create greater amounts of anabolic hormones, and less cortisol, we discover a key that opens aspects of our minds and bodies that we doubted we could access. It is a choice we can make which impacts things we thought we could not choose. We can *enhance* our bodies and minds with a stress-as-enhancing mindset, and render ourselves more heroic by telling ourselves a better story about ourselves.

Just as ideas and words willed new realities into existence, from industrial revolutions to suffragist movements, so too can the words we use to speak about our lives change them. We are not zebras: we can understand our worlds and fears, we can change our stories and narrate ourselves into heroism. It may begin with words for you, and the actions may follow. You may prefer, as I did as a teenager, to find adventure and see your worldview change. We need to understand the hard things and fears in our lives, not avoid or imagine them, and often the best way to understand something is to tell a story.

Whether you want to picture yourself as Gilgamesh, Moana or a Hobbit when you do, is up to you. It's your journey, and it's your life, so own and appreciate it for the heroic adventure that it is.

KEY TAKEAWAYS

1. Anxiety, and debilitating stress, are often the result of living in a constant state of arousal, where our brain is in an unending state of fear, perceiving and imagining threats which may never come to pass.

2. We can move from a 'threat' to a 'challenge' mindset by:

- Treating stresses as structured events – looking at their cause and effect

- Seeing the things that cause us stress as essentially manageable – thinking about our capabilities and how we can respond effectively

- Accepting occurrences that cause us stress are meaningful – they're part of life's journey

3. If we reappraise our stress responses as signs of our body doing what it *needs to do* rather than signs of rising panic, or threat, we respond better to the stressor.

4. Developing a 'stress-as-enhancing' mindset as opposed to a 'stress-as-debilitating' one makes us more psychologically secure, our outlook proactive and *even* primes our bodies to produce hormones that stimulate growth rather than those that signify psychological discomfort.

5. Narratives matter. Treating our lives as a heroic journey prepares us better for challenge and attunes us to potential opportunity. It may also encourage us to take adventures, leading to more growth. Your own narratives may be stronger than you think.

Be a hero.

3. Fear Is a Feminist Issue

Taking Our Fair Share of Adventure

It was not until 1988 that women were allowed to compete in track cycling events at the Olympics. The majority view was that riding around in a circle was too risky for our delicate bodies. This means that for the first eight years of my life, society could not even conceive of the person that I would become, let alone accept it. Which is striking. I don't say this to present myself as a trailblazer, or to shame the world of competitive cycling – I only bring up the fact to introduce a simple reality, of which you are probably already aware.

'What is possible' for women is often conditioned by what has previously been allowed, and our sense of 'who we can be' is constricted by all that has been hidden from us. When it comes to seeking out challenges or pushing ourselves outside of our comfort zones – as well as in so many other areas – a lack of representation matters. It is always more frightening to lead than to follow, and that is why we celebrate leaders, and firsts, because they pave the way for others to see that their fears should not be insurmountable.

Cycling may have caught up, but women are still generally thought to be more 'risk-averse' than men.[1] This view is culturally dependent and chock-full of assumptions,[2] but it is as limiting as it is pervasive. So I will provide some counterpoints to it, which centre on the idea that any difference in risk-aversion is broadly based on historical ideas about how men and women *should* behave[3] and is unlikely to be biological.[4] I will do so, because I would like to see more women enjoy the benefits of adventure, and I think the perception that it is *too high-risk* for us plays a role in our underrepresentation in adventurous activities.

Representation matters because as long as we mostly see men taking risks, and having adventures, it will be harder for women to feel they can do the same, and we stand to miss out on the joy, connection and growth that adventure can provide. I particularly want to look at why adventures – even everyday ones – can seem harder for women, and show how making them more accessible could have transformative personal and social impacts. I'll look at the barriers, at society's prejudice around women who don't stay in their lane, and what women in particular can stand to gain from embracing an adventure mindset. I'll discuss arguments from psychologists and sociologists who see the overrepresentation of men in fields like extreme sports (and, evidently, *track cycling*) as the result of social, rather than biological, factors. Then I'll make the case that adventure is only really associated with masculinity because, for a few hundred years, women were denied the right to do it. Once I have presented those arguments, I want to encourage you, whatever your gender, to go on a little adventure and take some sort of risk, because it's fun and because it's good for you. If you happen to be a woman, you may also enjoy the fact that you can undermine millennia of patriarchal misrepresentation simply by doing so.

Racing Against Men

The characterization of women and girls as fairer, softer or more risk-averse than men and boys came as a great surprise to me as a child. Alex and I thought of ourselves as twins first, individuals second, and a little boy and girl in distant third place. We certainly didn't consider that this seemingly superficial distinction would have any bearing on what we would be capable of or the activities we would be encouraged to do. I was therefore shocked whenever people in the wider world assumed my characteristics, and dare I say limitations, based on my gender. It seemed that the opportunities for active, headstrong girls were dependent on having an active, headstrong mother or father who could help them play sport or take risks. The difference in access was obvious, but I could also sense the more subtle differences in perception. I was good at sports, believed in the capability of my body, and used it with the conviction that is required for competition. I was certain, from my experiences with Alex in the garden, that this would be seen as a good thing. Yet throughout my school years it seemed to be *a problem*. People didn't want me to crash into tackles on the sports field, or run until I was a panting, sweating mess. It was somehow *unbecoming*. While I watched boys take a fast track towards social status through sporting ability, mine seemed to take me on a slippery slide towards oddity.

It made no sense, and felt deeply *unfair*. The approach my parents took to Alex and me was one of parity, but also fairness. We both got the same presents, similar toys and equal access to the world around us. As I got older, and went out into the world, the situation didn't always improve. There was the time I was told by a *national* coach that 'women's races were just there to fill time between the men's ones', or the many occasions on which I was asked by sports reporters about my plans for motherhood (rather than, say, a possible tenth world title). Needless to say, they were not asking my male teammates when they planned to become dads. These manifestations of societal unfairness – clear sexism – angered me in the same way when I was twenty-eight and the most successful female track cyclist of all time, as when I was eight and the discipline didn't exist yet. A lot changed, but a lot didn't. I haven't adapted to it, and I don't think I will until the world does too.

But I've never been one to let someone else set my limits. I'd rather grate against the world's expectations than change my expectations of myself. For example, at sixteen, after a few years of winning princely sums of up to £5 in girls' cycling races, I was told that there would be no more. There wasn't the demand for a junior girls' category and, as such, there was no ladder left for me to climb. I was told that the simplest thing would be to stop racing, or try a different discipline. This did not seem simple at all to me. I knew I was good at it and I liked that. In fact, it was stopping that seemed like the most difficult option, and as a result the hard path I chose seemed, then and now, quite straightforward. If there were no races for girls, then I would have to race against men.

There's no denying this was difficult, but those difficulties seemed temporary and paled into insignificance beside an alternative which involved closing down some part of myself. The easy way out may have involved less action, less blowback and fewer confrontations, but it would have entailed a great deal of internal disappointment. Option one, 'racing against men', meant losing, receiving strange looks and bearing a fair few critical comments. Option two, 'giving up', meant losing some part of myself and giving up on the one thing that made me feel capable. I could only conclude that the so-called easy way out would have been far harder on me.

So, I raced the blokes. It must have made for quite a sight. A passing observer who happened upon one of those muddy fields in an English backwater would have been confronted with a striking image. An objectively small teenage girl being given a minor head start in front of twenty large men in Lycra. The small girl would push off and pedal demonically in an attempt to hold off the stampede of wizened weekend warriors. They would watch something closer to a rabbit on a greyhound track, or a GCSE student wandering out in front of a herd of buffalo, than a Saturday race meet.

The aim was to try to keep ahead of them for as long as possible, to see how far I could push them, and then when their grunting mass (I could only hear them, there was not time to turn back and look) caught me up, I would tuck in my elbows and try not to get knocked off my bike. I did this for a good few months before I eventually *won*. Granted, this was a rare occurrence that could only take place in shorter races on particularly wet tracks where the men's extra weight pulled them deeper into the mud and slowed them down. To repeat, though, I *won* – and I felt great. I am not entirely proud to admit that I also loved the frustration it created. I revelled in the appeals the men made to stewards that 'it wasn't fair', that I got a head start or that they were held back by the conditions. All I could think was, *You're telling me!*

I loved winning, I still do, but I think I have always been more motivated by the opportunity to subvert expectations. The enduring sense, from my childhood, that it was wrong for people to assume women would be less driven, adventurous or motivated only gave me more of those things they thought I should lack. I knew I wouldn't go on competing against men (surely there would be a women's category at *some point*), but I intended to continue competing and living in the ways that I was told only men could. Drive, adventure and motivation simply could not be male traits, because they were cornerstones of exactly the sort of person I wanted to be.

Are Women *Really* More Risk-Averse than Men?

Let's start with a basic proposition that has been 'proven' in a number of studies: *Women are more risk-averse than men.* As we will see through numerous examples in this section, it is supposedly well tested and well understood, but when the feminist economist Julie Nelson reviewed decades of evidence with new approaches, she showed things were not so simple. Here are just a few of the assumptions and biases that she unpacked in her groundbreaking review, 'Are women really more risk-averse than men? A re-analysis of the literature using expanded methods'.

Firstly, we have to look at how risk is being defined in these studies. Risk-taking is an action that could either confer on us a benefit or a cost, an opportunity or a threat, and our evaluation of it is how we balance the two. As a result, this research has often taken the shape of a financial gamble, because this places reward and loss in clear terms.[5] [6] [7] For example, the question 'Would you stake £100 with an 80 per cent chance of it returning £200?' is a classic example of how risk appetite is often evaluated. The view that women are more risk-averse than men is often based on the greater willingness men show to make these risky investments than women. But very few studies discuss how financial advisors have historically *encouraged* women to be more risk-averse, with 'widows and orphans' (aka people *without* men) treated as a distinct investor category.[8] This group is not only considered more naturally risk-averse, but *advised to be*.[9] If we are assuming women are risk-averse because we make less risky financial decisions, it's worth keeping in mind that this is something we have been *told* to be.

Equally, these studies do not consider how cultural assumptions about the idea of an investor play into responses. The Austrian consumer psychologists Katja Meier-Pesti and Elfriede Penz[10] attempted to make this argument by priming men with an image of a male businessman or one holding a child before answering questions relating to financial and other risks. When they were 'masculinity primed' with the businessman, they showed a far higher propensity for risk than when 'femininity primed' with the baby. It could be that the image of the businessman *empowers* them to be risky or that the image of the child *reminds* them of the sort of responsibilities that women have traditionally been encouraged to consider when taking risks. Interestingly though, they did not find that 'being feminine' meant being risk-averse, only that 'being masculine' supported risk-taking.

Indeed, it's when analysis of risk-taking behaviour gets broken down beyond basic gender lines and starts to account for cultural ideas such as responsibility and security that more nuance emerges. For example, we see that a person's willingness to engage in risk-taking is highly correlated with how socially or financially insulated they are from negative outcomes.[11] Studies repeatedly show that wealthy, white men in the US are the great outliers when it comes to the willingness to take risks (Mark Zuckerberg's MMA career might be an example). This makes sense, as they are the group who are best insulated from negative outcomes (the Zuck can probably take the morning off for a doctor's visit and not worry about making rent). We don't just associate risks with wealthy men from politically influential groups because we have been shown enough James Bond and Iron Man films to last a lifetime, but because powerful men can actually better afford to fail, so their assessment of the relationship between opportunity and cost is different. They have the money to pay for treatments, time to recover if problems occur, and fewer dependents. A working-class single mother may have a very different attitude to helicopter-skiing than a billionaire playboy, because in the case where it goes wrong, her outcomes are materially more serious. This idea is borne out by findings on the 'White Male Effect',[12] which suggests that men from marginalized communities often displayed risk-aversion tendencies on many topics that were closer to females of any race than their white male counterparts, because of a combination of risks and a lack of insulation from them.

But the 'White Male Effect' is not the only reason we see women appearing more risk-averse in studies. Role models are well under-stood to be crucial to increasing participation and attainment for underrepresented groups, be that in work, education or sport.

Role models from our own social group help individuals envision 'possible selves' and navigate 'identity construction'[13] because seeing someone who looks like you doing things you have only dreamed of confirms that your goals are very real and possible. They also act as 'social vaccines'[14] against negative stereotypes because they offer a concrete counterpoint to the arguments that certain things are not possible for certain 'types' of people. 'If *she* can, *I* could' is a logical thought. Again, we see that because there are fewer historical precedents for women doing activities that are discussed in studies on risk (from investment to extreme sports), it follows that fewer women decide to take these risks. As with track cycling in the '80s, or many adventurous practices now, it's more difficult to imagine yourself doing something when you've never seen someone like you doing it.

In fact, the things we *define* as risk-taking and then use as evidence of gender differences are often the things that mainly men have historically done. But when we broaden the scope of what we consider to be risk-taking behaviour and include things like social risk (disagreeing with those close to us on important issues) or the willingness to take a small risk with the potential of a large (but unlikely) reward (like a lottery), we see women are as open to risk as men. When the psychologist Christine Harris and her team at the University of San Diego broke down risk into more concrete categories, the limitations of treating risk as a single thing became clear.[15] Men would take more financial risks (which we have seen could depend on the history of financial advice), recreational risks (again, extreme and adventure sports have a masculine history), and health risks (there is an argument that much of the history of the labour market is men risking their health for rewards), but in social situations women were equally open to risk. They also found that when it came to small risks with a large but unlikely reward, women were more likely to commit and more optimistic about the possibility of success, which is interesting because it is these final two categories that are less dependent on someone's 'insulation from negative outcomes'. It adds up that women have been treated as primary carers and so often only feel free to take risks that wouldn't compromise their families (social conflict or lotteries).

We simply do not have enough evidence on *very common* risk-taking practices, such as those that occur in the social world, and as such we are left with a very small, very specific account of the gender differences in risk-taking. And let's not forget, we are simply unable to quantify gender differences in risk perception when it comes to arguably the *most common* risk/reward calculation on earth: childbirth. I can't help but feel that factoring in many of the 140 million women who each year take a risk that has a 1 in 500 chance of killing them (globally, or 1 in 200 in Sub-Saharan Africa according to UNICEF's Maternal Mortality Database)[16] would provide a very different perspective on the risk tolerance of men and women to studies about imaginary stock portfolios (with the caveat that in many cases women do not have a choice).

Furthermore, it is important to acknowledge that there are other forms of risk which cannot be measured or analysed by economists, such as the risk of intimate partner violence (which is far more commonly committed against women) and the risks associated with being a woman in a public space. It is possible that the leap many people make from quite limited research to a view that women are more risk-averse stems from the observation that women perform more risk calculations to protect their safety every day. Factors like this should not contribute to any gendered idea of risk-aversion. They are safety calculations, based on real potential harms and the increased likelihood one group has of facing them versus another.

Finally, when it comes to the image of women as risk-averse

and more prone to cautiousness, we have to consider again what is idealized in terms of our behaviour. We present different levels of risk tolerance based on how we think we should appear and whether we feel we are presenting our gender in the correct way. A brilliant study by masculinity researcher Jonathan Weaver and his team in Florida[17] found that heterosexual men were far more likely to engage in risk-taking behaviours if they were primed by putting on scented hand lotion before the study (with some respondents specifying it was because it threatened their masculinity) and far less likely if they were primed by testing a power drill (which affirmed it). When they were 'made' to feel less manly, they decided to present as more risky, and when they were given the trappings of masculinity, they presented a less risky version of themselves. The difference between their self-described risk tolerance when they felt manly versus when they didn't was actually greater than the differences between male and female risk appetite in many studies which supposedly show that women are more risk-averse. This would suggest the difference between male and female risk appetites is in many cases about as strong as the effect of hand lotion or power drills on the risk appetite of this group of men. We can only wonder how many more variables there might be for women who supposedly present as more risk-averse.

This is a long way of saying that you should not be limited by cultural ideas about the risks you could take. You have control over your mind, your risk appetite and challenges. While history, social forces and a lack of role models may conspire against women taking the risks which may benefit them materially or allow them to enjoy the benefits of challenging, thrilling experiences, we have the power to recognize that this is not fixed. If women want to take some risks or go on challenging adventures, then we need not doubt our capacity to on any biological level – there is no evidence risk appetites are physically determined by sex and plenty of evidence of social constructs at play. Men, just be aware of what scented hand lotion could do to you.

What Women in Particular Can Gain from Using Adventure as Fuel for Happiness

We should also recognize that a lot of women may feel less comfortable with the idea of taking on adventures because of some ingrained ideas that adventurers are men (see the research on role models above). So let me say it now: women are innately no less adventurous than men; adventurers simply *were men* for a good few hundred years. This has led to a mistaken belief that adventurousness is somehow a masculine trait. Just as we should not assume the predominance of 'Great Male Artists' across five centuries reflects more innate artistry in men than women, but a set of social conditions which only allowed men to sell art, so too should we avoid associating adventure with masculinity because women were held back from it. Adventurousness is not innate, and the reasons we have far more male adventurers in our history books can be boiled down to three key factors:

1. The mistaken belief that adventure is about physical endurance and that this is for men.

2. The mistaken belief that adventure is about territorial conquest, i.e. for armies and that this means it is for men.

3. The institutions and organizations that funded adventures were, for the most part, made up entirely of men and only funded men.

Fortunately, these beliefs and circumstances have been rendered almost entirely redundant in time, and none of these three points should prevent women from taking on adventures.

Point I: Endurance

Countless women complete phenomenal feats of physical endurance every year, and it's actually in fields such as ultra-running that we see the least discrepancy between the physical performance of males and females. Athletes such as Camille Gerron, Jasmin Paris and Courtney Dauwalter actually win ultramarathons (100 miles or more) outright, beating all male athletes, and as a result we can safely say that compared to power events like weightlifting or short-track speed events such as sprinting, physical endurance is an arena in which women perform particularly well. There is also evidence that in competitive adventure sports tourism, there are fewer female participants, but a higher proportion of those female participants complete their objective[18] than males. Even if this could be explained by the fact that women who take on these challenges like expeditions are outliers, resourceful and committed because they have chosen to compete in a field where their presence is rare, it is still a fairly strong rebuttal to the assumption that women lack endurance.

Point 2: Territorial Conquest

Well . . . I don't think we're planning on conquering any territory, are we?

Point 3: Funding Committees

The sorts of adventures I am encouraging you to take do not need a funding committee. They can be free, local and require as little or as much time as you have spare.

When I look at these three assumptions about adventure, it's clear to me that there is significance in reclaiming it now. Every time a contemporary woman takes on an adventure, we create a new image of an adventurer that pushes back against outdated imagery. We can become case studies for future girls who would previously only have been shown Victorian men with trust funds when they looked for an example of an adventurer. You could go some small way to reclaim the practice from its colonial and expansionist framing, too. We may not undo any of the history of adventure as territorial expansion, but we can provide an alternative image for the record books, one in which the expansion is internal, of strength, agency, confidence or possibility. This may seem grand, and you are right to say that joining a women's hiking trip to Snowdonia won't knock Edmund Hillary off his perch or take Dr Livingstone's name off the numerous African landmarks he renamed, but it might at least help update our mental image of an adventure (or adventurer). If even some of us doubt our fitness to take risks or go on adventures because they have historically been male-dominated, your decision to present an alternative might be the reason some future girl believes in herself. That girl *might* inspire a thousand others, and in some way we can gradually reclaim the satisfying, healthy and *natural* practice of adventuring from its overtly gendered, colonial roots.

Or you may simply open up the space for one more person to use the adjective 'adventurous' to describe themselves. This is no small feat. As we've discussed, people often need to first see things in others before seeing them in themselves, and it may be your adventurousness that encourages someone to see their own potential. This opening up of space for self-identification is a powerful thing. We discussed the power of narrative in the previous chapter, and honed in more specifically on how framing our own lives as a hero story can make us more resilient to setbacks and more motivated towards goals. But many of us may need *permission* to frame ourselves and our lives in such a way, and seeing someone else do so might give that permission.

To recap, our adventures can:

1. Turn the dial on an image of women as necessarily risk-averse
2. Reclaim the mantle of adventurers from Victorian men
3. Show the next generation that *anyone* can be an adventurer
4. Allow those people to apply the adjective *adventurous* to themselves
5. Gain the benefits of adventurous play we described in Chapter 1, and the adventurer's narrative from Chapter 2

These factors alone would make setting out on an adventure worthwhile. But they're not all. They're not even the most important reasons.

The Adventure Advantage

Adventure is *good* for us, and all of the social and political motivations for adventuring rest on that fact. I would not want to reclaim adventurousness for the next generation of women if it were not fundamentally a good thing. Now, clearly, adventurousness can be a *useful* thing – we may make the friends of a lifetime, meet the love of our life, or find our dream job/hobby as a result of something that we call an adventure, but that is not my point here. I am saying that *even* if you did not find any of those good things in the space beyond your comfort zone, there is benefit in adventuring for adventure's sake. That the process *is* the outcome worth pursuing.

So what does this process look like? What is an adventure? First it may be useful to clarify what adventure is not. Adventure is not *necessarily* dangerous. Just as our image of an adventurer has been shaped by history to look like a Victorian man, so too has our story of adventure been shaped by history and tragedy. We learn about unsuccessful adventures (Scott of the Arctic) and successful ones where people overcome near-death experiences (Edmund Hillary, and *Touching the Void* by Joe Simpson) because these are dramatic stories, but we benefit just as much from broadening our scope of adventure as we do from broadening our idea of an adventurer.

Our adventures are as personal as we are. They can take us into uncharted psychological, social or geographical territory, but in my view they do not have to put us in danger. What they do have to present is a degree of unpredictability, some unknowns and some adaptation on our part as we adjust and adapt to novel (preferably natural) circumstances. The best description I have read of an adventure was given by the adventure psychologist Eric Brymer (who we will meet later in this chapter). He describes it as 'going knowingly into the unknown',[19] and while much of the research about the psychological benefits of adventure is drawn from studies on people involved in more extreme pursuits, I believe that the benefits of an adventure are relative to our individual comfort zones, experience and the knowledge we have.

So let's look at some of that research on the role of adventure in mental and physical wellbeing, and then consider the forms of adventure that may be the most impactful – and the most doable every day, with a particular focus on adventures that get us moving and take us outside. For example, a project at Nottingham University studied the effects of outdoor adventure projects on the wellbeing and self-efficacy of different groups of work colleagues. Repeatedly they found that these adventures took people somewhere new, and developed their sense of capability by encouraging them to adapt to these novel, uncertain situations.[20] Adventures offer us clear markers, events or milestones that allow us to track progress and personal growth, which is a means by which we can build self-esteem, strength and confidence. Equally, adventures are a reminder or a refresher course in how adaptable we can be. For many of us, throughout the course of our lifetimes, things become set – we do similar things, with the same people, and often start to believe we might be incapable of doing things differently. An adventure is a period of self-directed adaptation, where we take ourselves to a place we have never been before and remind ourselves of our ability to adapt to such novelty. This sense of our own adaptability breeds confidence in our ability to make changes in our lives. For the adventure psychologist Patrick Boudreau at the Ara Institute in New Zealand, adventure not only prepares us to *make* changes, but also *primes us* to see the changes that are forced upon us for the adventures that they are.[21]

Equally, adventures encourage us to practise excitement, awe and joy, because they promote those emotions, but also, in my view, because the simple act of calling something an adventure sets us up to focus on these aspects of the experience. That alone is a good enough reason to go on an adventure, as excitement, awe and joy are key components of an enjoyable life, but these emotions also become more natural to us the more we practise them. Just as repeated exposure to threats will make us see the world as threatening, so too can repeated experiences of joy and awe encourage us to see the world as joyful or awe-inspiring.

How to Have an Adventure

I have read a lot about what makes for an adventure, and experienced quite a few, and as far as I can see the following seven characteristics seem to come up a lot. Whether big or small, adventures seem to involve:

1. Novelty: Doing something new or out of routine

2. Uncertainty/Risk: Not knowing what will happen; perceived or real risk

3. Challenge: Facing and overcoming something difficult or unfamiliar

4. Agency: Choosing and owning your actions

5. Engagement: Being absorbed and present in the moment (flow)

6. Growth: Learning, mastery or transformation as a result

7. Remarkability: The experience is memorable or 'worth talking about'

We will look at these seven elements individually, but first it is important to acknowledge that these characteristics make space for adventures of different sizes. An adventure could take us around the world, or it could take us to the park. Genuinely. What matters is not the distance we cover or the danger we face, but the reality of the experience relative to our comfort zone. If we do not know what will happen, think some aspect might be difficult and know it is on us to see it through, we're halfway to an adventure. If we take the opportunity to do something new to us, if we learn something, lose ourselves and want to tell the tale, then we have done it all. We have had a complete adventure with all of the healthy fear and benefits to our confidence that come when we step outside of our comfort zone.

You may choose to have a *microadventure*. These smaller-scale experiences are the everyday adventures we have discussed; they still have the core elements of adventures, but take a smaller, cheaper and simpler form. I warn you that they can be something of a gateway drug to macroadventures, but I have no problem recommending them. (Just don't come to me if you become a so-called adrenaline junkie down the line!)

The term 'microadventure' was coined by the British adventurer, author and motivational speaker Alastair Humphreys, who spent four years cycling 46,000 miles around the world (this is very much not a microadventure). He wanted to create an accessible idea that offered people with busy lives and limited resources a way to access the benefits of adventure and encourage 'enthusiasm, ambition, open-mindedness and curiosity'. In his words, we only need to seek opportunities for adventure, rather than the constraints that get in the way, to begin our adventure journey. So don't just go to an improv class, call it your microadventure in comedy; put yourself forward for the *adventure* of a solo in your choir or stop going on holiday and start *exploring*. As we saw in Chapter 2, the narrative we create around our behaviours has the power to transform our attitude and their impact.

The Opportunities: The Anatomy of a Microadventure

So let's think about what one of these microadventures might look like based on the seven characteristics listed above. We're going to assume you don't have a great deal of time or lots of cash and live relatively near a town or city. Let's say you're a working mum, and live around Manchester. You would like something that you can do in an hour, that's exercise but not *just* exercise and that feels fun. Okay.

This is the Salsa Class Microadventure.

1. **Novelty:** You take a look at your routine. You feel, as you sometimes do, that it is a bit predictable. You would like something that feels a bit *different*, not always, but sometimes. You know that before you had kids you loved dancing. So you look up 'Salsa classes Manchester'. The lesson is an hour. It's near the train station. It's £8 for the lesson or £15 for three. That's doable for you. It's not free and it's possible the kids will turn the house upside down between 6:40 and 7:40 on a Tuesday, but it would be *novel* (the class, not the upside-down house – sadly that would be routine). So this ticks the novelty box. You check your partner can be home on time and then you book the three sessions. Everyone likes a deal.

2. **Uncertainty/Risk:** It's Tuesday afternoon and you had last night's curry for lunch. Was it too heavy? Will it weigh you down? There's a risk that you'll be too sluggish to salsa and everyone there is miraculously good. You don't know what the teacher is like, but you *do* know that you're not a gorgeous Colombian. You don't know anyone there. You do know that you are a nervous sweater. You stop, remind yourself that there's nothing to be done now, the class is booked and the husband is secured for parental duties. So you accept that you won't know anyone, will feel awkward at some point and will probably make some mistakes. You remind yourself that if you felt certain about it all then it would probably feel routine. The uncertainty *is* the fun, and it *is* the reason for the microadventure. The sweat you could take or leave.

3. **Challenge:** You arrive. Everyone seems to know each other. They're doing *warm-ups*. You don't know any warm-ups, so you do a sort of wiggle and shake. It actually feels all right and one of the *actual* warm-up people smiles at you. That was nice. The class starts and you get paired with the woman beside you. It's mostly women. You feel ungainly, uncoordinated and possessed with all the grace of a Maris Piper potato. You and your partner laugh each time one of you makes a mistake, but you commit to listening, learning and trying your best. You remember that the whole point is to learn. Twenty minutes in and you feel less like a potato.

4. **Agency:** You get paired with someone a bit better at salsa and less smiley. This part is less fun. You feel a bit self-conscious when you go in entirely the wrong direction at an important moment and would, frankly, like to leave. Then you say (internally) that you chose to do this, and you're already better than you were at the start (at the wiggling stage), so you must be doing something right. You aren't here to please your partner, but to do something new. And you're doing it.

5. **Engagement:** You do it. By *it*, we don't mean perfect salsa, or even a full correct set of moves, but you *dance*. You get into it and lose track of time. There is a state of something like flow where you are thinking only about the music, your moves and your partner's feet (not the one at home). This is probably exactly the moment that your house is being turned upside down. You feel great and the hour is up before you notice.

6. **Growth:** You are now prone to do a few salsa steps while stirring food on the hob. You add a little side step in mid-hoover. You feel a little bit proud when you tell your colleagues that you have to leave for salsa. Your boss says that sounds fun and says she's been getting her partner to try for ages and you feel even more proud when you say you go by yourself. At the class you now join in with the people who know how to warm up. You still wiggle a bit, and they do too.

7. **Remarkability:** At after-work drinks on Friday people ask you how salsa was. You tell them about being a potato and going in the wrong direction, then you show them a step you've learned. They smile, and you feel glad that you started – it's worth talking about. The next day you show your husband how to do a move while you're watching *Strictly*. You feel pretty good.

You have not trekked across a desert, or leapt out of a plane. You packed a pair of leggings on a Tuesday and got home by half-eight. You faced the fear that comes with doing something new and had a microadventure, and you might just feel a little bit better about your life, and the person living it.

Joy and Awe Every Day

Adventures are often our most direct route towards joy and towards awe. They are a means to practise these things in our everyday lives. While the most powerful adventures will often involve some engagement with the natural world, microadventures such as the Salsa Caper are still valuable on their own terms. We use the same brain on a mountaintop as we do on our commute, for example, and if our journey to work fails to inspire awe, joy or excitement, then it is up to us to provide our brains with other ways to access it. There *is* wonder to be found on the commute, and we may only be missing it because we are no longer priming our brains to see the world as awe-inspiring. In fact, the passage of hundreds of thousands of people to and from places every day *is* awe-inspiring. Nearly seven million people ride the Tokyo Subway every day, for instance, and that is objectively awe-inspiring – the interconnection, the logistics, the sheer movement (it's a bit like salsa . . . you know?) – but it feels mundane because we tend not to switch our perspective outside of it and we tend not to practise novelty, joy or awe. When we prime ourselves to experience these things, though, we see them in places we never expected, and when we reframe our perspective through adventure, we can see the very ordinary-seeming aspects of our lives in extraordinary ways. We need adventures from an everyday existence to rediscover quite how much of an adventure everyday existence really is.

We benefit particularly when that adventure takes place out into the natural world, and if we reconnect with the natural world, modern life can be reframed as extraordinary (rather than mostly a bit *annoying*). And adventure in the natural world is in *our* nature: our ancestors were the apes that decided to leave the trees, they chose the adventure of leaving forest for savannah and the savannah for the wider world. We could just as well give our species the name *Homo exploratus* as *Homo sapiens*, because what has defined us is a call to exploration and adventure in the natural world. At least, it defined us until the last few hundred years.

When I spoke to the psychologist Eric Brymer, one of the world's foremost authorities on the mental benefits of adventure, he was very keen to emphasize how *unnatural* our contemporary environment is. In fact, he went as far as to describe our modern human existence in a concrete world in terms of a tiger in a cage. Our minds and bodies are refined and attuned to the natural world, to walk long distances, see beyond the horizon and sleep beneath stars. He has consistently found health and wellbeing benefits to adventure, but many of them he can bring back to the natural components of the experience: nature is natural and adventure is in our nature. In his eyes, the human form of life is an adventurous one, and those adventures take place in the open air. I imagine that his decision to divide his academic placements between the open air of Yorkshire and Australia's glorious Queensland coast is a testament to that fact.

We also tend to associate adventure with dangerous risks, but Dr Brymer does not think we need to. Adventure may involve the unknown, but it does not necessarily involve danger, and our tendency to associate the two may be a mistake of framing. Those historical associations we discussed, between adventurousness and masculinity, cut both ways. We see men as more adventurous because of our history, but in fact we may mistakenly attribute a certain rugged form of masculinity to adventure. We set heavy-metal soundtracks to snowboarding expeditions, picture beards and boots, bros and badasses. This is not a necessary link; adventure can just as easily be peaceful as it can be extreme, and if we primarily locate the benefits of adventure in connection to the natural world, then we have even more reason to emphasize these peaceful aspects. To Dr Brymer, the most transformative adventures involve a process of attuning to the natural world. While the built environment we mostly move in has direction encoded into it – *these are steps, for walking up; that is a terrace, so you can sit there; this is a park, so play is permitted* – nature has no such direction. It is adventurous because we are free to engage with it on the terms we choose, and as a result it opens up our range of 'affordances' or possibilities. Adventure, and particularly adventure in nature, is an exercise in increased possibility.

It is also an opportunity to reframe our relationship with threats and stressors. If we think back to the 'threats' that underpin many of our contemporary anxieties, they revolve around other people's perceptions of us or hypothetical things that are unlikely to happen. When we adventure in the natural world, we engage with something that does not perceive us, does not lie, and presents threats that are open to our evaluation. It is an opportunity to live with a challenge, but without the threat of judgement, to engage with a space that does not require the social mind-reading which causes so much stress and allows us to decide which threats are worth caring about. There is no point worrying about avalanches on a surfing trip, or great whites on a mountain. In fact, there is no point worrying about such things even in places where they exist, only preparing for them. Adventurers, and people who engage in adventure sports (skiing, surfing, base-jumping), are calculating – they will usually have a far healthier ability to assess risk than people who do not engage in them. As Dr Brymer said, the characterization of such people as risk-takers is in fact misguided, for what they are is *capable risk-assessors.*

Neither are adventurers adrenaline junkies. In both my and Dr Brymer's experience, adrenaline is the last thing that someone should be running on during an outdoor adventure. Adrenaline is a sign that something has gone wrong, as there is rarely reason to fight or fly, freeze or fawn on an adventure unless there is an extreme and highly unlikely outcome to face. I feel like adventure and adventure sports have simply had terrible branding, run by a few frat-bros who think that they are more likely to impress people by presenting what they do as lethal. This is normal – young men like to exaggerate and they like to impress their friends by emphasizing the frightening and dangerous things they overcome – but it has resulted in a misconception about adventure itself. People talk about staring down death or conquering Everest, but as Dr Brymer put it, 'Everest doesn't even know you're on it, and there is no competition here.' Adventure, when presented through a hyper-masculine (and immature) framing of battles, conquest and death-defiance, misses the point. It is in fact more about peace, humility and life-preservation. Some may call these things feminine, but in my eyes they are simply some of the more laudable aspects of humanity.

The professor described adventure as more like a dance with the natural world than any sport or battle. No one tries to 'win' a dance – we simply enjoy it and the relational aspects between ourselves and our partner. If we try to dominate another in a dance, it becomes a wrestling match; if we try to win, it becomes a sport. We learn about what we can and can't control through adventure and this dance with nature, and that is a deeply profound idea that we will come back to at many points during this book. Trying to control things that we cannot and being controlled by things that we can is the basis of so much tension in our lives. Just as a kayaker knows they cannot control the river, but only try to move along with grace rather than friction, so too can we all learn about those aspects of our lives that are rivers and find grace. We cannot control everything in our existence, but we can learn how to differentiate between what we can and cannot, preparing when possible and seeking grace when it is not. Adventures are an exercise in reclaiming and ceding control, seeing we are capable of it when we need to be and flexible when the river takes charge.

The fear that we are not sufficient to face life's challenges can be approached from a number of directions, but all can begin with adventure. We can learn about what we are actually capable of, and see that we are enough. We can learn about challenges, so that we can better evaluate them and what they ask of us. We can see that in some cases the challenges cannot be overcome and accept that as part of the package. In the process, you may gain connection and trust with your body.

This is no small thing; we think of fear as a product of our minds, but neglect the fundamental reality that it is part of our body. It is our bodies that grow sick from stress-related illness. It is our stomachs where the butterflies live and our feet that tap restlessly. We pick our scalps and bite our nails and control our food because of this thing that we are told lives in our minds. We seek solutions through thought alone, and try to remedy a whole-body problem with only mental progress. There is room for the physical. Our minds move when our bodies do, our thoughts progress as we take steps and our horizons broaden when horizons broaden.

So try to seek an adventure, preferably in the natural world, for the sake of your mind and your body. You do not need to book a flight to Nepal or fire up a heavy-metal playlist (but you can, and I have), because the best change is gradual. Take a walk, somewhere safe, you have never walked before. Swim in the sea even though it's cold. Down the line, the gradients on your walks may rise and you may swim further, but that is for another day. What you can do this week, with the limits of time, money or dependents, is the perfect place to start. The career I had didn't exist when I was born, and the future you may grow to love might be beyond your imagination as you sit and read this.

Isn't that exciting?

KEY TAKEAWAYS

1. Women are no less adventurous than men. Just less represented in the history of adventure. By being adventurous, contemporary women have an opportunity to undermine this.

2. Adventure is anything that takes us outside of our comfort zone, internally or externally, but at best it will take place in the natural world.

3. It does not need to be dangerous, but it is an opportunity to better understand risks and rewards, our fears and responses to them.

4. Everyday adventures can help us see the adventure in the everyday.

5. Adventure gives us freedom to see what is possible, and we can grow this possibility gradually with small steps.

Don't fight; don't try to win. Dance.

4. Fear of Failure

What Are You Really Afraid of?

I learned to win quite early in my career. While it wasn't always easy, it was simple. I raced other girls at school or my older adversaries who sank into the mud, and if I pedalled harder, lasted longer or got luckier in my pursuit of the finishing line, I could win. Winning is a simple thing, sketched in black and white, a science that can be reduced to force output, friction and drag. Success can take seconds – but failing? Failing is the project of a lifetime.

I am still learning to lose and how to fail. It is no small project, because the simplicity of victory is matched by the complexity of failure and the many fears it generates. Just as a list of threats can be infinitely long and a set of goals or challenges satisfyingly short, the consequences of failure can seem endless. While we can package success, gift-wrap and tie it up with a bow, failure is liquid – it takes the shape of the fears that surround it and seems to flow outward. While success comes with a full stop, failure is an ellipsis.

That was a lesson I learned from the psychiatrist who changed my life, Professor Steve Peters. He was my rock within Team GB and the person who taught me the single most important truth about the fear of failure: that it doesn't exist. Fear of failure is an ellipsis because, as Steve recently reminded me, we do not fear failure itself, we fear its consequences; it is liquid because it takes the shape of the knock-on effects we most fear. It is not the missing trousers in the anxiety dream that embarrasses us, but the consequent laughter. So too it is not the split-second between first and fourth, but the disappointment you might generate, the value you might lose or the *failure* you might become. The moment in which we fail is not the problem, but what we all mistakenly believe will happen when it inevitably comes.

So I'm going to show you why the fear of failing should never be enough to stop you trying, and how accepting failure as a learning experience offers us the opportunity to better understand ourselves and to be proactive in our life, pursuing our dreams rather than avoiding our nightmares.

How I Successfully Learned to Fail

Our fear of failure grows in proportion to the view we hold of ourselves, the cruelty we imagine in others' hearts and the attachment to what it is we might lose, and that is why I never feared failing when I started out in cycling. Around the time I was tucking in my elbows to avoid the Home Counties buffalo, we received a call at home on the landline. These were not the days when you assumed such a call to either be incredibly serious or telemarketing (there is now no in-between when it comes to landlines); it was an ordinary thing. Or at least I thought it was. A national team coach had been scouring the back pages of *Cycling Weekly* and highlighted the name 'V. Pendleton', which seemed to keep cropping up in the results section. He liked the consistency with which my name appeared, and suggested that I come up to Manchester and do some physical tests. We were still a few years away from professionalism in women's cycling, so what now looks like the start of an illustrious career then seemed like a chance to move up into the ranks of elite amateurs. No matter how well the tests went, and the career that followed, I would still always be a part-time cyclist with another job, but that didn't stop us from driving up to Manchester like Charlie and his grandfather on the way to the Chocolate Factory. The tests were quite straightforward and my performance was good, if not outstanding. I could probably go on to have a good semi-professional career in either track or road cycling. We both knew which I would choose. Road cycling at that time was even less well-developed as a woman's sport than track.

At eighteen, I was accepted on to the national programme and invited to train with them at the Manchester velodrome a few times a year. That was quite a steep learning curve, literally, as the banks on a velodrome are far steeper and more perilous than any field in Hertfordshire. I took to it though, and had no sense of potential success or failure. I would do something I enjoyed, while studying at university, and it felt like all opportunity and no cost. Then things started to accelerate, and some of my fears did too.

By coincidence, the Commonwealth Games were taking place in Manchester that year and I was called up. The games themselves were fun; it was novel to be in a competitive environment and perform in front of a crowd, but while my teammates collected golds, I went out in the first round. I felt in some way I had disappointed them, which of course I had not. I was acting out an imagined consequence of failure, and if I were to counsel that young girl today, I would tell her not that she would go on to greater things, but that no one really cared. Ride your bike. Enjoy it. It's not a bigger deal than your happiness and never will be, no matter what many millions of people will seem to tell you some day down the line.

When I qualified for the Olympics in Athens, my sense of potential grew, as did the idea that people were investing and relying on me. Only then did I really start to feel the fear of failure and its consequences. Athens was another level to Manchester. An Olympic Games is an incredible thing – a sort of United Nations

Summit of (seemingly) superhumans; a collection of the most diverse but finely tuned bodies on the planet meeting in one place, coiled springs, a mass of tension, hope and expectation. (If you've ever watched a scene in a sci-fi film where an intergalactic federation of very different-looking aliens all meet under one roof, it's a bit like that. There's a 4ft 10 gymnast at a buffet beside a 7ft 1 basketball player and they are both ostensibly doing the same thing.) The hope was not something I felt, but the tension and expectation was. I was still young, my brain was still developing, and what would have seemed like a fever dream of opportunity only a couple of years previously felt like an even greater stage from which to fall. I didn't really think I could win, but I felt certain that I could lose in more consequential ways than ever before, and my focus was almost entirely on avoiding that.

Naturally, the worst-case scenario followed. I was knocked out in the first round after receiving a tough draw against a stronger, more experienced Russian, and this time I felt the world was watching. I was distraught and I wanted to give up, there and then, but it was when I returned home that I began working with Steve Peters and started to see the opportunity to turn my fear of failure into desire for success.

Steve is fatherly, kind and fiercely intelligent. He did not come into elite sport from the perspective of a coach or sports psychologist, but after a number of years working as a teacher and medical doctor (of psychiatry) in drug and alcohol rehabilitation. Steve did not speak the language of marginal gains, force output or performance optimization. He started from a place of compassion and a desire to know his athletes and help us to know ourselves. This is where the idea of a fear of the consequences of failure, rather than failure itself, came in. In Steve's eyes, we are much more capable of engaging with our fear of failure if we untangle the web of imagined consequences we perceive. If I said, 'I fear competing in front of a big crowd and losing', he would have to admit there was nothing he could do. I would compete in front of big crowds, and I *would* lose (this is true, whatever your work – whether it is a sale falling through, job application being rejected or customers leaving dissatisfied). The only way we could act upon my fear was if we looked at the consequences I was imagining, the beliefs that underpinned them and the mindsets I used to process them. The fear of losing in front of that crowd might really be a fear of the consequence that they would judge me or think I was foolish. That was up for discussion; I too had been in crowds and watched people lose, and I had never thought they were foolish because of it (just as you didn't think someone foolish when *you* rejected a job application or decided against making some purchase). So we moved past that. Then we dug deeper: what was it that I really believed would happen if I tried and failed? It became clear, through our sessions, that my core belief (a deeply held assumption that guides how we see ourselves) was that my success was the thing that made me valuable as a person. I assumed that I raced, and won, to *make* myself worthy. By extension, failing and losing publicly meant I lost that value. I did not fear failure, and I did not fear failing in front of crowds – I feared the loss of my self-worth, and that terrified me.

Core Beliefs

Our core beliefs are unique to us, but many of us do share similar ones. They may go back to our childhood experiences when we began framing the world, our value systems and our sense of self. It may be that we felt popular as a child, until we made a mistake in class and someone told us we were an idiot. We may then continue through our lives believing our value is somehow tied to being correct and go to great pains to remain correct even when it causes ourselves and others pain. It may have been that our families or social groups made us feel more appreciated when we did well at something, such as a sport or an instrument, and as such we embedded the sense that we must do well to be valuable, which was the case for me. We may believe that we have to be a peacekeeper, a model citizen or brave to be worthy, when in reality our very existence as humans gives us inherent value.

Our fear of failure is *deeply* predicated on our core beliefs about what makes us valuable, and it is only by understanding those core beliefs and the mistaken reasoning within them that we can see failure for what it is. A disappointment – but one that does nothing to undermine our inherent value as people. I told Steve that I wanted to race and to win to show people that I *could* do it. What he helped me understand was that I attached my self-worth, my basic value as a person, to capability. Failure entailed the consequence of incapability, and incapability meant I became worthless. I didn't fear losing; I feared being proved right, that I was somehow worthless. He helped me to engage with that core belief, to understand my intrinsic worth and to understand that it did not change with success or failure.

We discussed what I feared, in particular the core belief about a loss of worth, before discussing what I wanted. This wider project of helping me to understand myself was psychologically beneficial but also (sneaky Steve) profound in a sporting sense. It is only through self-knowledge that we can engage with our fear of failure, but it is also integral to first understand what success *actually is* to us. We often spend so much time fixating on the terrible things that might come from failure, that we never discover what we actually want. You may be well acquainted with the idea that you would be a failure if you were rejected for that job, but do you know that you would finally feel like a success if you weren't?

So remember to think about what you actually want. It is a powerful antidote to the fear of failure and a fundamental way in which you can start working back from your eventual success to the approach you'll take to reach it. The key for me is that it encourages proactivity rather than avoidance. When we tease out the consequences we fear, we begin to understand what we're trying to avoid, but when we think about who we are and what we want, we can begin to decide on the steps that we'll take to get there. Of course, this is a complex process, and there'll be many points along the way where we have to be reminded of our ability to do it, but it's really the best and only option if we are to pursue any meaningful goal.

EXERCISE: UNDERSTAND YOUR CORE BELIEFS

Step 1: Identify Automatic Thoughts

Begin by noticing recurring negative thoughts or emotional reactions in daily life.

Write down a recent situation where you felt distressed, and note the thoughts that went through your mind.

Step 2: Use the Downward Arrow Technique

Take one of your automatic thoughts and ask yourself:

O 'If this thought is true, what does that mean about me?'

O 'Why would it be so bad if this were true?'

Continue asking these questions (like peeling layers of an onion) until you reach a deeper, more global belief about yourself, others, or the world.

Example:

Automatic thought: 'I made a mistake at work.'

Q: 'If that's true, what does it mean?'

A: 'It means I'm not good at my job.'

Q: 'If I'm not good at my job, what does that mean?'

A: 'It means I'm a failure.'

Core belief: 'I am a failure.'

Step 3: Evaluate the Core Belief

Write down your core belief.

Rate how strongly you believe it (0–10).

List evidence that supports this belief.

List evidence that does not support this belief (even small exceptions count).

Step 4: Challenge and Reframe

Ask yourself:

O 'Is this belief always true?'

O 'Are there times when it's not true?'

O 'What would I say to a friend who held this belief?'

Try to develop a more balanced or compassionate alternative belief.

Example: Instead of 'I am a failure', try 'I sometimes make mistakes, but I also succeed and learn'.

Step 5: Behavioural Experiment (Optional)

Test your new belief in real life. For example, try a new task at work and notice the outcome. Gather evidence for and against your old and new beliefs.

Why This Works

This activity helps you uncover the roots of recurring negative thoughts, see how they shape your feelings and actions, and create space for more balanced self-understanding.

Research shows that identifying, questioning and reframing core beliefs can reduce distress and improve emotional wellbeing.

Taking Feedback

Most people exhibit something called 'negativity bias', which is essentially a tendency to pay more attention to criticism than praise.[1] Moreover, the extent to which we bias criticism is greater the lower our self-esteem. This is something to be conscious of when we are trying to understand success and failure, but also thinking about progress in general. If we are hurt by criticism (which we need not necessarily be – in many ways it is essential to progress), then we should be aware of our tendency to give it more weight than praise.

This was certainly a challenge for me when I took feedback. In part because of my core belief about my value (it wasn't solved in one conversation with Steve, and it remains a work in progress), I tended to accept negative feedback far more readily and deeply than the positive. I needed to do well to be of basic value, so affirmations just returned me to a baseline level of self-worth, while criticism retained the power to undermine any amount of positive feedback. If you need to do well to be good enough, then there is only room to fall. Steve recently reminded me of a time when a rival told me that I 'would never be the queen of sprints, always a princess'. Weird, I know. But at the time I took it to heart – I really believed it, and somehow it carried more weight than all of the other people who had expressed more positive sentiments. Steve and I worked on that, on the power that I placed in the hands of critics over supporters, and the relationship that held to my core belief about my value. He also used it to weaponize my incredible contrarian streak.

Steve knew, very early on, that I was deeply motivated by proving people wrong. This could stem back to my experiences of being told I was somehow not able to do the things boys were (when, as a twin, I had put that question to bed). He saw that I could be positively motivated by proving I was the Queen of the Track (my mechanics had nicknamed me QV – Queen Vic) and that this was worlds away from fearing I would be worthless if I failed. It was a goal, a challenge and a pursuit, rather than avoidance.

Thankfully, there are steps we can all take to help us move toward a mindset where we feel appreciated when praised and motivated by criticism or feedback. The key is to pay more attention to the praise that we often ignore, and feel less impacted (on a personal level) by the criticism we receive. So first, to praise. In professional spaces, praise or recognition is often so muted we don't even notice it. A good piece of work may receive a short 'thanks' or 'thumbs-up emoji', which is a shorthand for a well-done. At home we may receive the same reaction for a well-cooked meal (those of you with teenagers may *actually* get the emoji). The mistake many of us make is to think of these responses as evidence that we are meeting some minimum standard. We think we are doing as we *should*, when really the other person is telling us we are doing well. The more we can take a 'thanks' and tell ourselves 'well done', the more we are topping up our sense of value for the efforts that we make. Furthermore, we are preparing to see feedback not as a sign that we have dropped *below* the required level, but towards some ideal one.

This is where our response to feedback or criticism comes in. We all feel stung by criticism to some greater or lesser degree. My first tip is to separate that feedback from our self-worth as much as possible, and see it as a reflection of something we have made or done rather than who we are. The difficulty of being told 'this is not good enough' is something we can overcome, but if we take it as shorthand for '*you* are not good enough', then we risk having our self-image impacted by feedback that may in fact be productive. We will naturally grow defensive and miss out on the opportunity to improve whatever it is that we have worked on.

I was pleasantly surprised, when researching the subject of feedback and criticism, to find the work of psychologist and leadership consultant Nick Wignall, who discussed the importance of reframing criticism as an *opportunity* rather than an attack.[2] In his view, once we have separated criticism from our self-worth, we can always frame it as a question: 'What can this situation teach me – about myself, others, or the topic at hand?' The feedback we receive could be teaching us about our own way of working; it might highlight differences of opinion between ourselves and the person giving us feedback; or it could reflect genuinely useful insight about the specific thing we are working on. Our conclusion may be that we differ from our critics on what has been achieved or what we are trying to achieve, but we can be confident that we are learning something in the process.

So, starting today:

1. Note down the things you would like to praise yourself for, that no one else seemed to remark on.

2. Look for a moment when someone expresses gratitude (*nice one, thanks*) and elevate it to what it really is, praise and positive feedback.

3. Look for a moment when you feel you have received negative feedback and ask why. Is there genuinely something you could learn from it – about yourself, someone else or your work?

4. Recall a piece of feedback that hurt you – particularly because you took it as a statement that *you* weren't good enough, and try to separate it from your self-worth.

Neither praise nor criticism should change your opinion of yourself.

Proactivity vs Avoidance

Much like the ways in which we have distinguished between a 'threat' mindset and a 'challenge' one, in sport and life we can also separate out 'proactive' approaches from 'avoidance' ones. Steve realized early on in our work together that I was focused almost entirely on avoidance. This followed from my belief that failure held the consequences of a loss of self-worth, because why wouldn't we do everything to avoid that? We needed to reframe my outlook towards what I wanted to achieve (proactive, challenge, gold medal) rather than what I wanted to avoid (threat, failure, loss of worth). He didn't know that much about the technical aspects of racing on a velodrome, so he asked me to outline a race plan for him. My avoidant mindset presented itself almost immediately. In lines on a whiteboard I marked out my plans: if she does this I will do this, and if she goes here my plan is to . . . Steve stopped me. You've already lost, he said. All I was describing were reactions, reactions to the possibilities of losing and mitigations for that. What I needed was a plan for how I would win.

This is as true in life as it is on two wheels. We cannot thrive if our focus is on avoiding catastrophes, or reacting to the thoughts and actions of other people. We can only know ourselves, decide what we want and try to do our best to make it happen. I had to say that my plan was to win, to develop a strategy on my own terms which took me towards that, and be aware that if the plan was not working I had a back-up. Reactivity is great if it causes us to move from *our* plan A to *our* plan B, but it is no use if it is focused on moving around someone else's.

I had to commit to what I wanted, and I hope you can too. If we take the time to know ourselves and our desires, then we can create plans that help us realize them, but if we exist in a constant state of defensiveness, of threat and reaction, we are like a ship buffeted by life's storm. We cannot sail in a direction, but only try to stay afloat. I had to learn to see opportunities and not threats, and all of us can benefit from reframing our goals as choices. I chose to be a cyclist – no one was forcing me to do it and as such I had to see that I could not continue perceiving it as a series of problems and threats. It was my choice and it was my opportunity, so it was my place to decide on how I would take it.

Steve had to remind me of that after a particularly difficult incident at the European Championships early in my career. I took a horrific fall – my teammates said they watched me slide down the banks of the velodrome like a ragdoll, momentarily unconscious as my skinsuit disintegrated with the friction. I woke up the next morning, peeled myself off the sheets and knew that I wouldn't be able to race very well. I told Steve I didn't want to do it. His response was 'fine, you can go home then'. Whether it was my contrarian streak or the light of an epiphany that sparked in my mind, I don't know, but both seemed to be at play. I *could* go home. I could *always* go home. I chose this thing, this life of speeding in circles on steep banks, and it was only worth doing if I wanted what it offered. It was a choice, and it was only one worth making if I was deeply internally motivated by it. When you doubt yourself, or your motivation, feel free to tell yourself 'fine, you can go home then' and ask yourself whether you are truly choosing the path you are on. You will either find that you are committed and affirm your motivation, or realize you are not and should make better use of your energy.

In your own life, the decision to take ownership will be a powerful catalyst for motivation and resolve. Many of us choose a path and either a) spend a great deal of time complaining about it, b) wishing it were easier or c) thinking about how it could be different. In reality, our options are to a) accept it as it is, b) try to change it or c) do something different. The responsibility is ours, and although it can be frightening to admit that we are the only one in control of our life path, it is far more fulfilling to accept that fear and see the opportunity that comes with it.

No one can decide on your life for you. We often wish people would, that a fairy godmother or a rich dead aunt would appear one day and magic a new life into existence, but it doesn't really happen. When it does, we hear about it, because it makes for a good story and fairy tale we can fall back on when we struggle to create the life we want, but it isn't useful. All good things come with self-awareness. It allows us to know we want them, to make the choice to pursue them, and the motivation to continue, repeatedly trying and failing until we have them. We have to choose what we really want, based on what we know about ourselves, and with that choice we gain access to a reserve of motivation that we could not if we were doing it for money, acclaim or avoidance of the consequences of failure.

Intrinsic Motivation vs Extrinsic

This is the idea of intrinsic versus extrinsic motivation. Intrinsic motivation comes when we engage with some activity or pursuit because of the inherent satisfaction we gain from doing it, rather than any consequence. Extrinsic motivation, on the other hand, is involved in any activity where we are trying to achieve an outcome that is separate from the activity itself. Usually these are outcomes like praise, money or prizes. Extrinsic motivators can be quite effective in the short term – kind words or the promise of a pay cheque can often help us get through a difficult day – but they are not enough to keep us committed throughout a lifetime or any project that requires hardship or discomfort. If I had been extrinsically motivated by the idea of a medal, or the recognition of my peers, my commitment would remain vulnerable to events. An injury that stopped me from competing at my best would have left me unmotivated because those rewards would be off the table. On the other hand, intrinsic motivation, say the love of competing or the pride I felt in myself for always trying my best, could not be impacted by events. I could always love training and I could always try my best, so injury or bad luck could not throw me off course.

This is why it is so valuable to think about what inspires us intrinsically, and try our best to develop thought patterns around intrinsic motivation. One way to do so is to simply do things that we enjoy. This may seem relatively obvious, but for many of us it is no simple thing. The passage of time and the duties we have can make us lose track of the things that we like doing for no other reason than doing them. This is a shame, but it is rectifiable. If I asked you now what you *enjoy* doing the most, what would you say? It should be something that you would do even if no one else knew about it (because we don't do this for recognition or social status) or whether anyone else thinks you're good at it. Would it be singing? Dancing? Running? Watching French arthouse cinema? Think about it, because it is the first step to reminding yourself what inspires you internally, and if you know that, then you have the basis of a goal that you could pursue indefinitely. You will also have less to worry about, as your goal is your own, your standard is your own happiness and your success comes from achieving it. Other people's reactions, changing circumstances or unknowns beyond your control don't have to be sources of fear because they're not relevant to what you do, on your own terms, for your own reasons.

A second way to progress without fear of the consequences of failure is to develop labels for ourselves built around effort and progress: 'I like working hard to improve', 'I like getting better at things' or 'I like to learn'. All of these labels create an intrinsic motivation, not towards some specific activity, but towards intrinsic behaviours or mindsets that are good in and of themselves. If we are are, for example, *not* intrinsically motivated by weekly netball but *are* intrinsically motivated by the feeling of working hard to improve at something, then we can access the benefits of internal motivation by internal progress. In this case, even if our teammates at netball don't praise us or we don't make the greatest shot of the week, we can be motivated to return next time because we feel good about ourselves, within ourselves, whenever we do. Moreover, even when the *result* appears to be a failure, the *outcome* is still success, as we will have met our own standard of effort and progressed by having the experience.

We should try to focus on things that we like doing, and take time to appreciate ourselves every time we do something for purely internal reasons. Equally, we should be wary of those things we do for extrinsic reasons. Choosing something because it offers praise, external reward or recognition over something that we enjoy is not sustainable because we cannot guarantee these things will come and in the process we tie our core value and self-worth to other people's opinions. We cannot guarantee that people will always praise, reward or recognize us, so when we tie our self-worth to these external forces, we open ourselves up to the negative consequences of failure. Doing things on our own terms, for our own internal satisfaction, is sustainable. The things we choose to do may change, because we might, but our ability to choose them and stick with them will not, because we have become used to relying on intrinsic over extrinsic motivation. If we fail, it is a sign that we failed to meet our own standards and motivations, and the knock-on effect is that we must try harder next time or change our approach.

It is only in retirement that I have truly embedded these thoughts. Through my career I only ever grew to manage the fear of failure rather than thrive without it. It is often useful, when confronting the fear (of the consequences) of failure, to focus on the effort we have put in. If we try our best to prepare for any challenge, to maximize our potential and our skills, then we can separate out any failure from the potential consequence of shame. If we have done our best, there is really nothing more we could do, and our core belief about our value can be reinforced by the sense that effort was our true motivator all along.

Whatever the challenge I am taking on, I always return to the idea that I have prepared the best I could. If we focus on preparation, then any time a fear of failure or a doubt creeps up in our mind, we can respond that we have *already* done our best. There is no room to be disappointed by the outcome because we have put in everything we could. Any failure can be a success if we judge ourselves by the standards of our effort and preparation. Still, I wasn't impervious to that fear.

My Greatest Success Was My Greatest Failure

I was now a World and Olympic Champion, going into a home Games in London 2012. There was reasonable expectation based on my ability which mixed with the intangible expectation of a nation that seemed to place their hopes on me and a few others. I don't want to sound ungrateful – it's a beautiful thing to be cheered on by 60 million people, but it is also, without the proper psychological preparation, *terrifying*. The years in the run-up to London 2012 were some of the hardest of my life. The combination of a home Olympics, a difficult team environment, national expectation and thus potential disappointment were enough to make my blessing feel like a curse. What should have been the most golden of opportunities only existed in my mind as a threat.

All I could do was focus, train and try to reassure myself that if I did my best I could only make myself proud. As much as possible I had to push other people's expectations to the side, as they only reminded me of the potential disappointment that could be around the corner. Of course that was difficult – it felt like every billboard and TV advertisement proclaimed how important it was that I performed for the sake of the nation, and everywhere I turned there was some reminder of quite how *extrinsic* this task seemed to be. All I could do was focus on myself, and not become preoccupied with the idea that I could be a national disappointment. Of course, the reality was that the worst-case scenario *was* disappointment: people may *be* disappointed, but *I would not become a disappointment*. I had to separate that final statement, about my worth and my value from an experience. This is difficult, but it is something we have to be aware of. We can be disappointed without being a disappointment, just as we can fail without becoming a failure. Our identity is not fixed, for good or for bad, and it is vital that we protect ourselves against the belief that an action, a failure or a disappointment can change who we are. You may not get a promotion you go for, but it does not mean you are incapable, unintelligent or unworthy of respect. You may miss a target you have set, but that does not make you any less than you would be if you had reached it. We must build a self-image that neither rises nor falls, nor becomes stuck, with the events of our life. We must see ourselves as constant, valuable, and capable of trying and failing time and time again. A failure, like a fear, is not something to stop us but to encourage us forward.

The importance of this mindset is compelling when I consider my experiences at London 2012. I learned something new about failure there, which is this: We should accept failure because we learn from it, we should accept failure without fear of the consequences we imagine, but we should accept failure most of all because it can come to us *no matter what we do*. I prepared for the Olympics diligently, I won race after race in preparation and I could have done very little more than I did. Yet I failed, twice and in different ways. In the sprint race I made a simple error – losing my balance point as nerves took over. I was human, and I made a mistake. Unless we are somehow perfect, this will happen to all of us, and in the heat of the moment we can all mess up. We should practise failing, in preparation for these moments, because we cannot practise perfection. I had done almost everything correctly and still I failed, because the better we do, the harder things get. That is the simple truth of progress: there is as much failure once we have achieved mastery as when we are a beginner, because if we are not failing, we are not growing and we are not being tested. So we have to get used to it and we *certainly* shouldn't fear it.

In the team sprint, I failed differently. My teammate and I were disqualified in an early round for a violation of the track regulations which many people would argue was an error. I'm not fixated on that, because it's beside the point. My point is that sometimes we will fail *unfairly*; sometimes we will fail because of things outside of our control and because of the actions of other people. What both of these failures taught me is that we need to grow accustomed to failure because it can find its own way into our lives, and no amount of dedication, preparation or perspiration will make us immune to it.

I learned that when we try, we fail, and in doing so we learn how different our experience of failure is to our fear of it. No one told me I was worthless for losing in the ways that I did – in fact, people hardly seemed to notice. What people notice is the effort you make, the ways in which you grow and the successes you have, and they soon forget the ways in which things fail to go to plan. Most of all, though, people don't notice the challenges fear stops you from taking, because those challenges never take place.

In fact, many people fail to notice our failures, because we hide them. Most cultures fixate on success – we separate it from all of the failures that were necessary for learning about our task, for developing resolve and understanding our abilities. As Thomas Edison said of inventing the lightbulb, 'I have not failed 10,000 times. I have not failed once. I have succeeded in proving that those 10,000 ways will not work. When I have eliminated the ways that will not work, I will find the way that will work.' He configured those failures, which many lesser inventors may have feared, as opportunities, because our successes are not the opposite of our failures, but the product of them. That is why we have a duty, to ourselves and to those who will fail like we did, to tell their story.

In 2010, this noble idea motivated Melanie Stefan, then a postdoctoral researcher in computational biology, to publish a brief but influential article in *Nature* titled 'A CV of Failures'.[3] She had failed repeatedly to receive an academic position after her postdoc and struggled to shake the sense that she was *the only person* this was happening to. You may recognize this feeling, that your failures are somehow unique, pointed and profound. The more she thought about it, the more she saw that the opposite was true. Her failures were in fact *very common* – all that was unique was the fact that they were visible to her. Failure was happening all the time in academic circles, but no one spoke about it because CVs were a catalogue of successes. She realized that failure would be an isolating experience and a shameful thing, as long as we kept it hidden. So she wrote her 'failure CV'. It outlined the exams she had failed, the fellowship applications that were rejected and the papers that were never accepted. It described the *majority* of academic life, disappointments that were completely necessary (we could not get *every job* and ace *every* exam) but that were always kept secret. It was six times as long as her normal CV.

Soon, other, more decorated scientists did the same. These were the sort of people whose glowing, streamlined successes had once made Melanie despondent. Gradually, stigma reduced and Melanie realized that starting a conversation about her failures might just be her greatest success. If we are open with ourselves about our failures, and then open with the world, we may just be an example to others who think their failures are unique and personal. We do not become a failure by being honest, but an example of persistence and perseverance.

EXERCISE: WRITE *YOUR* FAILURE CV

I. Choose Your Categories

Structure your Failure CV similarly to a traditional CV, but focus on setbacks. Common categories include:

Education & Training (e.g., schools, programmes, courses not completed or not accepted to)

Job Applications (e.g., jobs applied for but not offered)

Projects & Ventures (e.g., ideas or businesses that didn't work out)

Publications/Creative Works (e.g., papers, books or art rejected)

Other Personal Goals (e.g., goals missed, skills not mastered)

2. List Your Failures

Under each category, list your setbacks, rejections and unsuccessful attempts. Be as specific as you feel comfortable – dates, names of organizations and brief context can help.

Example:
Job applications:

2022: Applied for teaching job; not invited for interview

2023: Applied for promotion to Team Lead; not selected

3. Reflect on Each Failure

For each entry, briefly note:

○ What did I learn from this experience?

○ Did this failure lead to a new opportunity, skill or insight?

○ How did it shape my later choices or successes?

Example:
2022: Applied for teaching job; not invited for interview

Learned the importance of tailoring my CV. Improved my application, which helped me secure a role at another school.

4. Look for Patterns and Growth

After listing your failures and reflections, review your Failure CV and ask:

○ Are there recurring themes or lessons?

○ Which failures were turning points for later achievements?

○ How have these experiences shaped your resilience, skills or perspective?

5. Optional: Share and Discuss

Consider sharing your Failure CV with a trusted friend, mentor or peer group. Discussing your setbacks can help normalize failure and inspire others.

Why Do This?
Normalize setbacks: Everyone experiences failure – making it visible reduces shame.

Highlight growth: Many successes are built on lessons learned from failure.

Build resilience: Seeing your journey as a whole fosters persistence and self-compassion.

This is vital, because the most frightening thing about failure is that it can stop us from trying, from growing or succeeding. The most terrible thing is that we can imagine our progress out of existence by never even starting. We can be so preoccupied with the consequences of failure that we miss this most startling fact, that the only certain failure comes when we fail to try. It is the *doing* and the *trying*, the intrinsic aspects of any experience, that make it enjoyable, and a focus on success or failure can distract us from that. If we can see failure as *necessary*, we gain the opportunity to learn from it; if we see our fear of it as a reflection of imaginary consequences, we take the first step towards understanding and re-establishing our core beliefs about what makes us valuable. Engaging with our fear of failure is an opportunity to know ourselves better, to get better, and to live more joyfully. Because a lifetime spent failing joyfully is incomparable to one in which we fail to try and live consumed by the image of what would have happened if we did.

So go on: start failing. It will come one way or the other, so we might as well get good at it. In the process, you might just find yourself succeeding, learning and trying. All of these things are built upon failure, and if you can learn to love it, then in many ways you'll never fail again. You'll just improve at it.

So how, then, can you fail today? Now is the best time to start, because as I've learned, becoming a successful failure is a lifetime's work.

- -

KEY TAKEAWAYS

1. We do not fear failure; we fear the consequences of failure.

2. Often those consequences are imagined, and usually they involve a core belief about what we must do to be of value.

3. Taking time to remind ourselves that we have intrinsic value, regardless of our success or failure, is a worthwhile effort.

4. It is better to be motivated by the joy of doing, rather than the results of achieving. When we are, there is no such thing as failure.

5. Value effort, not outcome.

6. Accept failure as necessary, and useful.

Failure is an ellipsis . . .

5. Fear of Change

What We Keep, Let Go and Learn

The first big change in my life was not one I chose to make. In 2011, I suffered my first real injury, and the tear of a muscle began a break with the identity that I had always known. The management had lost confidence in me and this was the final straw. Within a year I would be retired and everything I thought I had been – Cyclist, Olympian, Competitor (capitals intentional) – was taken away from me. Or at least I thought it was. What I have learned since, is that while the cycling may have stopped, the woman who cycled remains. I realized that in any great change, and particularly those where the change is thrust upon us, the core identity that made us who we were in one part of our life, endures in another. Our circumstances may shift, but we get through it and grow.

In this chapter, I'm going to look at how change – one of our most persistent fears – can actually be a force for good. Whether it's change we choose or change we don't, it gives us the opportunity to do many things: understand ourselves and who we are more deeply, take on new, exciting challenges and start new chapters in our lives, and, when we cope with it, even learn to embrace it, build strength and confidence.

Of course, when confronted with a change that *seems* to shake the bedrock of our identity, appreciating it as a source of growth is challenging. So it's no surprise that change is something we feel afraid of, something that takes us well outside our comfort zones. These changes could be your kids leaving home (*I am a parent, first and foremost*), losing your job or choosing to start a new one (*I'm a teacher, an accountant, a project manager*), or divorce (*I'm a husband or a wife*). For me, there seemed to be an internal logic to the idea 'I *am* a cyclist, and tomorrow I will not be, therefore I shall be something lesser', so I struggled to reach the viewpoint from which I could see that, in reality, I was everything *but* the bike. This is the challenge of any change, and of any moment in which we confuse who we *are* with what we do, particularly if we have done it for a long time or with great conviction. So it is useful to recognize that the pursuit of our goals, be they in our relationships, work or passions, can grow so large that it casts our enduring self in the shade.

That was true of me and my bicycle. Which, when I put it like that, sounds fairly ridiculous (as many all-consuming thoughts do with the benefit of hindsight). I had been a cyclist since I was sixteen years old. I had not really been much of a teenager (parties occurred the nights before races) and I had always felt more like an up-and-coming athlete than a young woman, so as I approached thirty-two and a looming retirement, half of my life had been spent building a single thing at the expense of all else. It appeared that the single thing I knew was being taken away.

This grand transformation took place across a year in which I prepared to scale my last and greatest professional summit. I prepared for my home Olympics and the almost unique experience of being crowned champion an hour from my birthplace (it was quite the commute) while I processed the reality that it was all about to end. I had to prepare to win while believing it would spell the loss of my everything.

The grand projects of our life require sacrifice. Long-term relationships, raising children or pursuing career goals all require us to forego things which we may have once loved in the name of something or someone else we are prioritizing. Most often we think about these sacrifices in terms of time or autonomy. We may forego our freedom to travel because we are dedicated to staying in the same place as a partner. The need to be dependable and consistent for our children may lead us to take fewer risks and make ourselves available to meet their needs over our own. The requirements of our job may make it necessary for us to give up certain freedoms that we may otherwise have enjoyed.

We give up some choice or autonomy in the pursuit of a goal. This is well understood, but we focus less on how often people give up parts of ourselves, and in particular the knowledge of what *we really want*, when we commit to satisfying other people's needs and expectations. A forty-year career or a twenty-year (minimum) commitment to raising children requires us to think first about what others need and prioritize it above what we might. While this is noble and often necessary, it's a sacrifice that can leave us in a difficult situation when circumstances change. If we grow comfortable with putting ourselves second, then we may find it uncomfortable to think, do and act in pursuit of our own happiness when those who have depended on us, depend on us less.

This, fortunately, can be relearned. The change that we fear is of losing some part of ourselves and of gaining a freedom which we have forgotten to use. With some awareness, we can see it as an opportunity to renew and relearn those things. I hope this chapter goes some way to explaining quite how much of you will remain through change, and the joy you can find remembering how to use the freedom it necessarily brings, because change can seem like a threat, but it is so often an opportunity.

When we lean into change, examine what it is we're really afraid of, whether with change that's enforced upon us or change that we choose, we see that what feels like a loss can really be a chance to grow, and to understand ourselves more deeply. As with so many things, the way in which we see it will often determine how we engage with it and how confidently we approach it.

I'm going to examine the idea of self-knowledge, and in particular how a sense of our 'core values' provides a vital source of continuity and empowerment in the face of change. Our core values are our principles, the things that matter to us because we believe in them and strive for them. While core *beliefs* can be dangerous ideas about what makes us worthwhile, our core *values* are about what we consider to be worthwhile. Just as understanding our core beliefs about what makes us valuable helps us remain steady in the face of our failures, so too can our core values provide the anchor that stops us drifting away on our fears in times of change, and later be the compass that directs us towards new goals. We will return to narrative and our choice to either frame change as a loss or an opportunity, an end or a beginning. And I'll discuss how the fears that come with change can be transformed into something beautiful by developing a growth (or learner's) mindset. I only learned in retirement that *getting better* was far more enjoyable than *being the best*, which was an important lesson. I drew far more joy from being a bad (but improving) surfer than a cycling world champion, which provided me with a vital sense of the value of progress over mastery – of journeys rather than peaks.

Finally, we will look at grit and resilience, the ability to endure even when the journey does not seem worth the peak and how it informs our ability to flourish amidst change. This may all seem very grand, but that is because it is. The universe (here I go) is nothing if not a process of change; life as we know it, or better yet – living, *is* change. So if we lean into the fear, and appreciate change for the joy it can be, we can better appreciate life itself.

Self-Knowledge and Core Values

Have you ever considered your core values? These are not skills or actions; they are your beliefs and your priorities. Your values are what matter to you. So, try it now. What do you stand for and against? Write down a list of principles that matter to you, as many as you can (but no need for more than say twenty). Now group them along some lines that seem right to you. For example, if you have honesty and diligence in your list, you can place those under a banner of 'reliability', or you may have empathy and friendship, which you categorize under 'connection'. Look at these categories and try to weigh them against one another. Which would you prioritize if pressed? Would you choose honesty over kindness? Would you choose to be connected if it meant being unreliable?

EXERCISE: UNDERSTANDING OUR CORE VALUES[1][2]

Step I: Values List Exploration

Start with a list of common values. Here are some examples:

Honesty	Spirituality	Curiosity
Compassion	Integrity	Wisdom
Achievement	Humility	Mindfulness
Adventure	Courage	Joy
Creativity	Gratitude	Openness
Family	Perseverance	Freedom
Friendship	Respect	Discipline
Health	Responsibility	Balance
Justice	Service	Contribution
Learning	Equity	Authenticity
Security	Stewardship	

Read through the list slowly. As you read, highlight or write down any values that resonate with you or feel important.

Step 2: Narrow Down Your List

From your highlighted values, choose your top 5–7. Ask yourself:

Which of these could I not live without?

Which ones do I want to be remembered for?

Which values have guided my biggest decisions or proudest moments?

Step 3: Reflect on Real-Life Examples

For each of your top values, write a brief example from your life when you acted in line with that value.

Value: Compassion

Example: I volunteered at a local shelter during a difficult time because I wanted to help others.

Step 4: Notice Conflicts and Priorities

Are there values that sometimes conflict (e.g., 'adventure' vs 'security')?

Which values do you want to prioritize more in your life right now?

Step 5: Create a Personal Values Statement

Write a short statement or paragraph that summarizes your core values and how you want them to guide your life.

Example: 'I value honesty, compassion and learning. I strive to approach challenges with integrity, help others whenever I can, and seek growth through new experiences.'

Note:

Remember that your circumstances will change, and your values can too. These values are core, in terms of importance, but they should never feel restrictive. Your core values are your core values and they are yours to adapt and develop through your life.

The articulation of our core values and the practice of self-affirmation (which we will describe) were first discussed fully in the 1980s by the psychologist Claude Steele.[3] A body of research already existed around how humans seek to maintain 'self-integrity' – the idea of ourselves as good, competent or moral people – but that this integrity was vulnerable if it was tied to things like status or recognition. If our value (our integrity) is tied to inflexible ideas, like 'I am a mother', 'I am a doctor' or 'I make a lot of money', then our self-worth can quite quickly be shattered by changes in our circumstances (medical diagnoses, or the loss of a job). On the other hand, if we can bring our self-integrity to rest on more flexible, dynamic ideas of who we are and why we are valuable, we can be much more resilient. In the cases of being a mother or being a doctor, we may shift the identification from the role to the disposition – I am caring. Or rather than identifying with making money, a person may instead choose to emphasize their willingness to work hard. In these cases a person can continue to be caring, or hard-working, even if circumstances change, and as a result their self-integrity is more durable.

That is why many psychologists use self-affirmations as a tool to help people adjust and thrive through change. These are positive statements about yourself which reinforce self-worth, confidence or resilience, such as 'I am worthy of respect and love'. When we are threatened by changes, it's often because we sense a threat to our sense of self (I am a cyclist/I am a parent/I am a spouse/I'm the kind of person who lives in a city) and feel lessened by it. By articulating positive or kind sentiments about ourselves, we can benefit from a powerful antidote to the psychological stress that we experience when change shakes our sense of self.

EXAMPLES OF SELF-AFFIRMATIONS

General Confidence & Worth

'I am enough just as I am.'

'I deserve love, success and happiness.'

'I trust myself to make good decisions.'

Resilience & Strength

'I can handle whatever comes my way.'

'Challenges help me grow stronger.'

'I've overcome tough things before – I can do it again.'

Self-Compassion

'It's okay to make mistakes. I am learning.'

'I give myself the same kindness I offer others.'

'I don't need to be perfect to be valuable.'

Motivation & Growth

'Every day, I learn and grow.'

'I am capable of achieving my goals.'

'I welcome new opportunities and learn from them.'

Health & Body Positivity

'My body is strong, capable and worthy of respect.'

'I treat my body with care and gratitude.'

'I am more than how I look.'

Relationships & Boundaries

'I deserve relationships that uplift and respect me.'

'It's okay to say no to protect my peace.'

'I bring value to the lives of others.'

This process leads us back to the enduring reality that we are not the sum total of the things we have done or do – there was a principled, believing person doing them who is capable of doing the next thing with the same guiding values that helped us get up to the point of change. For me, it was realizing that the values of diligence, being a learner, and fairness were as applicable to my new life after cycling as they were to my life within it. In fact, they were even more relevant, because being a diligent learner generates far more progress as a beginner than it does as a master.

Once I understood the depth and transferability of my values, I realized that they did not disappear with a shifting environment; they actually allowed me to flourish with a new identity and new pursuits. After I retired I saw new identities open up to me through the closure of the one that had previously consumed me. I could now go for a run, ski or surf, which were things that I was actually not *allowed* to do as a competitive cyclist. Think about any changes that could present a threat to your identity. Maybe your work circumstances could change, resulting in less disposable income, an older relative may become more dependent on you, compromising the freedom you have to do things which you feel identify you. Longer term, it may be retirement, kids leaving home or the end of a relationship. Now ask, what are the values that you have brought to your current state that could be applied in that new one? What things that make you a good parent, professional or partner would allow you to continue being *you* even in the face of change?

So, being clear on our values, and then articulating them through affirmation can remind us that, whatever changes take place in our lives, we remain the same person: our core identity is strong. But there is another scientific reason underpinning the effectiveness of this process, one that is also found in practices known as visualization or manifestation. While these practices are often ostensibly understood in somewhat unscientific ways, through the laws of attraction and more spiritual terminology, in fact they can be effective because of a fundamental way in which our brain works. 'Reticular activation' describes the process by which thinking of something makes it seem to appear more frequently in the world. Just as owning a new pair of shoes may mean you start seeing those shoes on *everyone*, or driving a Skoda somehow makes more Skodas appear, so too articulating our values makes the opportunities for applying them seem to appear more readily. If we tell our brain something matters, it will look for examples of it in the world. These are the brain patterns at the root of what is often called perception bias, which is often quite a negative phenomenon (e.g., you tell yourself the world is unfair and you see more unfairness), but in the case of manifestation or the articulation of our values, it can be used to positive ends. Manifestation doesn't make our goals happen; it makes opportunities to pursue them more visible, and the articulation of our values makes us more likely to see the moments when we can live in value-driven ways.

Finally, gaining self-knowledge through the description of our values protects and empowers us in times of crisis, helping us face our fears. Firstly, our negative stress responses are reduced when we remind ourselves of our values. The neuroscientist David Creswell and his team at Carnegie Mellon University[4] studied how people suffering from chronic stress performed on a series of cognitive tests, with and without the provision of self-affirmation exercises. Those who were supported with self-affirmations performed at the level of a control group of low-stress participants, which suggests that self-affirmation can buffer the negative effects of stress on cognitive performance. Meanwhile, studies conducted at Chongqing Cognition Lab have focused more specifically on how value affirmation affects our brain chemistry in stressful situations.[5] They found that affirmations actually alter the way our brain reacts to stressors – speeding up physiological recovery, supporting emotion regulation, and making us more resilient. It is interesting to note that they also studied how self-affirmations can help us develop a growth mindset – the sense that we can grow and improve – which is something that we will go on to discuss as a powerful driver of positivity in times of change.

We are also more likely to act defiantly against what we see as wrong when our values remain present in our minds. Sunita Sah is an award-winning professor of psychology at Cornell University and an expert on the subject of defiance. Her research finds that people who have a sense of their core values are far more likely to act defiantly against wrongdoing or injustice in the world.[6] Here we see that these values don't just help us thrive internally amidst change, but stand up against negative changes we see in the world.

So value your values, and see how they can help a process of change feel more like bouncing forward, rather than trying to bounce back. Progression is integral, because it is by looking forward that we see what is to gain, rather than what is lost in change. I didn't lose cycling; I gained mountaineering, skydiving and autonomy over my body. This is not to say we should be modelling some brand of toxic positivity. Loss does hurt, and that's fine – we need to make space within ourselves to accept and sit with that. What we often find, when we do sit with loss, is that there is always something gained. We may have lost the ability to do certain things which felt core to our identity – like me maybe you were injured and could no longer perform physical tasks which felt core to who you were. The only way, going forward, to come to terms with this is to see the time you have gained and the space you have made for new pursuits which offer different meanings and dimensions to your sense of self.

Maybe you have lost time itself. I know from friends that there can be complex emotions around the loss of time and identity which come from parenthood. There is the obvious gain of a new small person in your life, but there may be a sense that the freedom you once had and the self you were is gone. That is not entirely true. You are free to experience the world and relationships in different ways, the self that you were is changed, not absent. Even in moments when we wish we had not changed, we know really that we must, that living is changing and that to mourn a past life is to deny ourselves a better one in the present.

Which brings us to narrative, and studies which have looked at the power of the stories we tell ourselves when facing a potentially frightening change.

Narrative Effect

Madeline Toubiana, who holds the chair in entrepreneurship at the University of Ottawa, conducted ten years of interviews with people who had confronted drastic changes in their lives.[7] Alongside her team she identified the phenomenon of 'identity paralysis' to describe how people could feel angry, frustrated and hopeless after periods of change, and detailed approaches which help to overcome these feelings. Their interviewees included a number of people who immigrated to the US and left high-skill careers for lower-skill ones because they could not transfer their qualifications. They found that those who crafted stories that placed their ups and downs within the context of a broader narrative journey inevitably had more positive sentiments about their current situations. For example, one former engineer navigated his experiences as a taxi driver by thinking of himself as 'an explorer in a new land, learning the language and culture. Every passenger was a lesson in American life. This mindset helped me stay positive and eventually led me to a new career . . . where my skills were finally valued'. In contrast, another interviewee – a physician from South America – also faced the loss of professional status after immigrating. She struggled to see her journey as anything but a setback: 'I felt like I had lost everything I worked for. I couldn't get past the idea that I was a failure. I kept my story focused on what I'd lost, which made it hard to move forward or see new opportunities.'

We see that the ability to link between our past and present can either empower us (as in the case of our taxi driver) or hold us back (as per the physician). The key difference is the narrative structure that we overlay on that journey from past to present. This continued narrative can give us a sense of continuity, as our core values do, but it can also help us access the benefits of a heroic narrative that we described in Chapter 2. In a heroic journey, change is necessary and compelling; it is the driver of the narrative and it is in seeking change, adventurously, that the hero earns their title. A hero's journey is just a story about change, and it is usually one that begins with a hope, an ambition or a dream – whether that's of a better life or a stronger self.

A dream like this is a very positive way to approach change;

it's the mental image of a mountaintop that inspires a climb. This way of thinking is essential for leaning into risk and facilitating a change that you want, but it may also be useful in re-interpreting a change you fear. The room for dreaming is limited when we are fixed or comfortable. The distance between ourselves and achieving a dream is filled with potentially off-putting ideas of discomfort, but when we are already presented with the discomfort of an enforced change, we have the opportunity to dream more freely and imagine new adventures because we are starting anew. In fact, we can dream proactively. For those of us who grew up in British schools (or probably any schools, bar Finland, where everyone seems to have a lovely time), dreaming, or daydreaming in particular, was considered the antithesis of productivity. It was a sign that someone is unfocused, unready and unlikely to pursue meaningful things. Thankfully we are not at school any more, and the usefulness of a dream is that it focuses you on things you might want, through change. It readies you for it and it is essentially the first step in preparing for it.

A dream is an unencumbered form of self-exploration. It's seeing what you might value without the constraints of practicality or social expectation. Far from being something we only do when we're asleep, dreams can wake us up to all of the changes we might actively want to make in our lives, even where they involve taking risks and doing things that might scare us, at least a bit. They are effectively an exercise in visualization, which as we discussed, activates our reticular system to make things we may not have been aware of or have countenanced appear more regularly and in higher definition. This is a powerful form of self-awareness that can be combined with practices like journaling and meditation (both also well-evidenced ways of improving self-knowledge) to give us a sense of how we feel, which helps us deal with the stress of change, and what we want, which helps us see change for the opportunity it is.

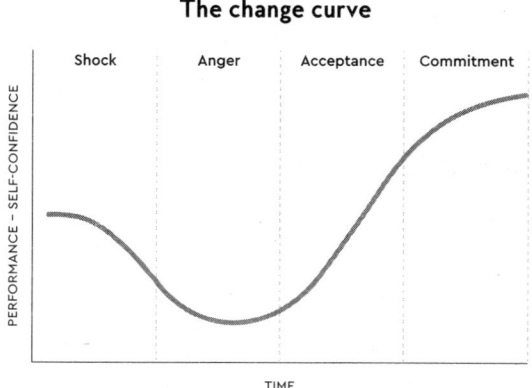

The change curve

| Shock | Anger | Acceptance | Commitment |

PERFORMANCE – SELF-CONFIDENCE

TIME

The Four Stages of Change

In management theory, change is often described in terms of a 'Four-Stage Curve' (image: University of Nottingham). The steps in this process mirror Kübler-Ross's influential model of the five stages of grief,[8] a framework describing common emotional responses to loss (denial, anger, bargaining, depression and acceptance), but I think it's useful for understanding the turbulent emotions that can come with any change. The first stage of change is shock (or denial). We all know that one – I felt it when I discovered I was injured. You may share these feelings if you've suffered redundancy or the unexpected end of a relationship. Our self-knowledge is vital at this stage for a simple reason: to *know* we have been shocked. This may sound like a low bar, but in many cases the experience of a shock is so disorientating that we struggle to connect what has happened with the feelings it has created in us. Until we know we have been shocked, we cannot begin to process it and progress towards some sort of action. In this model this is the second stage – anger or resistance.

Martin Luther King described his supreme task as organizing and uniting people so that 'their anger becomes a transforming force.' He saw that for all its power, anger often lacks direction, that it can be a disorganized form of motivation. When we work to develop self-knowledge, we can understand where we would like to direct that force. When we place that energy within a narrative that is directed forwards, towards the future rather than the past, we can use anger as fuel to drive us to the next stage of our story. My anger propelled me to the Olympics after my injury, anger at my body for failing me and anger at the people who told me I shouldn't compete or remain on the team afterwards (I was still the fastest, and certain that some regressive idea about women being less durable than men played into their assessment). I don't recommend this as an approach, only because I don't want to *encourage* you to feel angry for prolonged periods of time. However, if you are angry, then there are times where channelling it towards a goal will give you a faster track to stage three, of acceptance. If you are offered voluntary redundancy at work, it may be your anger that drives you to pursue your next project passionately, or some degree of anger at the end of a relationship that empowers you to prioritize yourself for the first time in ages. You will not want to remain angry, but it may be the first emotion that ignites your drive, so don't be afraid to think '*I'll show them*' when a change is thrust upon you.

Acceptance, the third stage, requires us to know what we are accepting and what the change means to us, and that relies on the type of self-knowledge that practices like journaling and meditation facilitate. At this point we no longer reject the change and have a chance to process it, to decide where we want it to take us and in the context of our heroic narrative. When this is done we reach the fourth stage of 'commitment'. Here, the focus of our change is no longer backwards-looking and we are not changing *from*, but *towards*, something. I changed from someone who no longer cycled into someone who began skiing. We may go from being a homemaker to a world traveller or a career woman to artist, and the same principles will apply. If, when faced with a change, we lean in to the risk of it, actively engage with our fears and grab the opportunity of using that change as a chance to do something new, who knows how far we'll go? Spending time developing our values and self-knowledge will allow us to choose the next phase of our life authentically, and seeing ourselves as the hero of our own stories might just give us the confidence to take that leap. With this mindset, we see that our fear of losing one thing is often the opposite (but essential) side of the opportunity to gain another – the loss is integral to the gain. It might just take some self-love, self-awareness and good storytelling to see it.

If you prefer a model which offers more room to move to cycle between stages, that sees change as a flexible process with steps forwards and backwards, you may find the 'Transtheoretical' model more useful.[9] It was developed by James Prochaska (who was later recognized as one of the five most cited authors in psychology by the American Psychology Society) in the late 1970s, as he attempted to help people quit smoking. As Prochaska reviewed hundreds of psychotherapy outcomes, he noticed something striking: no single method worked for everyone, and change rarely happened all at once. So he began mapping out how people actually move through change, step by step – not as a sudden transformation, but as a progression through stages: from not considering change (precontemplation), to weighing it (contemplation), preparing, acting, and finally maintaining it. What emerged was a model both elegant and compassionate: it didn't shame people for relapsing or hesitating; it saw those as part of the journey. The Transtheoretical model became one of the most influential frameworks in health psychology, used everywhere from addiction treatment to public health campaigns, because it honoured the truth that change is a process, not a switch.

While the Four-Stage Change Curve helps us to think about our feelings, the Transtheoretical model is more about behaviours and readiness. We can combine the two to help us understand our attitude to change and see the behaviours which advance us through these stages.

EXERCISE: USING THE TWO MODELS

Step I: Set the Scene

Imagine you've just accepted a job in a new city. You're leaving behind friends, familiar places and routines. This is a change many people experience, and it can trigger a range of emotions and behaviours.

Step 2: Map Your Emotional Journey (Four-Stage Change Curve)

Use the Four-Stage Change Curve to reflect on your feelings at each stage:

Stage	Typical Feelings/ Thoughts	Example Reflection Prompts
Shock/Denial	'Is this really happening? Maybe it won't be that different.'	How did you feel when you first got the job offer? Did you try to downplay the reality of moving?
Anger/Resistance	'Why do I have to leave? I'll miss my friends. This is unfair.'	What frustrations or fears have come up? Are you resisting packing or making plans?

| Acceptance/ Exploration | 'Maybe I'll find new favourite spots. Let's see what's out there.' | When did you start researching your new city or reaching out to new colleagues? What small steps have you taken? |
| Commitment/ Transformation | 'I'm building a new life here. I'm starting to feel at home.' | What routines or friendships are you forming? How are you making the city your own? |

- Write a journal entry for each stage as you experience it.
- Notice that you may move back and forth between stages, and that's normal.

Step 3: Track Your Behavioural Progress (Transtheoretical Model)

Overlay the Transtheoretical model to understand your readiness and actions regarding the change:

Stage	Example in Moving Scenario	Reflection Prompt
Precontemplation	Not thinking seriously about moving, ignoring the reality.	Was there a time you avoided thinking about the move?
Contemplation	Weighing pros and cons, feeling ambivalent.	What were your hopes and worries?

Preparation	Making concrete plans (finding housing, saying goodbyes).	What steps did you take to get ready?
Action	Actually moving, starting the new job, exploring the city.	What did you do in your first week?
Maintenance	Settling in, building new routines, staying connected.	How are you maintaining your wellbeing and connections?

- For each stage, jot down what actions or thoughts you had.
- Identify where you are now and what the next small step could be.

Step 4: Integrate and Signpost Progress

- Combine your emotional and behavioural reflections.
- For example: 'During the anger/resistance stage, I noticed I was still in contemplation, not ready to plan. Once I accepted the move, I shifted into preparation and started looking for apartments.'
- Use this awareness to normalize your feelings and motivate action.
- Recognize that discomfort is part of the process, and each small step is progress.

Self-Determination Theory

In my case, when faced with the reality that I would compete in one last Olympics and then retire, what I thought was a loss turned out to be an opportunity to experience autonomy, to build new and better relationships and to learn things that I never had before. These three things (autonomy, relatedness and competence) are the pillars of Self-Determination theory, a psychological framework created by Edward Deci and Richard Ryan (who we speak to in this chapter) as a means to understand what motivates people.[10] This is one of the most impactful psychological theories of the last fifty years, and a hugely useful tool when it comes to learning how to benefit from the increased risk brought on by change and how to foster personal growth by finding intrinsic motivation (see page 96). Richard Ryan told me that his area of study was not so much psychology as 'human motivation' and that in his years of work with individuals and teams who want to find healthy, durable ways to remain motivated, there are three key components:

- autonomy – the sense of control we have over our lives;

- relatedness – the satisfaction we draw from living that life in relation to others; and

- competence – the sense, not of being good at something, but getting *better* at it.

The theory has been applied in so many fields, from sports psychology to social and environmental theories, that Richard Ryan is currently the ninth most cited academic in the world. There is almost nothing upon which the values of autonomy, relatedness and competence cannot shed light, because in every pursuit, and every change, motivation is key.

Autonomy, as Dr Ryan told me, centres on the feeling that we have *chosen* our actions. Naturally this can be challenging in times where a change has been forced upon us. An enforced change creates the opposite sensation to autonomy, but, if we don't shy away from it, it can provide a useful opportunity to develop more. An enforced change is a moment in which new choices can be made, goals set and identities forged. I did not realize how little autonomy I actually had as a cyclist, and it was only when I had the choice to carry on doing it professionally taken away from me, that I was able to start choosing all sorts of new things. This is the case for all of us who have attached our identity and actions to a particular role – the range of possible actions we can choose is limited by the requirements of the identity we have built. Just as I could not ski as a cyclist and gained the autonomy of choosing to ski when I lost my cycling identity, so can parents gain the autonomy to become travellers/tour guides/masters students (choose according to what you know about yourself) when becoming 'empty nesters'. An empty nest is like a cyclist without a bicycle – it can either be thought of in terms of emptiness, of a *lack*, or in terms of new space. It is not only something that has been emptied, but that has created room to be filled.

The ability to see vacated space or time as something to be filled rather than something that has been hollowed out is harder in some circumstances than others. This will be personal to each of us, but broadly speaking when we can see a change as *necessary* or representative of progress, it is more easily seen as an opportunity. We can accept the end of our career as necessary, or the progression of our children towards independence. It is more difficult in those instances where we would really have loved things to remain, that they could have, and maybe even *should* have.

This is often the case when we face a painful break-up with a person we continue to love. Autonomy may seem unappealing because we *preferred* dependencies with someone we loved. Any new relatedness may seem worthless given we have lost the one relationship we value over all others. Our competence may feel completely compromised as we have 'failed' to retain a love that matters so much to us. There is no doubt that this is particularly difficult, but we know it is not impossible, and many of us experience difficult break-ups and grow happier.

First, we must work to value the autonomy we gain. It is only by practising self-knowledge that we can appreciate the freedom that our independence gives us and value the compromises that we no longer need to make. This may be as small as our choice of television programmes and as large as our autonomy to live in new places, but both are forms of self-determination. We can become related in new ways. The life change you feared will open time and space to build new relationships, romantic or otherwise, and the energy you directed towards your previous partner can take new shapes, your love new forms. Your sense of competence, at first seemingly mortally wounded by a break-up, is actually in its greatest state of potential growth. You have a chance to rebuild yourself on your terms, and this may mean growing in ways that you could not have imagined within the security of a couple.

We also, through any kind of change, gain opportunities to decide *who we want to change with*, as most involve some changes in relationships. I went from seeing the same coaches, physios and teammates almost every day for fifteen years to almost never again. This is strange, and can feel like a loss, but it is also an opportunity. The simple fact is that the people we have built relationships with through our work, community, or any aspect of our now-shifting identity, are not the only people we could have powerful relationships with. It is unlikely that they are the *only* people we could bond with and highly unlikely that, by fate and circumstance, they were the single best people in the world for us. I found that, for all of the people I loved in the world of cycling, there were others outside of cycling who I could build profound relationships with, be they at all-women surfing groups or on hiking expeditions. Cycling had been my life, and the people within it 'my people', but in truth I just hadn't lived another life or had the time to meet those other people. Our relationships are profoundly important to our wellbeing and motivation, and when things change, we benefit greatly from retaining connection to those we can, and rediscovering the joy of building new ones.

This can seem *frightening* at first, but to return to a point that we have discussed previously, starting out, beginning, *not knowing*, is both the most frightening and most enjoyable part of many experiences. First love is not just powerful because people are young, it is because it is new. The very same things which make experiences frightening make them exhilarating – the novelty, the sense of adaptation, the reality that this could either be a dud or the start of something more beautiful than we ever realized. Starting again, whatever the circumstances, is a moment in which our present is loaded with all of the opportunity and potential energy of the future that it could grow into – 100 per cent of the growth and the progress is there to be tapped into, and that is a powerful driving force. As Dr Ryan told me when we spoke, 'competence is not the feeling that you can do something, but that you can grow. There is no better time for growing than after a change.' In fact, this is the pattern of the biological world: some environmental change, some apparent problem, dictates that species need to find a solution, and they progress. Competence and our ability to develop it in moments of change could just as easily be described, then, as evolution.

The important thing is to see change as an opportunity to grow gradually. Just as facing our fears involves steadily doing greater things we believed we could not, so too the ability to thrive in change involves the scaffolding of steadily growing competencies and strengths upon one another. We need a dream from which to hang our finish line, and a series of steps to get there. So in the case of an empty nester who may become a world traveller, we have a dream, but first we may have a local walking group, book club or Zumba class. These are all steps which build our sense of capability, and each step we make gives us the strength to see the next one as possible. With the self-efficacy and sense of autonomy we gain, we may go on a walking trip outside of the area in which we live, we may read out a piece of poetry we've written at an event, or take on a more challenging exercise activity. Each progression builds on the last and creates that sense of confidence which motivates us towards our next step. In time we arrive at the place we once only dreamed of, confident in our ability to choose our actions, conscious of the power of the relationships we have built along the way and stronger in our competence. I never learned this as a cyclist, only as a retired one, and that I think reflects the reality that a change which presents as a loss may just be the start of true learning.

Growth Mindset

Learning is something we often deny ourselves as we mature. In some way our identity becomes fixed to capability or mastery and the idea of being a learner or a beginner becomes embarrassing. I was lucky – I had always been a committed learner and I had internalized the sense that if I listened to expertise and tried my best, I could get better, no matter how hard it might be at the start. You too may have that sense, and if not, you can develop it. Think about your life, your heroic journey and your improvements. What have you improved at through your life? You will have grown socially, professionally or practically in any number of ways, and reminding yourself of that will be incredibly powerful as you start a new period of change and growth. It will aid you as you try to develop a learner's or 'growth' mindset.

In the late 1990s, Carol Dweck was studying motivation, personality and development as part of her psychology programme at Stanford University. Through her work she realized that the ways in which we respond to challenge and failure might just hold the key to unifying and understanding the three. Our personality, or outlook, is what allows us to remain motivated and develop, or continue to be motivated even when our development slows or stalls. While a great deal of her research took place in schools (they are the perfect setting because progress is already being tested) and its impacts have been particularly profound in education, it has gone on to influence workplaces, social psychology and the study of wellbeing across many fields.[11]

The 'growth mindset' is contrasted with the 'fixed mindset'. In a fixed mindset, we believe our abilities are static; they are connected to our intelligence or innate physical traits. But with a growth mindset, we see ability as something that grows with effort. Dweck's work began with students, and the stark contrast she discovered was that students with fixed mindsets, regardless of their supposed ability, were more likely to give up when encountering difficulty. Students with growth mindsets were more likely to continue and improve, even if they had less traditional aptitude for the subject. In many studies these students continue to *outperform* other students regardless of their socioeconomic status or initial ability.

A growth mindset is an incredibly powerful thing, and it is also, wonderfully, something that we can learn. Students who are *taught* about a growth mindset, about the malleability of our intelligence and the plasticity of our minds, not only develop a growth mindset, but grow their minds accordingly. So too can we adults introduce the benefits of a growth mindset at any point in our lives. In Dr Dweck's research, a change in mindset could be brought about by adding the word 'yet' to any statement about our capabilities. Try it now. Is there something you would like to be able to do that you cannot yet? For me (and yes, I know it's extreme), that thing would be freediving.

A fair assessment of my current ability would be: **I cannot freedive.**

An even fairer, equally honest but altogether more empowering one would be: **I cannot freedive yet.**

I am hard-pressed to think of two statements that are so similar in their contents but so different in their outcome. The first describes a past, of not learning to freedive and a present in which we cannot as a result. The second describes those, as well as a future in which all of that could change. The word 'yet' is a transformer, loaded with possibility and imbued with the sense of a growth mindset that could be applied to all manner of new challenges in our ever-changing lives.

A growth mindset allows us to bring all the possibilities of the future into our present actions, which is powerful when making a change that could otherwise be focused on the past and our losses. It helps us to move forward and remain conscious of potential progress, but it also protects us from becoming stuck or giving up. This process is often defined alongside resilience or 'grit' in psychological literature, which is a concept in psychology that refers to a willingness to pursue a task or goal for a long period of time. Much like the theory of growth mindsets, grit was developed by a theorist who began looking at how children succeed. Angela Duckworth was a seventh-grade teacher in New York City who noticed that some children with high ability (according to IQ and baseline assessments) didn't do as well as expected, while others with supposed 'lower' ability flourished and progressed. What she noticed, in schools and later in her research with high performers from Military Academies to tech companies and even spelling bees, was that grit or perseverance correlated more with progress than ability. 'Success didn't go to the smartest people. It went to the *most determined*.'[12]

The shorter-term component of grit is self-control – the ability to resist immediate temptation in the pursuit of goals. And this is important when we think about how we respond to change, and how we can manage our fear of it, because periods of change tempt us to dwell only on what we've lost. We may not immediately consider this focus as temptation, as temptations are usually *nice* things, but it is, because it's easier to think about what we've lost than to do the work of concentrating on what we might gain. Nostalgia is more comfortable than leaning into what we fear, taking a risk and embracing whatever comes after the change, but it is far less satisfying. It would have been easier for me to stare at the medals on my wall or stew over the harsh treatment I received from people that I believed incorrectly pushed me to retire, but it was harder and eventually more enjoyable to start doing completely unrelated things. Whether you have experienced an injury, a lost job or a break-up, you might recognize this. Our desire is to dwell on what went wrong, the unfairness of it or what was lost, but we all know that progress only begins again when we recognize our fear and choose to embrace the opportunities our new situation offers us. There is a level on which we want self-care to be soft and forgiving of these impulses, but at certain points we have to be firm with ourselves in the pursuit of happiness. Responding to change by dwelling on the past is an easy way out, and while it may involve a lot of 'self', it is eventually the opposite of 'care'.

Resilience

In many ways, giving ourselves allowances, going easy on ourselves and capitulating to the reflexive tendency we all have to fixate on past losses, is the crueller option. Failing to make a break with the past and the hardship of that loss means the pain of it is likely to stick around for longer, and go deeper than it would otherwise. Instead, actively engaging with our fear of what life will be like when things change, and doing so with a certain degree of firmness, helps, and there is a reason that such firmness is connected to the notion of resilience. Resilience, in material science, is about durability, strength and flexibility. There needs to be room for both adaptability and strength. Mental resilience is no different, and it is something that can be developed. Resilience has been cited as a key factor in coping with stress and maintaining mental wellbeing, and in many ways, through this book we have already been discussing how to build it. Penn State University in the US offers a popular resilience-building programme,[13] and you will recognize some of their approaches from what we've been talking about over the last few chapters. Key components of the prestigious course involve working with participants to develop optimism about the future, helping reframe fear and catastrophic thoughts by replacing them with constructive thoughts and a developing sense of our fear as a powerful driving energy source. They encourage people to develop a sense of control and take gradual small steps to feel more capable in the face of things we are afraid of.

The project of building resilience is one and the same with facing fear, developing a growth mindset and gaining confidence in our ability to pursue life's opportunities rather than avoid threats. These are the pillars which underpin our ability to live life more proactively and joyfully, and they are pivotal in progressing positively through change, because life is a series of changes.

The greatest life changes often take place after the longest periods of stability, of sameness. This is the source of both their threat and their opportunity. When we have lived a certain way for a long time, we have become more fixed than ever in that way of being and in the sense that it forms our identity. But, in fact, we will also have changed far more than we realize across that stable, seemingly consistent time. I thought all I had been was a cyclist for sixteen years, but in fact I had gone from being a sixteen-year-old girl to a grown woman. The cycling had remained the same and it gave me a misguided impression that I had too. When I woke up and realized that I had grown, I saw that I needed that change in my circumstances, actions and identity. After sixteen years, I needed to determine a new path, one fit for the person I was now rather than the person that I had been. If you are in a marriage that is ending after forty years, just think how different you are to the person who came into it and how strange it would be to believe that you are losing a single fixed identity from that time. You have become a different person, and changed long before 'the change' itself became forced on you. If you are ending a career, try to see how the person who gets to make the choices about the next steps is not the professional 'you' that you left behind, but the person who you have become, now. Life change is sometimes the moment at which we realize that *we* have changed, and that is exactly the sort of self-knowledge that we require to choose new paths, gain new relationships and begin scaffolding an upward trajectory of competence in something we *really want to do*.

There is a fantastic series in the *Guardian* newspaper called 'A New Start After Sixty'. It is a series of short-form interviews with people who have decided at sixty years old to do something completely new. Something strangely, brilliantly, different. There is an engineer who retired from her job at British Rail to become an award-winning wildlife photographer, a saleswoman who did her first pull-up as a pensioner and became the oldest contestant on *Ninja Warrior*, and a renowned creator of stained glass who took seventy years to find her inner artist. What I see when I read those articles, are people who have had enough time to *know themselves*, and choose their next steps in far more joyful and personal ways than they may have done when they were younger. Sometimes a life change forces them to look at themselves and the wide expanse of options that are open to them; sometimes it is the simple fact that they have lived long enough with the person we all call 'me' to understand better what they want to do. They do not lose all of the lessons of the life they have lived; they use it to inform the one they are living. They make a choice based on more intimate knowledge of what gives them meaning, and that knowledge only becomes available to us with reflection, change and a few shocks along the way.

We do not bounce back from life events, or changes – we bounce forwards. When I thought about bouncing back in the days before and around my retirement, I thought about finding a long-lost French ancestor who could get me a passport and allow me to compete for a different team. I thought about new ways of doing the same old things because they were what I knew, when in reality all of the joy I have experienced since has come from learning things I didn't. Bouncing back would have taken me to where I was; bouncing on forward has taken me far beyond it.

The first great change of my life was the one I feared and one I did not choose, but with it came an opportunity to finally choose my life.

KEY TAKEAWAYS

1. Life is a journey of constant change.

2. Your core values, the things you stand for, will remain through life's changes.
   If a change brings a loss, it also makes space. You can choose how you fill that space, which is a form of freedom.

3. A learner's or growth mindset allows you to think about what you cannot do *yet*.

4. You have *already* changed a lot up to this point in your life, and you will continue to change in the future.

**The change worth making is the change
that could make you.**

6. Fear of the Unknown

Reframing Uncertainty

We tend to think of *uncertainty* and the *unknown* in mostly negative terms. Those words, even just written on the page, conjure up notions of anxiety and peril. If they were images, 'uncertainty' may look like a rickety bridge and 'the unknown' the depths of some dark ocean, but this is not a given. We could just as easily view them through the prism of excitement and curiosity. We are rarely excited when we are certain, and we are not curious about things we already know. Uncertainty, then, is not a rickety bridge, but a library and a question. The unknown may refer to that deep dark ocean, but it also describes a journey to the stars.

Fear and excitement or anxiety and curiosity may seem as far from one another as the ocean and the stars, but they are closer than we think. What's more, we have the power to adjust our relationship to uncertainty and the unknown, moving it from one of fear to one of opportunity. This is a project worth undertaking, as uncertainty and a lack of knowledge are, in some ways, present in almost every moment of our lives. And on a wider societal and economical scale, it doesn't seem likely that uncertainty is going anywhere. It may feel counterintuitive (although possibly not, this far into the book!), but actively engaging with uncertainty – something so many of us are scared of, something that feels so full of risk – can build strength and confidence, and reduce our anxiety.

One way to reframe uncertainty and the unknown is to look

at their opposites. If uncertainty is bad, then surely certainty is generally good, right? But when we look closer, that's not the case. We can be *certain* that we are a disappointment, that we *always* mess up or that we will *never* be able to do something. In such cases of negative, permanent certainty, the ability to undermine our supposed knowledge would be a blessing and uncertainty could start to look like *possibility* by another name.

In my better moments, that was how I approached the uncertainty that came with my retirement. I saw the possibilities that it brought, and the uncertainty as a welcome change from my increasingly suffocating life within British cycling. It was in that mindset that I agreed, a year and a half after retiring, to compete against professional jockeys for a day. This was, and will never be, something that people recommend. The work of a jockey is dangerous, the training arduous and true expertise a result of a lifetime of practice. I had never been on a horse, but I was hungry for a challenge. So, when a company reached out and offered to pay for my training to race at Cheltenham, I took them seriously. Others took me seriously too – enough to say, 'seriously, don't do that'. In the eyes of the world, and particularly those with intimate knowledge of the complexities of horseracing, my decision was foolish to the point of quite serious danger. It was also very exciting. So I responded to the publicity team that had made me the offer and said I would need a few weeks to mull it over, but if they could introduce me to the trainer that I would work with, that would give me some more information upon which to base my decision. That trainer was Yogi, and it didn't take long for me to be sold.

Horse (and Vic) Whisperer

Yogi Breisner was the sort of coach that I had been looking for my whole life. He was clear, honest and kind, and much like Steve Peters before him he helped me to see myself and my sport in a new light. A cheerful, direct Swede, he is something of a horse whisperer, and his ability to read and calm animals seems to extend to humans too. This was vital: I was moving from racing on an inanimate object to competing alongside a conscious half-ton creature, so what I knew about speed or strength would need to be matched with a new appreciation for psychology. Yogi had that, but when we met I was most struck by the lack of cynicism with which he approached our project. Many experts (and he is a true expert, having coached multiple Olympians and champion jockeys) might be offended by an upstart from another field assuming they can jump in to theirs (then jump on and jump the course), but he treated me with the utmost respect. It was humbling, and a courtesy I expect many doyens of British cycling would fail to extend to a retired jockey who decided to race in the Olympics.

He was optimistic about it all, which was a welcome alternative to the pessimism that I received when I raised my plans with anyone else. I was terrified, but thrilled in equal measure. I didn't know how it would go but I was willing to appreciate that uncertainty. The strength and magnificence of the horses was genuinely awe-inspiring and I quickly gained enough trust in Yogi to follow his lead into the unknown. If he believed I could do it, and I wanted to, I would do it. So I told him, 'our agreement is that if you ever think I won't meet the standard required, tell me and I will stop. Until you do, I will listen, learn and strive to be better every day.' He agreed, and gradually we saw improvements. In his eyes it was actually better that I had *never* ridden before than if I had ridden a bit and learned bad habits. I was a blank slate, but I had a clear goal and some of the attributes for being a passable jockey. I was calm, coachable and possessed a good appetite for speed (and competition), and in Yogi's eyes those could be more difficult to learn than the technique of riding with a horse.

He was the first person who told me I was courageous. I fell in training one day and he suggested, as all horse people do, that the best thing would be to get right back up and start riding again. So I did and it was fine. At the end of the session he told me he was impressed by my courage, which was something I had never been told in my life. I had been told I was capable and been feted in newspapers with all manner of (often inaccurate) adjectives, but I had never received a compliment like that. In the last years of my cycling career, the one thing I had been was courageous, and it was only when he said it that I realized I was more proud of my courage during that difficult time than any victory. Someone will always beat your records, but courage stays with you for ever.

So I learned from Yogi and I learned from the horses. After a lifetime spent in a meticulously controlled sport, one where data models could predict down to the tenth of a second how fast you *should* complete a race (if you don't mess up), my control was now more limited. Riding a horse, unlike racing a bike, feels like life; you don't try to win, but to move with it gracefully. Just as a kayaker cannot control a river, you can't really control a horse – it is not your energy to control, but to harness. I had to control what I could, accept what I could not and learn to spot the difference.

This wasn't always easy, as horse-riding is a partnership with limited communication. As much as possible you try to maintain the flow when things seem to be going well, and maintain perspective and focus when they are not, but you cannot always tell when things are about to go wrong. A horse is a complicated creature that can be scared into wild behaviour by something as simple as a crisp packet on the wind. This was beyond my control, but I knew that I would be better placed to ride it out if I kept cool. We all have to submit when we're confronted by forces of nature. Just as we do not actually 'conquer' Everest, or swim *against* a riptide, we cannot expect our small human hands to ever *really* control a thoroughbred, so with some humility we must submit. All we can really try to do is know ourselves well enough to react in ways that improve the situation rather than make it worse, and believe in our ability to see it through.

So we trained and I fell, I got up and I rode again, and in the process I got better every time. Until there was no time left and we prepared to go to Cheltenham. It was only long after the race was done that I found out a *lot* of people were very nervous about my performance. Much of the horseracing community was concerned about the publicity my race was getting, and the way it would turn if I was unseated (as I had been in a practice race) or my horse was injured. It was not only me that was going into the unknown.

As I mounted my beautiful horse Pacha and waited with him in the paddock, I tried to relish the private moment between the two of us. I held my palms to the warmth of his neck and felt his rhythmic breath, the calm before the storm. I tried, as much as possible, to be one with him. Great horse-jockey combinations create a sort of hybrid creature, unified and more like a centaur than two very different animals – the more connected the runner and the rider, the better the outcome. Unfortunately prior to the event my focus was interrupted by two stewards, who separately reminded me that I could pull up whenever I wanted to. Some part of them wanted to protect me, but all I heard was their lack of belief. They didn't know whether I was capable, and in their uncertainty they had turned to protective behaviour, paternalistic prodding that presented as care, when really it was thinly veiled fear. They were wrong, and they were right. I was in danger – all jockeys are, in any race. Their sport was at risk too – if myself or my horse got injured it would draw a great deal of negative attention and publicity to a pursuit that has to justify its moral existence. In their eyes, if I was unprepared, then everyone would be better off if I just pulled out. They were wrong because I knew all of that, Yogi knew it and we had decided, based on my training and our evaluation of the risks involved, that it was worthwhile. I knew the danger I was in, and I had decided to face it just as all the others would, so there was no more reason for me to pull up than there was for anyone else.

I wouldn't, and from the moment we emerged into the paddock in our silks, through the final discussion of our race plan, I felt comfortable. It felt familiar, the expectation and the risk, and this time I felt the added incentive to project calm for Pacha Du Polder, my horse, partner and friend. When the bell rang, I swung up and found the stirrups, took a deep, slow breath and reminded myself that this was exactly where I wanted to be.

The race itself flew by in a glorious blur. I was in a state of pure 'flow', of clarity and focus, without much sense of time. Flow is what we experience when completing a challenging task of which we know we are capable, and we switch off all aspects of our mind that are not relevant to completing it. I stayed with Pacha, hoof step by pounding hoof step, jump by jump, connecting with him rather than directing him. When we reached the finish line, in a respectable fifth place, I was exhilarated and satisfied. I didn't know if I would do it again, but that was part of the fun.

I had stepped out into the unknown, faced the fear and uncertainty that came with it, and enjoyed myself. Our ability to engage with uncertainty is multi-faceted. I seem to have developed a fair tolerance for unknown challenges – the risks and the uncertainties of adventure – but that does not mean that *all* unknowns are comfortable to me. We will discuss soon how a period of anxiety left me unable to leave my own house. I felt out of control, surrounded and overcome by a heightened sense of risk. I could race a horse but I could not ride an underground train without feeling panicked and claustrophobic. I say this because I want to be clear that uncertainty is not the same for all of us, and we will all have different experiences that make us feel more or less uncomfortable. The knowledge we can gain about uncertainty, however, will benefit us in whichever situation our discomfort happens to arise. I did not need to learn those tools to be comfortable in the uncertainty of a race, but I needed them later when I learned again how to re-enter the world.

Uncertainty Intolerance

So let's begin with the ways in which an intolerance of uncertainty can make us fearful and unhappy, and then discuss the patterns of thought and perspectives that allow us to grow more tolerant. Uncertainty is any experience that contains an element of unpredictability, and as such the unknown is as personal to each of us as the life we have led up to it. We grow uncomfortable in a moment of uncertainty as our brain defaults to a negative, defensive and protective state. This is a product of our early evolution, where an uncertain threat was often mortal, and as a result, assuming the worst-case scenario was a reasonable and essential survival approach. In our modern world, uncertainties are more prevalent and less acute. That is to say that we have more things to think about than a zebra does, but far less to be threatened by. So we should try to adopt a more thoughtful response to uncertainty. If we do not update our uncertainty tolerance and improve our ability to reason through it, we are bound to assume the worst in any uncertain situation. This tendency to assume that uncertain scenarios = worst-case scenarios is what leads us to develop what psychologists of uncertainty call 'safety' or 'avoidance' behaviours. The following are (some) safety behaviours which any of us might use when faced with uncertainty:

- Excessive reassurance-seeking: Frequently looking for advice, opinions or confirmation about choices
- Over-preparation: Excessive preparation in the hope of eliminating uncertainties or negatives

- Avoidance: Failing to even engage with things that might seem uncertain
- Escape: Leaving situations where uncertainty is present
- Compulsive behaviours: Repeated actions that we believe reduce anxiety
- Distraction: Diverting our attention away from the uncertain situation

Most of us struggle with some or all of these reactions to uncertainty. I am a worrier and a warrior, so at some point in my journey, I have personally displayed *all* of the behaviours above. How much we rely on them will be determined by the extent to which the uncertainty causes us discomfort, but the 'safety' behaviour can also cause pain which is potentially greater than we might have experienced if the uncertain outcome had come about. This reflects the way in which people will often choose a known discomfort rather than remain uncertain about one that may or may not come. This was demonstrated succinctly by a landmark 2016 study at UCL,[1] where participants were given a 50/50 chance of receiving an electric shock. They were told to wait until it came, but were given the option of pressing the button and administering the shock to themselves. Many participants pressed the button, choosing an immediate and guaranteed form of pain over an uncertain one that may or may not come. They would rather painfully avoid the uncertainty than remain uncertain but free of pain.

Humans are wired to avoid uncertainty. We have discussed how our brain developed to respond to threats in the animal kingdom and when we employ them in the modern world we take any uncertainty as a sign of threat. If we can learn to overcome this wiring, learn to tolerate uncertainty rather than run from it or fight it, we can be happier and healthier. In fact, the 'Intolerance of Uncertainty Index' is a tool that the psychologists Michel Dugas and Robert Ladouceur developed in the 1990s to evaluate how comfortable we are with uncertainty.[2] They were researching the mechanisms behind Generalized Anxiety Disorder (GAD) and found that individuals with GAD often struggle deeply with uncertainty – worrying excessively about future events, even in the absence of specific threats. So they created a tool to measure different people's relationships to uncertainty and study the impacts that different forms of support and therapy could have.

Our score on the index is determined through a series of questions that help us to understand our view of ourselves and of uncertainty itself. These measures include:

- Our need for closure – how we deal with ambiguity and how open-minded we are about ambiguous ideas.

- Our emotional relationship to uncertainty – how positive or negative it makes us feel.

- Our self-efficacy – how far we believe we have the tools to deal with uncertainty or how much we believe we could learn them.

The more capable we are of being open-minded, seeing uncertain situations as potentially positive (rather than only negative) and trusting ourselves to overcome uncertainty, the higher we will score. More importantly, these dispositions are broadly consistent with mental wellbeing and personality traits such as openness, durability and different forms of bravery. Political extremism is correlated with a low uncertainty tolerance, as is the membership of cult organizations and a willingness to trust dictatorial figures, while uncertainty tolerance is associated with lower levels of prejudice and mental flexibility. If we can learn to be open-minded in uncertain and unknown situations, we not only protect ourselves and our values from manipulation, but we get to experience excitement and curiosity where we may have experienced fear and anxiety. We will also be more creative, intellectually flexible and hopeful. The ability to see that the unknown is not always black and white, and to remain uncertain (especially in place of seeking false certainty), allows us to take more time to consider different points of view and combine ideas that may seem contradictory. As F. Scott Fitzgerald said, 'The test of a first-rate intelligence is the ability to hold two opposing ideas in the mind at the same time, and still retain the ability to function.'[3] Which sounds to me like a tolerance for uncertainty.

It's clear for all these reasons that developing a tolerance for uncertainty is a worthwhile undertaking. It can make us less fearful, more resolute and perceptive, but the question is: how? You may not be surprised that the answers, in different ways, revolve around knowledge of ourselves and developing belief in our ability to cope with the fear that we face, rather than run away from it.

If the problem could be described as:

A. Sensing the unknown and feeling threatened
B. Taking the feeling of threat as evidence of threat
C. Believing that we are incapable of dealing with the evident threat

The solution could be

A. Understanding how and why we feel threatened
B. Realizing that such a feeling is not always actually consistent with a threat
C. Understanding the reality of a situation
D. Knowing that we are capable of overcoming both the feeling and whatever the reality happens to be

The Real Sixth Sense

If we can learn to read our responses (self-knowledge) and truly believe that we are capable of dealing with uncertain outcomes (agency), we will be less likely to engage in damaging and life-limiting safety behaviours, but we also access the myriad benefits that come with self-knowledge and agency themselves. I spoke to Katherine Templar Lewis, leading cognitive scientist and co-author, with Sam Conniff, of *The Uncertainty Toolkit*,[4] to find out more about how uncertainty influences our health and happiness. She introduced me to 'interoception', a fascinating concept that looks at these benefits. Katherine is an incredible researcher and an even more amazing communicator, so when she described interoception – which she termed 'the *real* sixth sense' – I was enraptured. Interoception is the ability to recognize what is going on *inside* of our body. While the traditional five senses generally deal with our ability to take in and process information from the external world, interoception gives us crucial information about our responses to it. It is through this sense that we evaluate the physical sensations in our body which are indicators of psychological responses we might not have been consciously aware of. Butterflies in our stomachs, cold feet or the tingle of intuition – these are all physical sensations which describe knowledge that our conscious mind may not yet recognize. Our emotions are physical things.

This may sound speculative, but it is well evidenced[5][6] that our ability to read physical cues in our bodies allows our minds to make better decisions. Interoception – this conscious assessment of the cues our body gives us – provides a way for us to feel the physical sensations that arise in the face of uncertainty and leverage them towards curiosity and excitement rather than panic. If we can recognize a feeling, we are less likely to be overwhelmed by it, but we can also be positively guided by it. And this too is backed up by the research. One such example comes from a study[7] conducted on a London trading floor which found that the interoceptive ability of bankers was linked to longevity in financial markets. Throughout the study, the team monitored the heartbeats of traders, and at different intervals asked them to make a judgement of their current beats per minute. Those who judged their own heartbeat more accurately were found to have better outcomes and keep their jobs longer. That is to say that bankers who demonstrated an ability to read their bodies also performed better in their minds.

It's all in Your Body

This should not necessarily be surprising. Self-knowledge is a valuable thing, and the ability to take information from another sense and feed that into our reasoning should be useful, even when that sense is looking inward. We only find insight like this surprising as we tend to separate out our bodies from our minds. Knowledge of our physical state has historically been assumed to be irrelevant to our psychology or intellectual performance because the two have been treated as independent for hundreds of years. This is something that the psychologist and neuroscientist Antonio Damasio called 'Descartes' Error' in his 1994 book of the same name.[8] In the seventeenth century the philosopher Descartes argued that our mind did not have a physical basis and that unlike other animals our soul was what allowed us to behave rationally. Damasio, nearly three hundred years later, countered with something quite different. He provided ample evidence that our rational thought and decision-making processes have a basis in our physiology and that our minds and bodies are not so disconnected as Descartes suggested.

More recently, researchers have extended Damasio's argument to describe how we can approach our minds through our bodies, and our bodies through our minds – often landing on the importance of the 'sympathetic nervous system'. This system is not so much physical *or* mental, but both, and this is significant, as it can explain both how exercise changes our minds and mindfulness transforms our bodies.

The sympathetic nervous system is the part of us that regulates our responses to stress. It determines whether our heart rate increases, our pupils dilate to improve vision and our airways expand to improve oxygen intake. It is always active in some form, but when we are psychologically stressed this physical system changes our bodies in such a way to be ready to respond to a threat. You may recognize it as a subject we have discussed in terms of the psychology of fear at various points – it's what's readying that zebra to flee from the lion. We discussed moving from a threat to a challenge mindset, how narratives about our life journey can create a sense of adventure rather than fear, and how knowing our values can help us with change. All of these techniques are implicit ways of developing a better understanding and control over our sympathetic nervous system. But there are explicit ones we can tap into, too, and they're of particular value when embracing our fear of uncertainty.

We have spoken at length about the role of self-knowledge in any attempt to reframe our relationship with fear, and knowledge of how our bodies feel and express themselves is an important part of that. Practices such as breathwork involve focusing on a physical process to help us to feel more physically aware, and in the process open us up to the physical feelings that coexist with (or are synonymous with) our psychology. Breathwork offers a *direct* way to calm the sympathetic nervous system, which is responsible for the anxiety in our minds. By choosing to breathe in certain ways, we can not only learn about how our body is feeling, but direct that feeling away from threat and anxiety towards calm.

This is important because, when it comes to uncertainty and fear of the unknown (say, worrying about all the things that *could* go wrong on an upcoming trip, or imagining a social event that *might* be awkward), many of us feel anxious or threatened by things that we consciously know are not threatening us – or at least, they are not doing so right now. In such experiences, our sympathetic nervous system is acting as if the threat is real and immediate and as a result we *feel* very threatened, even if we knew initially that the threat was unlikely. By intercepting this process and going directly to our sympathetic nervous system, we can interrupt the process that leads to panic, catastrophizing or the constant hum of low-level anxiety by engaging the very physical process that *is panic*. As Damasio said, emotions are physical phenomena, and that means that we can learn physical practices that regulate them.

EXERCISE: BREATHING

1. Box Breathing (Square Breathing)

How to do it:
1. Inhale slowly through your nose for 4 seconds.
2. Hold your breath for 4 seconds.
3. Exhale slowly through your mouth for 4 seconds.
4. Hold your breath for 4 seconds.
5. Repeat for 4–6 cycles.

Why it helps:
Box breathing calms the nervous system, reduces stress and improves focus. It is used by athletes and the military to manage anxiety and maintain mental clarity. Research shows[9][10] it can lower heart rate and blood pressure.

2. 4-7-8 Breathing

How to do it:

6. Inhale quietly through your nose for 4 seconds.

7. Hold your breath for 7 seconds.

8. Exhale slowly and fully through your mouth for 8 seconds.

9. Repeat for 4 cycles.

Why it helps:

This technique relaxes the body and mind, making it easier to manage stress and fall asleep. Studies show[11] it activates the para-sympathetic (rest-and-digest) system, reducing anxiety and promoting relaxation.

3. Diaphragmatic (Belly) Breathing

How to do it:

10. Sit or lie down comfortably.

11. Place one hand on your chest and one on your belly.

12. Inhale deeply through your nose so your belly rises (not your chest).

13. Exhale slowly through your mouth, letting your belly fall.

14. Repeat for 5–10 breaths.

Why it helps:

Belly breathing increases oxygen flow, helps you relax, and can reduce symptoms of anxiety and stress. Research shows[12] it lowers cortisol (the stress hormone) and improves mood.

Making the Unknown, Known

In some sense, our fear of the unknown is best remedied by access to 'the known'. We cannot ever entirely remove uncertainty from our lives, but we can get to know the part of ourselves that processes it and learn to reassure ourselves. Mindfulness works along these lines, and there is good reason that it's often grouped alongside breathwork as a practice that allows our conscious mind to think freely by calming our unconscious one. Mindfulness practices (which often involve meditation) in which we place our mind inside of our body, scan it and see what's going on, are a powerful way to improve our interoception. They also encourage us to view our thoughts from one step's remove. This, again, offers us a way to separate out our conscious mind from the unconscious. When we sit with our thoughts and watch or note them, we gain a means to disentangle our conscious thoughts from unconscious feeling, but also from an activated sympathetic nervous system. It allows our mind to take a moment and see that our *body is panicking*.

When we understand that our body is acting on a threat response (which is the basis of fear, or anxiety), we open up space for our conscious mind to make decisions to calm it. This can feel impossible when our thoughts feel like necessary continuations of our stress, but we can break the chain. If we can see that our emotions and our physical processes are one and the same, we gain self-knowledge, self-control and a very specific entry point to calm our subconscious and improve our conscious experience.

EXERCISE: BODY SCAN MEDITATION[13]

Get comfortable: Sit or lie down in a quiet place. Rest your hands by your sides and gently close your eyes.

1. Focus on your breath: Take a few slow, deep breaths. Notice the feeling of air moving in and out of your body.

2. Begin the scan with your light: Imagine your attention is a warm, gentle light.

3. Start at the top of your head. Shine this light on your forehead. Notice any sensations – tingling, warmth, tension, or even nothing at all. There is no right or wrong.

4. Move the light slowly: Gradually move your light down, illuminating each part of your body in turn:

   - Your face
   - Your jaw
   - Your neck and shoulders
   - Your arms and hands
   - Your chest and back
   - Your belly
   - Your hips and pelvis
   - Your legs
   - Your feet

   Pause for 20–30 seconds on each area. Let your light gently reveal any sensations, comfort or discomfort. If your mind wanders, simply guide the light of your attention back to the area you're scanning.

5. Acknowledge and accept: If you notice tension or emotion, imagine your light softening and warming that area. Breathe into it, and as you exhale, picture the light helping to ease any discomfort.

6. Complete the scan: Once your light has reached your feet, take a few deep breaths and imagine your whole body bathed in this gentle, warm light. When you're ready, open your eyes and return to your surroundings.

The Effect of Emotions

When we struggle with fear, and particularly fear of the unknown, we are effectively operating an alarm system that looks for intruders and takes steps to up our defences in response. We can either train that system to differentiate between friends and intruders more effectively (which would be the conscious process of reframing threats of all kinds), turn the system's sensitivity down (interocept to see how sensitively it is attuned and use breathwork or mindfulness to calm it) or look at the defence mechanisms the system employs. This third option entails engagement with the emotions that our unconscious mind throws up and practising ways of thinking which in turn calm our unconscious mind back down.

It is in this way that the self-knowledge of our emotions acts as a powerful tool when it comes to improving our relationship with uncertainty and fear of the unknown. The active practice of questioning our emotions allows us to approach these experiences with curiosity rather than outright fear and panic (*why does meeting my partner's parents make me feel this way?* Or *what is it about holidays that makes me feel nervous?*). This in turn may allow us to even develop some degree of excitement about the unknown that we are approaching. Katherine Templar Lewis made the vital point that excitement and fear are very similar physical processes in our bodies, but that the 'valence' – i.e. the pleasantness or unpleasantness of our emotions – is different, excitement being good and fear bad. The fact that the two are so closely related as physical processes allows us to shift one to the other with relatively small actions, and questioning our emotions is one of them. If we think of the example of riding a rollercoaster (exciting) versus falling off a cliff (terrifying), we see that both involve hurtling through the air, both engage the same physical responses, but one is deeply enjoyable (okay, admittedly only for some), while the other is awful. The difference is that we know we are safe on a rollercoaster. What could be fear is excitement because we know we are safe, we believe there is a degree of control over the situation, and we have knowingly decided to engage in it.

EXERCISE: HOW TO QUESTION YOUR EMOTIONS[14] [15]

Example: Fear of Making a Mistake at Work

Step 1: Notice and Name the Emotion
Emotion: Anxiety or fear

Thought: 'If I make a mistake at work, I'll get in trouble or even lose my job.'

Step 2: Question the Thought
Ask yourself:

What evidence do I have that one mistake would lead to serious consequences?

Have I made mistakes before? What happened then?

How do others at work handle mistakes?

What is a more realistic outcome?

Step 3: Gather Evidence
For: 'My boss has pointed out errors before. I've seen colleagues get feedback when things go wrong.'

Against: 'I've made small mistakes before and was able to fix them. I've never seen anyone fired for a single mistake. My overall performance is good.'

Step 4: Reframe the Thought
Original: 'If I make a mistake at work, I'll get in trouble or lose my job.'

Balanced: 'Mistakes happen to everyone. If I make one, I can address it and learn from it. My job performance is generally strong, and one error is unlikely to define my career.'

Step 5: Notice the Change
Emotion after reframing: Less anxiety, more self-compassion, and a sense of perspective.

When we engage in the practices discussed throughout this chapter, from mindfulness to questioning our emotions, we become more capable of reminding ourselves that we are actually safe in the here and now, that we are in control and have agency about the choices we make. The future is uncertain, and there may be threats and dangers, but we cannot weigh our present down with those hypotheticals. Understanding that an uncertain future and a safe present can coexist can be the difference between uncertainty feeling like a fun rollercoaster, or falling off a cliff. This is vitally important, because the way we feel about uncertainty influences our mental wellbeing across our lives, not just in uncertain moments. The researchers who developed the Intolerance of Uncertainty Index found that patients with GAD could experience significant progress by engaging specifically with their intolerance of uncertainty. Over twelve weeks, this group learned to challenge the negative beliefs they formed in uncertain situations, they went to eat in new restaurants to test the idea that 'uncertainty ruins everything' and practised coping with uncertainty without reassurance. This allowed them to gain a greater awareness of their feelings around uncertainty, to see where they diverged from reality and to address the safety behaviours they turned to. This process, of developing self-knowledge and strategies that promoted agency, reduced their experience of GAD both in and outside of uncertain situations. It also impacted their experiences of worry and depression and made the case that working on our tolerance of uncertainty can make us happier across a number of dimensions.

The interventions that these researchers used were mostly based in cognitive behavioural therapy. This involves looking at our thoughts (almost like mindfulness) and questioning them impartially. It provides a means to create understanding, and something closer to certainty, about how we react in uncertain situations. It provides knowledge and agency, but mostly helps us *not* to focus on the worst-case scenarios that could arise from uncertain situations. This is a vital intervention in terms of treatment for mental-health conditions, but there is also room to learn about how we *can* prepare and forecast in uncertain situations. We can grow less afraid of the unknown by getting to know ourselves, but we can also make ourselves better at approaching the unknown knowingly.

Jane McGonigal is a visionary games designer, writer and researcher who argues that our ability to imagine (plausible) futures allows us to prepare for them through scenario planning and future forecasting.[16] This means thinking both about the future we want and potential negative scenarios, as this allows us to be proactive rather than reactive about both. There is room for dreaming in such an approach, but not for catastrophizing. A worst-case scenario might be worth considering, but it should receive no more attention than the best-case or many middling-case scenarios in-between. This builds a future-ready mindset, in which we are comfortable with the fact that the future is unknown, but confident that we can approach it in an informed and strategic way. So she encourages us to list possible events in our futures (particularly in line with what we would like to achieve on our journey) and consider the best- and worst-case scenarios. We use our imagination actively and we develop a skill that increases our sense of agency. Whereas many of us use our imagination mostly for catastrophizing, this practice recentres imagination as both the ability to picture the good and the bad that can come with life and prepare for it. In the process, we see that we are capable and as much in control as we could reasonably be.

EXERCISE: IMAGINING AND PREPARING FOR POSSIBLE FUTURES

I. Choose Your Time Horizon

Decide on a specific point in the future to imagine, such as five or ten years from now.

2. Identify a Key Area of Life or Work

Pick an area that matters to you (e.g., your career, health, community).

3. Imagine a Positive Future

Close your eyes and vividly imagine the best-case scenario for this area.

Ask yourself:

- What does my life look like in this future?
- What steps did I (or we) take to get here?
- What skills or resources did I develop?
- How do I feel in this future?

Write down your vision in as much sensory detail as possible. Imagine not just the facts, but how it feels, sounds and looks.

4. Imagine a Challenging or Negative Future

Now, imagine a plausible worst-case scenario.

Ask yourself:

- What went wrong, and why?
- What challenges am I facing?
- How am I coping, and what support do I have?
- What actions could I have taken earlier to prepare or prevent this?

Again, write down this scenario in vivid detail, including your emotional and physical responses.

5. Scenario Planning: Identify Signals and Actions

For both scenarios, list:

- Signals: Early warning signs that this future might be coming true (e.g., trends, news, behaviours)
- Actions: Steps you can take now to move toward the positive future or to prepare for or prevent the negative one

Consider: What can you do today to increase your readiness and agency, no matter which future unfolds?

6. Reflection and Sharing

Reflect on how imagining both futures makes you feel. Do you notice more optimism, agency, or calm?

If comfortable, share your scenarios with someone else. Discuss what actions you might take together to shape your preferred future.

McGonigal treats future planning and imagination as a skill, and in the context of processing the unknown, our fear is the first sign that we might need to develop certain skills. Self-regulation is a skill that is often studied in this context, and I know about it from the perspective of sport. It is usually centred around how we regulate focus, manage negative thoughts and think about new situations (unknowns) in terms of the task and the demands. When we can understand a task, and the demands, we are more capable of devising strategies that create a greater sense of agency and ways to monitor how we're performing. In short, we face an unknown, we focus, consider what is required of us and decide on the best response. This is a framework that has benefitted numerous sportspeople – for whom every competition is just another unknown – and allowed them to do their best in high-stress situations. We all need strategies to turn to when stress is high because it is at these times that we are least capable of acting rationally, but through frameworks for decision-making we can provide ourselves with a degree of certainty in situations with a lot of unknowns. Certainty about how *we* will respond.

If we bring together the practices described in this chapter and others, we can see how a strategic response to stressful events could work. The stressor could be anything – a comment from a colleague, a difficult demand from a child, or a broken boiler – but the strategy could remain constant.

Stressor: It occurs, your colleague is dismissive or patronizing

Body Scan: How am I feeling about this in my body?

Breathing Exercise: Ten seconds to calm your body before your mind gets to work

Question Your Emotions: Think through how you feel. Question whether this feels more damning because you have a core belief about your value which is being undermined (I need to be respected). Question that core belief – this allows you to go from 'I am less valuable when I am patronized' to 'it is not my fault if someone else has a tendency to be dismissive'.

Self-Affirmation: Return to your affirmations to remind yourself of all the ways in which you are valuable and then approach the problem with a calm body and the security to see it as a challenge rather than a threat.

A strategy, whether you are on an Olympic race track or in a shared office, can be the difference between an unforeseen event derailing you and taking it in your stride.

Uncertainty Immunization

In the same way that in Chapter 1 we discussed 'stress inoculation' by introducing small fears and stressors into our lives, so too can we train ourselves to make decisions in uncertain situations by introducing small amounts of uncertainty into our day-to-day. Playing sports, visiting new places or taking on hobbies all provide us with novel experiences in which we practise decision-making, but our practice doesn't even need to be that formal. Any of the following would be simple ways to improve our uncertainty tolerance:

1. **Try something new without over-researching.** Order a meal at a restaurant you've never tried before, or pick a film or book at random instead of reading reviews or seeking recommendations first.

2. **Make small decisions quickly.** For example, choose a route for your walk or commute without checking traffic or weather apps. Accept that you don't know if it's the 'best' option.

3. **Allow plans to remain open-ended.** Agree to meet a friend without setting a specific time or place right away, and see how it feels to leave details flexible.

4. **Limit checking and reassurance-seeking.** If you're tempted to check the news, weather, or your calendar repeatedly, pause and notice the urge – then wait a little longer before acting on it.

Gradually we find that decision-making itself becomes easier and we gain a sense of our ability to remain in control even when all aspects of a situation are not known to us. The fear of the unknown can in many situations be boiled down to the belief that events, circumstances or new environments could overwhelm us, and that we do not have the resources to control our outcomes. We have to practise planning and decision-making, get used to the experience of novel situations and decide on the best way to understand and utilize the feelings that they create in us. Then we can make good decisions based on our goals rather than doubts.

We all have control, not over the world or all of the events in it, but of ourselves. If we know ourselves and the ways in which we think, we are never truly facing the unknown because everything is mediated through knowledge of ourselves. Everything good is unknown before we picture it or pursue it, whether that is a better world, the answer to a question, or a future version of ourselves. If we can accept the unknown as a prerequisite for progress, we are able to see it as a positive, plan for it, and do so with a body and mind that we understand. We can reframe the unknown as an opportunity rather than a threat and value optimistic uncertainty as a healthy alternative to certain pessimism.

The people that told me to give up before I raced at Cheltenham were certain that I would be better off quitting. I was uncertain about whether I would succeed, but confident in my ability to adapt to the uncertainty I faced. I knew how to engage with an uncertain mind and I felt my agency to act. These two things can be the difference between facing the unknown as a threat or as an opportunity in which our fear is just another energy source.

Because, really, the 'unknown' is just another word for the future, so there will be both threats and there will be opportunities. What matters is that we know ourselves and regulate ourselves well enough to remain calm in the face of those threats and motivated in pursuit of opportunities. If we do, then the future is something that we can manage and a place where we can thrive. We can step up to the unknown, and face it with strength, confidence and self-belief, then we can make it known. It is only then that the future we may have feared can become the present we are looking for.

- -

KEY TAKEAWAYS

1. We often mistake uncertainty for unrealized catastrophe, and try to protect ourselves.

2. If we understand how and why we feel this way, and develop tools to evaluate uncertainty, we will feel more confident and capable in uncertainty.

3. Uncertainty tolerance makes us happier, more creative and less likely to be manipulated by people who pretend to present certainty.

4. If we can practise techniques that calm our bodies, we will have calmer minds.

5. We cannot control outcomes, but we can control our responses. We cannot avoid unknowns, but we can always know ourselves.

6. Uncertainty can become excitement. The unknown can breed curiosity. Fear can become an opportunity.

**The only thing worth knowing,
certainly, is yourself.**

7. Fear as Avoidance

From Everyday Anxiety to Breakdown

I've spoken a lot about narrative and how it can determine the shape and outcome of events in our lives. How belief in our own strength can show us opportunities where once we saw threats, how a learner's mindset can create beginnings out of endings, or how stress, reframed, can feel like fuel rather than the fire that may burn us out. The truth is that this *can* cut the other way. So in this chapter I want to take a moment to tell you the story of a time in my life when I decided to put my strength to the test as a way to avoid sitting with how weak I felt. How I created a false beginning in the hope that it would make an ending less real. How I sought a challenge to hide from the fact that in my day-to-day life I was burning out.

This is the story of how I hit rock bottom at 10,000 feet and everything I learned about the difference between chasing a dream and running away from reality. I call it a story, because I want you to learn, as I did, from my experiences first and then expertise later. It's a cautionary tale, but one with a happy ending. About how fears can provide our greatest opportunities, but also the risk of relying on their power to avoid deeper issues. As with all questions around our fear, knowledge of our true motivation and purpose is what makes the difference between pursuit and avoidance.

In 2017, my marriage, a partnership of over a decade, was coming to an end. I had retired, competed at Cheltenham and skipped through the pages of a new chapter in my life. I had not stopped and evaluated, and I had not entirely come to terms with my new existence. I had 'bounced forward', but I hadn't truly stopped to ask what would make me happy. Without reflecting on where I was or where I had been, I progressed – on autopilot.

Many of us, in suffering, compromise the joy of our present moment by believing it's the future that will make us happy, or our past that makes us sad. I have always been firmly in the future-focused camp. For a long time, as a competitive athlete, I had understood that the here and now had to be painful and it should feel hard. Blood, sweat and tears were the price you paid for a future victory and if I felt good at the end of a day, then training had not been hard enough. This is often called 'deferred gratification', and while it's integral to the pursuit of a goal, it alone cannot make for a satisfying life. I sacrificed a potentially wonderful 'present' at university, exploring my independence and social life, in service to a future where I made it onto a national team. I spent those years in the national team, not growing to understand the adult world and my own happiness, but striving to *become* an Olympian. Once I was an Olympian, I ignored the joy of being one because I needed to focus on winning the next Games.

My present was a means to pursue my future. This meant that I spent very little time cultivating aspects of myself that did not contribute to my future goals. I thought very little about my relationships, or my happiness, 'understanding' on some intuitive level that joy in my present could be at odds with the goals in my future. I grew to believe that the pursuit of a future challenge could *always* justify present discomfort.

Avoidance vs Presence

A challenge mindset can make us happier than one that perceives threats. What I am arguing is that there have been instances when

I have believed I was running towards something, when in fact I was running away. Where I *was* perceiving a threat and, rather than engaging with it, created a separate challenge to avoid it. The key difference is in the avoidance. If we are engaging with our threats and fears as challenges, we can grow and gain greater control, but if we are challenging ourselves as an avoidance tactic, then we can give up even more control of our happiness. We can engage with challenges and learn more about ourselves while also gaining the tools and skills that will help us to deal with threats, but relying on them as distractions? Well, that's dangerous territory.

The unravelling of my marriage and retirement left me feeling disconnected and out of control. In Chapter 5, we spoke about 'self-integrity' – how our idea of our self and value through time can be threatened if we tie it to specific titles or achievements, like 'wife' or 'Olympian', rather than values. I think my self-integrity was tied to the fact that I had a stable life, and that I was a competitor who always looked forwards, so when my life felt unstable and the competitions stopped, I experienced the double jeopardy of sadness at the instability and loss, along with a threat to *who I was*.

My response to this threat, what psychologists call 'self-defence', was to take on a challenge that helped me avoid my pain and reinforced my identity as a competitor. I decided to climb Everest, not for joy or self-knowledge, but to avoid my sadness and put off the moment when I confronted the fact that I didn't appreciate my *real* core values, which were so much deeper and enduring than the labels I had relied on. I only see now, with the benefit of age, experience and reflection, that I was not running towards a challenge, but away from the shame that my life was changing and the pain of losing (I believed) an identity that was built on achieving.

I try not to beat myself up for learning this so late. As I said, I had been taught that pain in the present was necessary for future success, and as a result I made the mistake of believing that the introduction of an imagined future success would justify my painful present. This was avoidance. Of course, my nature was also at play too. If I look back at the compulsive behaviours of my teenage years, I see that I have previous experience of creating a separate controllable action (hand-washing, to avoid a future in which I made people sick) as a means to avoid my uncomfortable present (as an anxious, insecure teenage girl). So I can understand why I agreed to go up Everest rather than engage with the grief I felt at the passage of time, the end of a relationship and a body that would not always feel capable in the same way it always had. It was Everest that forced me to stop and to learn, that exposed my vulnerability and the sadness I was running from.

What Is Progress Without Self-Knowledge, Direction Without Location?

My decision to go up the mountain was impulsive. I was sitting beside the adventurer Ben Fogle at an event and he invited me to join him on the expedition. I said 'why not?' and began two years of training for one of the most challenging endurance feats in mountaineering. I prepared diligently, first travelling to Austria to learn the basics of climbing. I focused on using crampons and an ice-axe, going up the great mountains of the Alps as a first step on my journey to the Himalayas. From there I went to Bolivia to do some high-altitude training and adjust to the experience of physical exertion in low-oxygen conditions. Bolivia took my breath away, quite literally, as I flew into La Paz – the highest capital city in the world – at 3,640m above sea level. It is an incredible country made up of opposites and what feel like contradictions; the might of the Andes paired with the flattest landscape in the world at Uyuni; endless-seeming salt flats that make you feel like you exist in an optical illusion; deserts that morph into rainforests and lakes that form in the sky (Titicaca, at 3,800m). I was surrounded by such beauty and yet the contradiction, the opposition in my life, was that I couldn't really appreciate it. I hid from the descending reality of my divorce and isolation by travelling and ascending, missing both the sadness I was running from and the joy that Bolivia's surreal beauty should have inspired. I remained in a blinkered state that focused on the challenge of the mountains ahead of me rather than the glory of those around me or the reality of the life I left behind, where the ground seemed to be falling away beneath my feet.

I hardly considered how others who cared about me might feel about my decision to take on the challenge. I was selfish, as many high performers feel they must be, prioritizing my goals ahead of the needs of people who cared for me. This is something I feel regret for – but understand – when I look back at my career. The life of a competitor is defined by the marginal gains you have relative to your competitors; you are encouraged to think first about your performance goals and the needs of those around you second. I think in some ways this is necessary, but it does not lead to a balanced and happy life. A certain degree of selfishness is required to remain single-minded in pursuit of individual success in elite sport, but it has limits and often comes at the expense of personal growth. I did not spend much time in my twenties or early thirties thinking about my relationships, or how to balance my priorities with those of the people I loved. It was assumed that whatever led to improved performance was right for me.

I took that mindset into my decision to become a committed mountain climber. After spending time in Bolivia, my husband and I exchanged divorce papers, and instead of taking stock, I focused entirely on Everest. I can best describe this drive, and the problems it created, in physical terms. As a cyclist, my training was all about building muscles that propelled me forwards. There was very little focus on developing strength in those parts of my body that might help me to take a step back, move sideways or slow down. In the human body, this can create imbalances, and injuries occur when one part of the anatomy is strong and others are weak. In a sense, this describes my psychology too. I had only ever trained the part of my brain that moved forwards, and my ability to think laterally or stop had never grown alongside it. This meant that I continued forwards when a moment's pause was called for, and I moved upwards when I needed to take a step to the side. In fact, I kept going forwards until I could go no further. It was only when I was forced to stop by the magnitude of a mountain that my learning and growth could begin.

So I travelled out to Nepal with a team, connected by a common goal and knowing that we were all individually responsible for each other's safety. We had to be conscientious and present if we were to survive. Those first weeks of the expedition went well, and we made it to Base Camp, which at first seems like some strange mountain mirage. Bright tents are marked out like traffic cones against a sky so blue it could be a dream, and the freshest air on planet Earth mingles with wood smoke from the tea houses. Wind whistles constantly in the background, as if waiting to decide whether it's going to be a friend or foe, while the booming cracks in the nearby Khumbu icefall leave you in no doubt as to the nature of *that* relationship. It was cracks in the ice and the movements of winds that we had to listen to and respect as we waited for a weather window that would beckon us towards the summit. We thought we would be there some time among the yak bells and pack animals, but without notice a weather window came. It was early, and we were told that once it passed it would not come again for weeks or months. So, in haste, we continued upwards, sooner than planned and far sooner than is safe for a novice mountaineer.

I have been told by many experts that I should never have continued up the mountain. It takes a good deal of time to acclimatize to the extreme environment of the upper Himalayas, and I had not had it or the experience to fall back on. Only an experienced

high-altitude climber, or people raised in such mountain conditions, could safely continue to the summit with so little time. I did
not stop though. Like my muscles, which had only been trained
to push me forwards, my mind moved onwards and upwards and
I decided to accept the 'accelerated preparation' for the summit.

As we climbed, I fell into myself, just two legs and a bag of
supplies padding rhythmically through powdered snow. Extreme
mountaineering is quite the opposite of hiking or hill climbing.
Whereas those pursuits offer a lot of time to look out into the
distance and appreciate the experience and company, Everest is
a much more isolated experience. You focus on putting one foot
in front of the other and you do not have enough oxygen to speak
to your team as you climb. I could not look into the distance and
I could not share in the experience. So I retreated, disconnected
both from home and from the very thing I was doing.

Then I ruminated, and thought only about the mistakes I might
have made in my relationship. I asked myself if the divorce was
my fault, grieving at 20,000 feet without the oxygen to think
clearly or the experience that would tell me that my life was in
danger. So I continued to hike even as I began to grow ill. My
body was entering a state of hypoxia, when your body isn't getting
enough oxygen and confusion leads to nausea, loss of consciousness and even death. Yet, even as every one of my cells lacked
the oxygen they needed to survive, I did not stop; I was too starved
of air to really think and too used to suffering discreetly to see
that this pain was serious. So I pushed on far past the point of
safety, and it was only a few days later that my crew noticed I
was growing quiet and losing coordination. They ordered a
medical assessment and then the truth became clear: I might die
if I continued, and at the very least I would leave my crew with
the dangerous and arduous task of getting me down from the
mountain. I was shocked by the words of the medics, in part
because I had grown so used to discomfort but also because

hypoxia doesn't create the type of pain that we can read effectively. It's not like a broken leg or a torn muscle – there's no sharpness or ache, just a slowing down of the system towards failure. If it had been only me, I would have continued, but my team explained that if I grew more sick, it would put them at serious risk.

That I could understand and, begrudgingly, I accepted my responsibility to make the sensible decision for the team. This was an actual life-and-death decision, and even though my ego had pushed me towards the mountain, now that I was on it, I could not let it put other people at risk. So, slowly, we retreated, and I now mourned the loss of a very different kind of relationship – with my body. I felt as if it had failed me, and as such, another of the key calculations upon which I had built my identity was thrown up in the air. I had always believed that if I put my mind to something, and remained consistent and committed, my body would follow; it would go where my mind led. But after descending that mountain, I felt for the first time that this might not be true.

I lost trust in the one part of myself that I had ever truly believed in. Here, all of the pain that I could've felt in retirement came through me with the force of a burst dam. Many sportspeople feel they lose some part of themselves in retirement – the thing they're good at, the ability to put their body to use in the way they've trained it. I had navigated that by seeing that my physicality could still be useful in other regards, now I was confronted with the fact that it might not be. I felt as if I had lost some self-efficacy, and I mourned the body that I had relied on even when my relationships, my mind and my career had felt unreliable.

I see now that this was not a correct assessment. My body had not failed me; my mind had. I had tried to make it do something impossible, and I did so because I lacked the self-awareness to see I was putting myself in danger, as well as the ability to pause when all I had ever known was progress. As I look back now, I see that my body was simply the last thing to give up when I faced emotional and personal realities that I wouldn't confront. The only thing great enough to make me stop and take stock was Sagarmatha (Mount Everest), and that is a testament to just how far my forward drive would take me to avoid sitting with myself.

How to Start Again from Nothing, and the Opportunity that Awaits

When I got home, I confronted all of the changes that I'd never prepared for. I was divorcing my partner, and feeling separated from my body and the natural world, both of which I had always trusted. This confrontation took place amid the profound physical and psychological trauma of hypoxia. The condition has been shown to bring on symptoms of depression, and although I think I was facing depression of one form or another either way, it probably did accelerate or deepen them.

Into my mind I went. My armour was pulled back, the spikes that I'd grown through years of competition were removed and I emerged, weakened and vulnerable. I had spent my adult life building defence mechanisms to feel less vulnerable to the ups and downs of elite sport and the harshness of the people that operate within it. When I failed on the mountain, I saw what was left. A woman who had sacrificed connection, and the self-knowledge that it takes to maintain it, for the sake of her physical performance. In this lack of knowledge, I had taken my body to a place it shouldn't be. Then that body felt broken, and I was left to start rebuilding from the floor up.

It was clear that I was very unwell. I stayed on my own for a short time, but doctors advised that I should move in with someone who could keep an eye on me, so I lived with my mum rather than be hospitalized. She gave everything to bring me back into the world, but I had almost totally withdrawn. I didn't eat, I hardly slept and I passed four months in a tranquillized daze. I didn't trust my body, and I didn't trust my mind, doubting constantly whether I had any joy left to live for. My love, my body and my belief in the very relationship between effort and reward felt broken.

It was a few months before I began eating properly and behaving lucidly enough to be allowed back home to live on my own. I spent a few days readjusting to the place I had shared with my husband and my past self, before I made a drastic decision. I would leave and go to Costa Rica. I understand that this is not an option that everyone has when diagnosed with severe depression, but I can only describe life as I lived it. A friend of mine, a deeply wise and insightful surf instructor, Monty, was based out there and insisted that I get on a plane and join him for a week. He had been through a divorce, and he had known what it was to live through depression, and thought that the sense of presence that came with surfing, and the sense of connectedness that the natural world inspires, might be able to help.

I only half-believed him, but I couldn't see any other option. I was so desperate to find some joy in my life and surfing somehow presented a chink of light in that dark tunnel. Looking back now, I think the fact that it was an activity that I had relatively recently started learning and exploring was an important factor. Something in me told me that I had to start again, to step into a learner's mindset when it came to my whole life, and surfing was the last thing that I'd enjoyed starting anew. Mostly though, I didn't want to be in my home, and I wanted to make decisions that the happy version of me might make, so I took him up on his offer.

Monty woke me up every morning and rallied to get me into the surf. It'd been some time since I'd seen any reason to get out of bed, but I accepted his calls. He fed me, finding the most nutritious local food and serving it to me after I exhausted myself battling the waves each day. I surfed through that rainy season amid thundering storms, paddled hard to stay afloat among black waves and then returned to my room afterwards to sit alone and listen to the sounds of the jungle. I did so every day, eventually staying for a month, and most days I felt as if I was paddling for my survival.

One day, towards the end of that month, I sat on the shoulder of a wave with two fellow surfers. I remember the moment vividly. I looked from the sun to the trees along the beach and then across the water until my line of sight fell on my hands and the two people beside me. I *do* want to be here, I thought. I *want* to live. For the first time in a long while, I felt present, and I wanted to be. In fact, remarkably, I felt like I *could be*, happily. Up until that time I'd assumed that because I couldn't fight my way through unhappiness ('muscle-through' in the language I was used to), it must be something that wouldn't pass. In fact, it was my very belief that sadness was something to be fought that had been holding me back. My life and my depression were not things to be fought or races to be won, but parts of life to be *experienced*. Running and fighting had failed me, so I had to learn to sit – with myself, with my fear and in my present.

It may not be clear how this experience pertains to fear, or anxiety, but in a number of ways I believe it does. First, a great fear of mine has always been sharing and vulnerability to criticism, which goes back to the days where I lived in fear of being misinterpreted by the British media. I had been honest on a few occasions, and it had rarely gone well for me. So, what you have just read is me being honest and facing that fear of being judged, in real time.

I believe what I experienced also introduces the subject of anxiety and other connected forms of mental anguish because of the role of avoidance in my unhappiness and of presence in returning me to a happier state. It was only when I stopped running, sat within myself and understood my sadness that I felt present with it. It was only by being present with it that I could learn about myself and my situation and, as we will see, avoidance vs presence is at the heart of the distinction between anxiety and fear.

Anxiety vs Fear

Anxiety differs from fear because it doesn't have a clear focus or resolution. It's a state of being, but the opposite of presence. If a friend tells you they're afraid, you might ask, 'of what?' But if they say they're anxious, the causes – and responses on offer – are less clear. Our fear makes us present; it places us in front of its cause. Whereas our anxiety dissociates and misdirects us.

That is why the story of my attempt to be absent from my pain bears more resemblance to my anxiety than it does my confrontations with fear. Fortunately, I've learned that fear provides opportunities to access the presence, approaches and resources that help us stand above, rather than beneath, our anxiety. To confront it as *a* problem, rather than feel we are *the* problem.

The distinction between fear and anxiety is well evidenced, with different fields saying much the same things in their own language. The adventure psychologist Eric Brymer, whom we met in Chapter 3, maintains that fear is an emotion, but anxiety is a *state of being* – and as such the two differ in certain important ways. While emotions (fear) pass, states (anxiety) can continue indefinitely. While fear has an obvious, direct relationship with our experiences and environment, anxiety does not. Anxiety is disconnected from events, and from time, causing us to regularly shift between the past, present and future. It is also dislocated in terms of the impact it has on our bodies. While fear generates physical responses that are equivalent in scale to their cause, anxiety is disproportionate. This can make it much harder to reason with it by focusing on the nature of its causes. We can rationalize that a fear may be greater than whatever caused it, but the vague and distant roots of anxiety make it harder to figure out. It either comes over us in waves or exists as constant tension in the background of our anxious state of being. Fear is the 'pragmatic force' which brings together our thoughts and skills so that dangers can be addressed effectively, narrowing and focusing our attention towards the source of danger. Anxiety only makes us less focused and less pragmatic at a time when pragmatism is all that will help to untangle it.

Dr Brymer studies these differences in terms of their role in adventure and argues that while anxiety is of no use in adventure, fear is. Compare the anxious thought, 'what will people think if I don't complete this hike?' with the fear 'I am not sure we have sufficient supplies'. Only the latter encourages action, such as rationing or foraging, and it's those actions that will determine whether or not you finish the hike. Fear is present when we are actively coping with a perceived threat, whereas anxiety results from a feeling of threat without an active means of coping. In the case of my breakdown, I didn't have an active means of coping. In fact, what I displayed was more similar to the 'avoidance behaviours' that we discussed as a response to uncertainty. It's ironic, I'll admit, to go up Everest as an anxious response to the unknown rather than the active pursuit of fear, but it's not inexplicable. On some level I decided that it would be easier to confront the great, knowable fear of mountaineering rather than live in the state of unknowable anxiety that surrounded my home life, but because I did so in avoidance, it became only an anxious act. I ran away rather than confront, and in that sense we see its basis in anxiety rather than fear, even if the setting was one we associate with an adventure. My outcome was not the adaptive fear response, which generates new approaches and growth, but the self-destructive sickness that comes with anxiety and avoidance.

I also didn't learn anything from my anxious-avoidant journey up Everest. While we could expect a mountaineering journey of this sort to teach us profound lessons about our resilience, motivation and focus, I suffered the physical and mental pain of trying to avoid reality. I couldn't have gone any further or any higher to get away from myself, but, unsurprisingly, I was still there. I needed to understand my life situation and reconnect it with my mental anguish, to be with my pain and take a moment to marshal the resources I needed to rediscover what I wanted and learn to enjoy life again.

Self-Talk

Of course, adventure, pursued for the right reasons, teaches us the very skills that I couldn't practise in my anxious mind state. Self-knowledge, presence and self-efficacy are grown through adventure, and it's these skills that help us dial down anxiety. If we start with self-knowledge, we see how important 'self-talk' is in both reducing anxiety and our motivation for challenge. You've probably said 'I can do this' or 'I am capable' in some moment where you had to build yourself up towards a frightening challenge. This is an exercise in positive self-talk. It's conscious, but that doesn't mean it's disconnected from the (often unconscious) anxious self-talk which presents as feelings of 'I can't do this' or 'I'm not capable'. The self-talk that simultaneously underlies and overlies anxiety is something we can reshape both in terms of broad self-identifications (I am capable) and the more specific phrases which we *have* to practise in adventure and challenge, such as, 'Take it one step at a time' or 'I've handled challenges before'.

Adventures are very useful for recalibrating our sense of what's useful and what's not, because we have very real challenges that require very pragmatic thinking. It's clear that, 'I'm not good enough' serves no purpose when facing a frightening aspect of a challenge, whereas 'keep going, you're doing great' really does. This sounds simplistic, but I think it's profound. Genuine challenges shed light on what's rational and what's not, and this is often just what our anxiety needs. It endures in some part because it's internal and private and thus exists like a hypothesis that cannot be tested. It's only by reconnecting the focus of our anxiety to outcomes that we can see it's not relevant; it's only by tying it to experience that we see it offers us no help.

Imagine a challenge, we can say mountain climbing as we've discussed it already, with your own internal guide. That guide is either practising the sort of self-talk we associate with facing fear, or that which we associate with anxiety. One internal guide tells you to 'take it one step at a time', reminds you of how far you've come and often recalls times when you've previously overcome challenges on your route. The other says, 'maybe you aren't good enough', stops every few metres to say 'imagine there was an avalanche' or 'we could die up here'. It's very clear which is more useful, and it's only by doing the hard things that we can really see the difference between the value of our own internal guides. We are much more capable of saying 'this is really not helpful' to our internal guide when we're doing something that stretches us.

The challenge gives us a clear-eyed view of what self-talk is useful, and usually it becomes evident that it's the sort that affirms us and increases our sense of self-efficacy. We see how our output and outcome changes when the self-talk is positive and compassionate and we learn how to talk to ourselves positively and proactively going forward. We may learn the skill on a mountain, but we can apply it when faced with all manner of day-to-day challenges, fears or frustrations.

The negative self-talk, which is a cornerstone of anxiety, does not make hard things seem any less hard. In these challenging moments we are much more ready to grab on to anything that will make our challenge feel easier, and this gives us a good opportunity to practise positive self-talk for the sake of our life outside of it.

It's as if anxiety is a weight we carry around with us all the time, we have grown used to it, but it is only when we make ourselves go uphill or run that we see quite how much of a handicap the weight really is. Self-talk can be a burden or a fuel and we are much more capable of seeing the difference when we put ourselves in situations that benefit from our lightness or energy.

Antonis Hatzigeorgiadis is a professor of sport psychology at the University of Thessaly, Greece, whose research has been pivotal in demonstrating how structured self-talk strategies can enhance confidence, reduce anxiety and improve athletic performance.[1][2] When given prompts for motivational self-chatter, subjects in tests are able to go longer and feel less exhausted by it, with less fatigue and less perception of fatigue too.[3] I think this is also true of anxiety in daily life. Positive self-talk, which we can practise through challenges, improves our self-regulation and resilience, which can be the difference between ordinary life feeling manageable and feeling exhausting. If we change how we interact with ourselves, we can change how we interact with the world.

This is just as applicable to how we perceive risks and threats. Chronic anxiety is consistent with a heightened sense of risk in our everyday life, which leads us to exist in a constant state of perceived threat. This perceived threat can be re-evaluated, because it's essentially a misunderstanding. If we can, through challenge, learn to better perceive risk and threat by facing fears and evaluating them, we gain this skill in our daily life. Adventure is an exercise in evaluating risk and deciding on safe and manageable approaches, which offers us tools that help us evaluate our anxiety and the disproportionate sense of threat that arises when we're consumed by it.

Cognitive Reappraisal

Both these practices, improving our self-talk and learning about how we perceive and evaluate threats, can be grouped under the banner of 'cognitive reappraisal'. In the *Handbook of Emotional Regulation*,[4] the Stanford psychologist James Gross defines this as a process of 'construing a potentially emotion-eliciting situation in a way that changes its emotional impact' by thinking about how we are thinking. When we engage in cognitive reappraisals, we develop a greater ability to monitor, regulate and control our cognitive processes. This is integral to developing a better relationship to anxiety because in many ways anxiety is the process of feeling threatened and not being able to understand why. It's a state of uncertainty and a feeling of a lack of control or efficacy. If we can evaluate threats, see when we are overestimating them and speak to ourselves supportively about our ability to process whatever it is that our anxiety is tied to, we make it into a known controllable. It becomes more like a fear, which creates energy and encourages action.

EXERCISE: COGNITIVE REAPPRAISAL TECHNIQUES

Activity I: Perspective-Taking Reappraisal

Goal: Practise shifting your perspective to reinterpret an emotionally charged situation.

1. Recall a Recent Emotional Event

Choose a situation from the past week that triggered a strong emotional response (e.g., frustration at work, a disagreement with a friend).

2. Describe the Event

Write down what happened and how you felt.

3. Perspective Shift

Now, imagine you are an outside observer (a friend, mentor, or even a neutral stranger).

○ How might they interpret the situation differently?

○ What alternative explanations could there be for what happened?

○ What might they say to you about it?

4. Reappraise

Write a new interpretation of the event, based on this external perspective.

Example: 'Instead of seeing my colleague's curt reply as disrespect, I can see it as a sign they were overwhelmed that day.'

5. Reflect

Notice how your feelings about the event change with this new interpretation.

Why this works:
Perspective-taking is a core mechanism of cognitive reappraisal, helping to break the cycle of negative emotional spirals by broadening your view of the situation.

Activity 2: Reappraisal Through Scenario Building

Goal: Build new, emotionally neutral or positive interpretations for challenging situations using imaginative scenario construction.

1. Identify a Triggering Situation

Pick a recurring scenario that often triggers negative emotions (e.g., being ignored in a meeting).

2. List Initial Thoughts

Write down your first interpretation (e.g., 'They don't respect me').

3. Generate Three Alternative Scenarios

Challenge yourself to invent three different, plausible explanations for what happened.

Example:

'Maybe they were distracted by a personal issue.'

'Maybe they didn't hear me.'

'Maybe my point was unclear and needs clarification.'

4. Choose the Most Helpful Reappraisal

Select the interpretation that feels most empowering or least distressing, and write a short plan for how you might respond next time.

Practice: The next time this situation arises, remind yourself of your new interpretation and observe any changes in your emotional response.

Many of these approaches will be familiar from discussions we have had about processing fear, and that's because we practise mindsets in approaching fear that equip us to understand and manage anxiety. Anxiety, when approached with the tools we learn from facing fear, can be broken down into singular issues rather than one all-encompassing state of being. Once we've done this, we can approach those individual issues with the pragmatism with which we have approached fear. Fear is manageable, but anxiety is not, and in some sense we need to make anxiety look more like fear: concrete, time-limited and potentially useful. Only then do we have something to act on, instead of actually *being* the problem itself.

All of these approaches, and my experiences that I recounted, can be better understood through the prism of 'presence'. It's a difficult term to describe, because it's so defined by *being* instead of *thinking*, but presence means feeling the sensations of where you are, rather than imagining how you could feel differently elsewhere. It's about experiencing the moment you're in, rather than dwelling on the past or imagining the future. It's feeling, without words and experience, and without judgement. Ironically, it's by cultivating presence that we are then able to make informed choices about what we will do that make us happy. When we're present, we have enough time to develop self-understanding, we can determine effective strategies for dealing with problems and we can decide on courses of action that make our present enjoyable. When we're absent, as anxiety renders us, we're consumed by overwhelming feelings, we fixate on problems not solutions, and we exist from one anxious present moment to another while fixating on the future or past.

It's 'presence' that mindfulness and connection to the natural world affords us. These experiences teach us that our consciousness is not the same thing as our thoughts, and that our thoughts can be consciously untangled. This comes back to the idea of anxiety *making us the problem* rather than allowing us to look at anxiety as a problem. When we practise mindfulness, we gain the ability to look at our thoughts with a degree of distance, to see those that help or hinder us and appreciate where irrationality leads to pain.

My irrationality quite literally led to pain in my experience on the mountain, but my presence, in my emotions and in the natural world, allowed me to process that pain and move past it.

If we can pause, as I did only after I was forced to stop, we have the chance to observe what's happening in our minds. If we can calm our body and look at our mind, we often see what we're going to such pains to avoid, and determine whether that avoidance is worth that pain. If we've learned (through chosen challenges, where we have embraced our fear for the right reasons) to assess risk, feel capable and speak kindly to ourselves, we'll be able to evaluate and act on our anxiety much more effectively.

We can run towards those things that need confronting, and avoid those that need avoiding, because we can tell the difference. We won't end up on a mountaintop when we really need to look inside ourselves, and we won't find ourselves constantly looking inward when we'd be better off taking action. There is a time for thought and there is a time for action, but action can teach us new ways of thinking, and thought can teach us plenty about how we're acting. If we are present in ourselves, we can be confident in our ability to determine what is called for in each moment, to take our fear and make it an opportunity.

KEY TAKEAWAYS

1. A challenge is a means to understand ourselves, not avoid ourselves.

2. Fear is proportionate to a threat; it marshals our resources and encourages a response. Whereas anxiety is disconnected; it drains us and leaves us with very little idea of what we must respond to or how we should respond.

3. Challenges and adventure connect us to ourselves and help us access mindsets and approaches that we can use to manage anxiety.

4. Adventure can facilitate presence and nature connectedness, which both help us to develop a sense of 'presence'. Given that anxiety is dislocated and makes us feel absent from the causes of our feelings, we can benefit from increased presence.

5. It also provides us with a starting point for engaging with our feelings, reasoning with those that are causing us unjustified pain and focusing on the joy of the moment rather than past regret or future worry.

**Happy, sad or afraid – if you are present,
then you are in the right place.**

8. Fear of Being Different

Why Our Fear of Standing Out Is an Opportunity for Connection

Our fears are as personal as our dreams – unique combinations of our circumstances and our character that over time come to define our choices. For many of us, the fear of standing out is primary among them. A lifetime of socialization, from school to communities and workplaces, convinces us that being different would be the worst possible outcome in any situation. To stand out would be to suffer; to be odd and recognized as such might well be the end of us. But what opportunities can we find in our fear of being different, and how can we channel them to build a happier, healthier life?

To find out, we need to go back. Way back, because this fear relates to the deep evolutionary roots of in-group dynamics, the subtle rules and behaviours that determine who belongs within a community.[1] Among early humans, these dynamics shaped decisions about who was worthy of sharing food, protection and resources. Archaeological and anthropological evidence suggests that factors such as cooperation, reciprocity, shared rituals and even visible signs of group identity (like adornments or language) played a role in who was accepted or rejected. Those who contributed to the group's survival, demonstrated trustworthiness or conformed to its norms were more likely to be included, while those seen as outsiders or as threats to cohesion risked exclusion.

The shadow of this ancient insecurity still lingers in our modern minds, making the desire to fit in feel urgent – even when our survival no longer depends on it. It's in our nature to try and fit in, but it's not always in our best interest.

My view is that when we really face up to our fear of being different, we realize that what we're really afraid of is isolation. This is a more sensible fear, the one that our evolution has taught us to avoid because it genuinely presents threats to our health and wellbeing (even if, today, these are more to do with loneliness than the fatal risks that affected our ancestors). It's also sensible, and useful, because it can motivate us to *act* in favour of connection rather than simply moderate our behaviour. We can control the extent to which we connect with other people in a way that we cannot control the ways in which we fit in (as styles, norms and people change).

So, in this chapter I want to give you a good understanding of the reasons you should avoid the oppressive stress of fitting in and fear of standing out and instead pursue the opportunity of looking to find connection. Rather than feeling threatened by the possibility of being marked as an outlier or outsider, I hope you can see that it's much more enjoyable to pursue new forms of connection based on an understanding of what makes you happy as a unique, and possibly different, kind of person. If it's as true for you as it has been for me, then this could be your moment to reframe a fear and see a world of opportunities.

How I Learned To Stand Out

Of course, we are *all* different. I've always been comfortable with standing out, and as I look back over the experiences I've recounted in this book, I see they are basically a catalogue of my oddities and a testament to my willingness to embrace them. The girl who ran laps around the school grounds when she wasn't allowed to play sports and who decided to spend her weekends among a grunting mass of middle-aged men was not one who hungered for the embrace of the in-crowd. I still had to make the choice, though, to stand out in the name of pursuing a life that was authentic to me. In this sense it's important to be aware that we can thrive through connection to others, but also connection to ourselves. Self-censorship for the sake of fitting in can chip away at that connection to ourselves, and in our attempt to avoid isolation, we can suffer the discomfort of being alienated from ourselves. If you have ever gone along with a cruel joke or misrepresented your values for the sake of fitting in and then felt awful later, you'll understand this type of alienation.

So, I was fortunate to have a disposition that allowed me to make uncomfortable but authentic choices, and then see that they could be rewarded. Those playground laps were the basis of the cardiovascular strength that I applied when racing, and those Saturdays were a vital experience in teaching me to lose. They provided valuable skills, but most of all they taught me the value of difference, that standing out is often necessary in pursuit of a goal. This doesn't mean it was always easy to commit to my difference. I felt the odd one out as the teenager who couldn't attend parties because of Saturday morning's commitments, or as the uni student who was never seen at the clubs. I was told by a professor quite early on that, of the three options – a 2:1 degree, qualifying for the Commonwealth Games and socializing – I could really only choose two, and that meant that I never really got to be part of the undergraduate scene. I didn't fit in at school, on the weekends or at university later on, but all of that was necessary to be the best I could be.

Once I was a cyclist, I had to continue in my pursuit of 'sore thumb' status. I moved from a well-recognized training establishment and senior coach two years after my breakthrough because I wasn't sure it was benefitting me. This was unconventional and unpopular, and I suffered for it. Or I could point to the run-up to the London Olympics, when I often had to create my own agenda without the support of the 'in-group'. If I'd feared standing out, I would never have won medals at those Olympics because I would've done what the in-group expected of me and retired in 2011.

Why We Should Face Our Fear of Standing Out

These are quite specific examples from my own life of how standing out was necessary to progress, but it's important in many walks of life, not least when we're seeking to improve the world around us. A willingness to stand out is not only a prerequisite for personal fulfilment, but principled action as well. If we look at heroism throughout history, whether it be women's suffrage, the civil rights movement or campaigns for decent pay and rights in professional settings, all have required people to break with established convention and expectation. Change at a societal level requires people to stand out (and, of course, to grow connected through collective action), but recent research suggests people are broadly becoming more fearful of doing so.

In 2024, the social psychologist William Chopik at the University of Michigan decided to try to evaluate the willingness of Americans to defend their beliefs publicly and see how they balanced the very natural desire to be a unique individual with other people's opinions about them. His team evaluated data from over a million respondents over the past twenty years and found a clear decline in people's willingness to defend their beliefs in public as well as greater concern about other people's opinions of them.[2] There could be a number of explanations for this, but given my focus on the importance of connectedness as an antidote to fear of difference, I would argue that many people feel their social position is more precarious than ever. People are less connected and identified with their core values, and less confident in their community or society to protect them if they exhibit 'unconventional' behaviour. Dr Chopik remarked on how often people discussed their fear of ostracization or 'cancellation', and although the latter is often a murky term, I think in this case it points to something important. Cancellation is impersonal; it's something we can do to those with whom we are not connected. We don't cancel neighbours, or family members, because we appreciate the interdependence we share. Our fear of standing out is actually a result of a lack of connection, of community, and a reflection of a growing distance between people.

A fear of standing out impacts our society, but also our well-being. The experience of moderating our behaviour and denying genuine self-expression in the name of conformity is an anxiety-inducing experience, but it also limits us from living in ways we might enjoy. So many recommendations from experts across this book start with self-knowledge as a means to understand the goals and approaches that can make us happy. That may be described through ideas like Richard Ryan's 'autonomy', or the value of motivation based on internal factors over external rewards, and even the call to rely on 'core values' in times of change in Chapter 6. What all of these ideas share, is that a connection to ourselves provides understanding of what makes us happy and the bravery to act on it. None of the psychologists or neuroscientists we have spoken to argue that we should pay more attention to what society thinks of us.

There is also an argument that conformity is often *ineffective*. This may come as a surprise to those of us raised in the British school system, where one-size-fits-all (baggily and unflatteringly) approaches are seen as the epitome of efficiency, but both research and practice contradicts this view. When psychologists at the Israel Institute of Technology created randomized controlled trials to compare the outcomes of high-conformity groups versus less conformist ones, they found that in unstable situations and changing environments (aka most of the world) the freedom to disagree and differ made teams more adaptable and efficient.[3]

In 2012, Google began 'Project Aristotle',[4] an ambitious research initiative at their headquarters in Mountain View, California. Named after Aristotle's notion that 'the whole is greater than the sum of its parts', the project took two years, analysed 180 teams and aimed to uncover the hidden conditions and relationships that make some teams excel while others falter. They expected that the answer would be in the quality of the team members – that the better the qualifications, expertise or experience, the more successful a team would be – but they found no evidence to support this. Instead, what they found was that *how* people worked together was more important than *who* was working. In fact, an idea called 'psychological safety' turned out to be the greatest predictor of team success. Psychological safety is defined as the ability to express ideas and opinions, admit mistakes, ask questions and challenge the status quo. Teams that made people feel comfortable to stand out in these ways collaborated better, had higher morale and made better decisions. Individual autonomy created the conditions for better team performance. This is another reason I prefer to reframe the 'fear of difference' as the goal of connectedness. Our connections are stronger when we're more psychologically secure, our difference is valued and the diversity of opinions and outlooks contributes to a broader perspective.

So, a fear of standing out is bad for us, and getting worse, while the freedom to differ is good for us, our workplaces and our society more broadly. I hope that gives you some encouragement to see that the fear of standing out is actually an anxiety that is as relevant to our contemporary lives as the zebra's fear of lions. When we stand out, we are not left to suffer on a savannah; we are standing up for the complexity, diversity and *efficiency* of human groups.

So what, then, are we really afraid of? And what is the opportunity we can find within that fear? I think the answer is in connection.

The Power of Connection

We fear isolation, not difference, and what we desire – quite reasonably – is connection, not conformity. The error we make is to believe that difference and isolation are the same thing, that connection *requires* conformity. When we commit this error, we fixate on the fear of difference, rather than the power of connection, and as we will see throughout this chapter, connection is too important to our wellbeing to be misunderstood in this way.

We are right to feel a certain amount of discomfort about a lack of connection, because isolation, disconnectedness and loneliness (they are sometimes studied independently but broadly refer to similar experiences) amounts to a major public health problem. One in three people in industrialized nations are deemed to suffer from the condition of chronic loneliness and it is estimated to result in a 26 per cent increase in mortality.[5] Loneliness, in a world of 8 billion people, is as confusing and disorientating as it is sad, but on a physical level is a silent killer. In part this is because human connection is good for our health, but also because loneliness is associated with addiction and poor mental health. The psychologist Bruce Alexander's 'dislocation theory of addiction'[6] frames addictive behaviours as a coping mechanism or adaptation to the painful realities of a disconnected and fragmented society. He emphasizes how rates of addiction rise in societies where social bonds break and how effective recovery programmes focus on the development of human connections as much as they do abstinence from any substance.

In these regards, disconnection makes us sick, but greater connection can make us healthy. This is borne out in research from diverse contexts. LGBT community groups in Ireland were studied[7] and proved to not only offer the joy of creative or sports activities, but crucial mental-health benefits for marginalized individuals. In Chiapas, Mexico, the effectiveness of health initiatives themselves were improved when they were connected to the presence of a community health worker because medical support was tied to social connection.[8] A study from a refugee camp in Greece which evaluated the impacts of community music projects for Yazidi children displaced by conflict in Iraq highlighted how one of the greatest impacts of music on their wellbeing came from the connection it fostered between the individuals, their community identity and the history they shared.[9]

A number of the discussions we have had in this book also point to the value of social connection which *starts* with a connection to ourselves, through self-knowledge and authenticity. If we look back at Dr Ryan's self-determination theory, we see that he started with autonomy – the sense that we are choosing our own path – and matched it to the value of 'relatedness' (the need to feel connected to others). In short, we thrive when we feel we have chosen our own path and take it in the company of others.

When we confuse our desire for connection with a fear of difference, we risk placing our autonomy and relatedness at odds with each other. We could seek belonging by trying to connect emotionally with other people, or we could seek the social safety of appearing to think and do things in the same way as them. We can express ourselves authentically and connect with others who value our honesty, or we can suppress our opinions that differ from the crowd to create an inauthentic version of ourselves. We could pursue a satisfying, authentic life, or run away from social stigma. Again, as is so often the case, the pursuit of something positive proves to be healthier and more satisfying than the constant avoidance of something that frightens us.

Dr Watts and the Three Pillars of Connectedness

Far from being a two-way street, more research is being done into how a *multi-dimensional* idea of connectedness can help us to flourish. The three dimensions that I would like to hone in on were introduced to me by the brilliant Dr Rosalind Watts, and I think that they neatly capture the process I went through in recovery from my deep unhappiness:

- **Connectedness to Self:** The extent to which we feel comfortable to sit with our emotions, experience and understand our feelings and feel aware of sensations in our bodies.

- **Connectedness to Others:** Whether we feel welcome in communities, and connected with strangers and acquaintances, friends and family.

- **Connectedness to the World:** Whether we feel purposeful, in touch with the natural world, the breadth of our perspective and our sense that the world is an interconnected space where love exists.

Dr Watts is a kind and perceptive clinical psychologist who facilitates the ACER (Accept, Connect, Embody, Restore) community, while also conducting clinical and therapeutic research. ACER is a network in which members strive to connect one another with their emotions, people and the natural world from which we have distanced ourselves. They have a community calendar which is built around the passage of the seasons and the growing cycles of the natural world. This ancient way of organizing people and time relocates people in our environment and social group in a profound and beautiful way. The idea is that the more we can locate ourselves in natural time, the more connected we are to our environment and ourselves, and our calendar becomes a reflection of our progress through the years, rather than something that drags us from one responsibility to another.

Dr Watts is also the originator of the eponymous 'Watts Connectedness Scale'. This began when she was a member of the team at Imperial College London who studied the use of psilocybin for treatment-resistant depression.[10] Dr Watts found that the theme of connectedness kept coming up in the descriptions participants gave of their depression (as a state of disconnection), the limitations of the psychiatric and pharmaceutical interventions they had been offered (which only made them feel more disconnected) and the positive impacts of psilocybin-assisted therapy (through increased connection to self, others and the world). Her experiences reflected the findings we mentioned earlier on the causes and responses to addiction, that disconnection seemed to be the cause of suffering, and reconnection an integral part of their progress.

The researchers were not surprised by this. For many years disconnection has been seen as a key feature of the experience of depression and other major psychiatric disorders, and effective treatments have often focused on helping people to reconnect. So when respondents in the study described their progress through psilocybin therapy in terms of a process of reconnection, it appeared that a new tool was achieving the sorts of results that therapeutic approaches had strived for, and pharmaceutical ones had failed to achieve.

So the Imperial College team set out to formalize the way we understand connectedness. There were already some good measures of things like 'social connectedness' (how well and happily we are connected to others in our community) and 'connectedness to nature' (the extent to which we feel in touch with the natural world), but there was not yet a measure that brought together these forms of connectedness alongside the idea of connectedness to self. This was important, as many participants reported feeling reconnected to their values, pleasures and hobbies as well as more integrated, embodied and at peace with their backgrounds. They saw this form of connection as related to 'the self' and considered it foundational to how we can connect to others and the world. So Dr Watts set out to determine how we could measure connectedness to self *alongside* our connectedness with others and the natural world and in relation to them.

While Dr Watts and her team's research initially centred on how psychedelics can help people suffering with depression, the findings on the importance of connection are being applied more broadly. They certainly resonated for me, given how effectively the idea of 'disconnection' characterized my path into depression, and how three pillars of reconnection guided my journey beyond it. I also think there's a great deal of crossover between many practices we have described in this book and the project of building greater connectedness. If we look at our discussions about appreciating our inherent value, practising self-compassion or using physical awareness to understand ourselves and our emotions, we can see that they fit into a framework of self-connectedness quite easily. We've discussed how mindfulness or journaling allow us to re-establish a connection with ourselves and how that connection provides the pivotal self-knowledge which transforms our fears of change, the unknown or failure. I believe many of the interventions we have discussed in relation to both anxiety and fear, start with connection to self.

Those interventions then often give us the courage to build new connections with others and the natural world, and it was this interplay between the three pillars of connectedness that motivated Dr Watts to create a scale which incorporated them all. In many ways they exist as a single form of connectedness, and each contributes to one another in different ways. For example, when researchers enrolled study participants in a programme of 'loving-kindness meditation' in which they intentionally projected thoughts of love and kindness out towards others, respondents regularly reported finishing the programme with a greater love and respect for their own selves.[11] Equally, research on 'flourishing' shows that efforts to become more socially connected are impactful to our own happiness and self-connectedness.[12]

What's more, connection to nature impacts our relationship to ourselves. A landmark meta-analysis by Colin Capaldi at Public Health Canada[13] looked at a range of projects evaluating the impact of nature-engagement and found we are consistently happier and kinder to ourselves when we engage with the natural world. When another team at the University of Calgary took this forward to test whether it also impacts our connection with other people, they found similar results. Their study with a large group of undergraduates found that an openness to nature reflected positive attitudes to their fellow humans and non-human animals. Openness to new experiences and honesty were also correlated with nature connectedness, which harks back to our discussion of uncertainty tolerance. People who connect with nature seem to be similar to those with a tolerance for uncertainty in that they are accepting of outsiders (here explained because nature encourages an idea of one human family), honest and humble (which fits with the idea of being able to process different viewpoints) and open to new experiences. I have found the results of both of these studies to be true in my own life. After time spent in nature I often leave feeling kinder to myself and a better friend and partner to the people I love. In reverse, love and appreciation for ourselves can draw us into that natural world.

EXERCISE: PRACTISING CONNECTION

I. Connectedness to Self: Mindful Self-Reflection

Activity:

Set aside 10–15 minutes daily for mindful self-reflection. Sit quietly, close your eyes and focus on your breath. Gently bring your attention to your thoughts, emotions and bodily sensations without judgement. Afterwards, journal about what you noticed, especially any moments of self-kindness or self-understanding.

2. Connectedness to Others: Intentional Listening and Sharing

Activity:

Arrange a conversation with a friend, family member or colleague where the focus is on deep, intentional listening. Each person takes five minutes to share something meaningful while the other listens without interrupting or offering advice. Afterwards, switch roles. Reflect together on how it felt to be truly heard.

3. Connectedness to the World: Nature Immersion and Gratitude

Activity:

Spend at least 20 minutes in a natural setting (park, garden, forest, etc.). As you walk or sit, consciously notice the sights, sounds and smells around you. At the end, write down three things in nature that inspired a sense of wonder or gratitude.

The beauty of Watts's three-pronged approach to connectedness is that you can choose to build whichever form of it feels most comfortable for you and see progress across the board. It may be that your first project is growing more connected to yourself. This is wonderful, and everything from the small adventures we have described to the practice of articulating your core values will help you to build it. The process of going from 'I would like to do that' to 'Could I even do that?' along past 'I did that' is a means to grow connected to ourselves. We engage with ourselves by engaging with our doubts, connect with ourselves by articulating our goals and re-enforce it all by pursuing them. A challenge is not an isolating experience, but one in which we grow closer to and more confident in ourselves.

You may choose to build connectedness through community. Many of the adventures and challenges we have discussed in this book, from joining a book club to going on a hike, take place in the company of others who want to do the same. The image of an adventure as an isolated experience is as outdated as our image of an adventurer as a Victorian man or a frat-bro on a snowboard. Joining a community is *in itself* an adventure, because we can never predict who we will meet or what we will learn.

If that community takes you out into the natural world, and if you have chosen that community based on an authentic and connected idea of yourself, then you have the potential to unify all three forms of connectedness and experience the broad benefits they offer. Still, if you choose to simply enter into the natural world alone and notice it (noticing it is all there is to do), then you should not doubt that this will impact your self and social connections too. All of these forms of connections connect us to ourselves and one another, because naturally, they do not exist in isolation. And neither do we.

My Story Through the Lens of Connectedness

If I look back on my experiences after Everest, they are best described as losses of connection. First, I was disconnected from myself. I felt alienated from my identity as a woman who trusted her body and saw challenges through. I felt disconnected from my body, which had always been an ally and now felt like something upon which I could no longer rely. I lost my social connections. To the people that I still knew and loved in cycling and to my family who could not cure me of my own alienation. Finally, I lost connection to the natural world, which I had always trusted implicitly as a place of pure comfort. This was a more profound loss than I first realized; unlike people in the social or professional world, nature had always felt trustworthy and understandable in its clear and consistent grandeur. Where once I had only felt hope in nature, on Everest I experienced it as suffering. For some time I could not connect with it as I once had.

When I apply the lens of connectedness to my journey back from depression, one I continue on even now, I think the three pillars interact in the following way. I was disconnected from myself, from others and the world. I connected with myself just enough to know that I needed to be somewhere, *doing* something that gave me meaning. That small realization opened me up to the social connection that my surf-friends offered. Through them, I reconnected to the natural world, and with that reconnected more deeply with myself and my enduring desire to stay alive. While I did begin to rebuild social connections with all the other people around me, it was clear that this was the pillar of connectedness that I would have to work at more slowly.

I can understand that, on a personal level. My connection to myself, which was built up through many years of challenge and growth, motivation and mindfulness, had a core strength. It was challenged by my life experiences at that time and by my depression, but it was there to reconnect with. So too my relationship to the natural world had a foundational quality. Looking back to my childhood games with Alex or the camping trips we took as a family, nature, in the form of the hills we rode down or the woods in which we found shade, was like another member of our group. As I recovered, I realized it was more like a friend with whom I'd had an argument than an adversary, and we were ready to reconnect once I understood that it had never tried to hurt me. I had taken it for granted and used our connection with the wrong intentions.

Social connectedness, the final pillar, has always been more difficult for me. I am naturally shy, I was often different to my peers and I lived a professional life which gave primacy to individual excellence over connection. Whether I was the schoolgirl doing laps or the Olympian training alone for London, I had embedded an idea that it was me against the world. This meant that it would take more time to rebuild that connectedness, but rebuild it I did.

In fact, the rebuilding process that began on the waves continued in the strangest possible place, the television programme *SAS: Who Dares Wins*. This is a UK reality show where celebrities are put through a series of intense physical and mental challenges that are based on the selection process for the British Special Air Service (SAS). The irony here is not lost on me: I rediscovered myself and social connection (which we are describing as counterpoints to the fear of standing out) in an intentionally hostile, conformity-driven environment that is designed to break recruits down. Before I describe what happened, it's worth remarking on one more aspect of Dr Watts and the Imperial team's thinking, which might actually reflect differently on the conformity of the SAS (an elite British Military force). We've discussed how a better response to our fear of standing out isn't trying at all costs to fit in, but is, instead, looking to forge connections. The military, and, in particular, elite divisions like the SAS, demand conformity and in fact they represent one of the fields in which it clearly offers an operational advantage (as opposed to somewhere like Google, where we saw it as a disadvantage). The interesting thing, in my eyes, is that the conformity they prescribe is *not necessarily* at odds with the connectedness that the Imperial team describe. If trying not to stand out can make us unhappy, how could such a conformity-driven environment make people happy?

The Imperial team actually describes *ego* as the counter-force to connectedness. In their research, connectedness was intimately tied to the view that we are individually no better than others, that our own issues and concerns are of no greater import and that the joys of unity provide a greater satisfaction than those that come with self-advancement. The SAS may be conformist, but it is certainly connected. The elite operators I have met did not *fear* standing out; they *pursued* the benefits of unity. One of the highest compliments a member of the SAS can offer is to describe you as 'grey'. This means that you neither seek to stand out above others, nor fall beneath the standards expected. You are not white or black, because you dissolve into the collective. It is a place where there is no room for ego.

I am sure that the researchers at Imperial would be surprised to see a connection being made between the work they did and the British Special Forces, but I see relevance both in theory and in my experience. Without realizing it at the time, I went on *SAS: Who Dares Wins* to reconnect to myself, and in particular to rebuild the foundational connection between effort and progress that is a core part of my self-identification (*Value:* I try my best to improve). When I suffered on Everest, I internalized a view that this relationship no longer held true for me, that my efforts might not result in progress and in fact they could result in physical and psychological pain. I sank into a state of passive pain, unable to make any effort and feeling uncomfortable in that state.

I came back from Costa Rica with a belief that simply making it to the start line of the programme would constitute reconnection with that value. I had said no to almost everything and everyone since my mental health deteriorated, so I decided that saying yes to something was a reflection of my returning belief in the relationship between effort and reward. Of course, this was, in *everyone's* view, a *terrible* decision. The recommended second step in recovery from physical and psychological stress is not going on television shows where Special Forces Operators try to physically and psychologically stress you. The general view of my decision was summed up by Nicola, my very protective and (thankfully) forgiving sister, who told me she would never speak to me again if I went through with it.

In my eyes, though, I had been so passively uncomfortable for so long, the idea of *active* discomfort seemed like progress. Being able to choose a challenge, for my own reason, felt more like the version of myself that I wanted to be. I would just try to make it through the first day, I thought, and that would be good enough for me. Then, at the end of that day, I decided I might as well try and find the strength to make it through the second. In no time at all, we had reached the final. All the while, I had a sense that I was *putting myself through* a challenge, which was such a stark contrast to the alienating challenges of my depression, which felt like it *sat upon me*. Somehow the chosen hardship felt knowable and understandable, and in turn it helped me to reconnect with that key part of myself that values effort. I had regained some trust in my body before the show, but now I regained the sense that, alongside my mind, it could endure and it could flourish.

I left feeling more connected to myself, and that left me only to start rebuilding my connections with others. I think that the former gradually gave me the strength to do the latter. About six months after the filming of the show, we were doing publicity around its release. In a quiet moment when the cameras were off, I turned to Jason Fox, one of the *SAS* directing staff, and said, 'You must have some hot single mates.' I was joking, but also, I wasn't. What I was actually doing was admitting to myself that I felt more ready than I had in a long time to reconnect with people, and in reaching out, I showed the progress I had made.

I'm so glad I asked him that. He introduced me to Louis, who had been in the Special Forces. We met and started dating. Four months later, he broke his kneecap into eight pieces jumping off a cliff (he was *just* my sort of person), so he moved into my house rather than sleep on a camp-bed in his office. While this may sound a bit like the plot of the film *Misery* (a horror), it was a romance, and six years later we are still together.

We're a good match. A journey that started by reconnecting with myself just enough to realize what could make me happy led to a reconnection with the world, and eventually him. In a virtuous cycle he has given me the psychological security to be myself and grow closer to myself. He is happy for me to spend hours with my horse and I have no desire to escape my reality with challenges. Now I challenge myself to see reality, and myself, more clearly.

A FIVE-STEP PLAN TO REBUILD CONNECTION

If you find yourself at a low ebb, then you might benefit, as I did, from improving your sense of connection. Here is a four-step plan to help you move through this process. You can adapt it however you like, focusing on those aspects which feel powerful for you.

Part I: Inner Reflection

Sit comfortably. Read and reflect on the following prompts, then write down your responses, freely and without judgement.

Self – Connection to Inner World

1. What signals is my body giving me right now (tension, energy, fatigue, comfort)?

2. What feelings are most present for me today?

3. Where in my life am I acting in alignment with my values, and where do I feel a gap?

4. How do I speak to myself in moments of difficulty – like a critic, a friend, or something in-between?

5. What activities or environments reliably make me feel alive, creative, or grounded?

And Looking Forwards?

1. What qualities of myself do I most want to cultivate in the months ahead?

2. What kind of inner dialogue would help me feel stronger and more compassionate towards myself?

3. If I imagined a version of myself who feels balanced and authentic, what daily habits or practices would they have?

Others – Connection Through Relationships

1. Which relationship(s) feel nourishing right now, and which feel distant or strained?

2. How do I tend to show up in relationships during stress – withdrawing, leaning in, or something else?

And Looking Forwards?

1. What kind of relationships do I want to welcome into my life going forward – supportive, playful, inspiring, collaborative?

2. What qualities do I want to embody as a friend, partner or family member?

3. Who in my current circle could I deepen a connection with, and who might I need to step back from?

World/Nature - Connection to the Larger Whole

1. When do I feel a sense of belonging or awe in the wider world – in nature, culture, or creativity?

2. Where do I feel most grounded – in natural spaces, spiritual practices, community, or beauty?

And Looking Forwards?

1. What kind of communities or environments do I want to be part of in the future?

2. What causes, values or traditions do I want to connect with more deeply?

3. How would I like to expand my sense of belonging in the months ahead?

Part 2: Map Your Current State

Draw a triangle with three corners labelled 'Self', 'Others', 'World'.

At each corner, rate both:

Current connection (1 = very disconnected → 5 = deeply connected).

Future aspiration (1 = I don't desire this much → 5 = I deeply desire this connection).

This shows the gap between where you are now and where you'd like to be.

Part 3: Seed Actions (15 min)

Choose one small, doable action for each pillar to try in the next 1–3 days, linked to both current needs and future direction.

Examples:

Self: Begin a 'kind voice' journal where you rewrite critical thoughts into supportive ones; or add 5 minutes of physical movement into your life daily.

Others: Message someone you want to grow closer to; look up a group/class aligned with your values.

World/Nature: Walk in nature with curiosity; research a local community group, cultural event or volunteer opportunity.

Part 4: Reflection Cycle (after 3 days)

Return to your triangle map.

Re-rate your current sense of connection.

Ask: 'Did my actions bring me closer to the kind of connections I want to build in the future?'

Adjust your next actions: reinforce what worked, try a new small step where there's still a gap.

I have found that in reconnecting with myself, I better understand the ways in which I want to connect with the world. I am not afraid to admit that I don't particularly like parties or big events, or that I sometimes prefer the company of horses to people. I don't fear standing out in that way because difference in and of itself is not something to fear. I discovered a virtuous circle: by connecting to myself, I better understood how to authentically connect to others and the natural world. As Dr Watts suggests in her research, these connections only made me feel closer to and more secure in myself. With that security, I continue exploring and connecting.

So, remember: your difference need not be your isolation. The things that make you unique, the ways in which you rebel and the perspectives which could only ever be authentically yours are the solution, not the problem. By being yourself, you can find connection on your own terms and experience the joys of community and relatedness, without the struggle to give up some part of yourself. You do not need to change your shape to fit in; you just have to find others whose pieces connect with yours.

Because we do not fear difference, we desperately crave connection. I hope I have shown you just how powerful that connection can be, when you share it with people who appreciate your authentic self as much as you do.

KEY TAKEAWAYS

1. What we think of as a fear of difference is in fact a desire for connection.

2. We can think of connection as a project of self-knowledge, community connection or natural immersion. Each of these three forms of connectedness help us feel more connected in the other regards and form virtuous circles.

3. Spending time in nature may help you feel more connected to yourself and your values. This self-connectedness could lead you to approach the community on more satisfying terms. Those positive social connections may take you back into the natural world.

4. Choose a path that suits you, but see the fear of isolation as a motivation for connection, not anxiety about whether you 'fit in'.

Stand up, stand out and stand for something.

9. Fear of Death

And How to Appreciate Life

I have tried to approach the subject of fear, its many faces and opportunities, with self-knowledge as a guide. It only seemed right to ground the science in my own story, given the power of self-awareness to turn our fears from a drain into an opportunity. As with any story, the parts we focus on leave other things unsaid. The lessons I learned from the fears that pushed me forward could have been illustrated with another perspective – and a life story, as we know by now, can appear very differently depending on how we choose to tell it.

I could have told the story of me and my brother, my twin and my other half. It was our story that introduced the question of how children play and learn through fear. That made sense, but when it came to understanding the fear of change, the unknown, or failing and falling, our relationship was not the aspect of my life that would shed most light on the research. Our connection was too consistent, our knowledge of one another unfailing and without loss. Our steady, joyful partnership was not the illustration that would explain the value of facing our everyday fears. It is only now, as we speak about the fear of death, that it becomes illustrative once more.

Had I illustrated this book with stories about Alex and I, we would have learned less about finding power in our fears and more about the power of our relationships. We would have started with those games we played on bikes and then talked about our first day at school when I felt no fear because my home was always right there beside me. I could have discussed all the times he talked me through my disappointments and helped me see them in a new light. Or when I felt an uncanny urge to call him and discovered that he had been waiting for my call.

I could have told you how he was always by my side when I failed or how he wore a 'Team Pendleton' T-shirt and flag for the London Olympics when I won. How he embraced change in his own life, leaving a good job in graphic design in his early thirties because he found something that he would rather do, for less money and recognition. How he was brave enough to put himself at the bottom of a ladder he wanted to climb rather than stay halfway up one he didn't.

Who knows, perhaps I would have described the fear of standing out differently if I had focused on the strength that I drew from the fact that, with Alex, I didn't. We were always united as one. Doubtless the ideas of 'connection to self' and 'connection to others' are something quite special when you believe from day one that you are as connected to another as you are to yourself.

I didn't want to explain the power of fear with reference to Alex because these lessons are universal and what we had was unique. Moreover, I want you to leave this book confident in your ability to stand alone, connected but self-sufficient, and so I had to lean on what fear taught me when I was alone. I needed to describe how you can stand up to the challenges of your own life, by describing the challenges of mine. Our life, the one Alex and I shared, was something else entirely.

That life started when we met each other a few months before we were born. My mother always remarked that we had known one another longer than anyone else had known us, as we had been sharing food and sound, light and darkness before the world had even seen our faces. I was, and am, a twin first, an individual second and the public figure whose story you have so respectfully read, third. That is why I could not finish this story without telling his, *ours*, and without discussing everything I learned about life through him and through his death.

So much of that life was shared in our early years. While many twins strive for individuality in difference, we thought we were perfectly unique as a pair. There was no pair like us, and for all the similarities in our dispositions, I think that the greatest similarity was in our experiences. Non-twins may find it hard to appreciate, but everything that happened around us or in the world for our first eighteen years, happened to both of us at the *same time*. That felt deeply formative. *Where were you when . . . ?* Questions inevitably lead us to the same answer; historical events, milestones and family fallouts all took place when we were exactly the same age, and we revelled in the fact.

It might seem like a shared perspective is less than two separate views, but I see something different. Our twin experience meant that at any moment, as adults or children, we were able to lean on a second pair of eyes with a similar outlook but none of the baggage or limitations of ego. If I had a problem, he could see it just as I did, but he would not approach it with the anxiety or weight that can come with being trapped in your own circumstances. We could think for the other in the way the other would think if they were not constrained by their own situation.

We leant on that in later years, but only after we parted ways. At eighteen, I went off to university and he dedicated himself to art, training to be a graphic designer. I still have the birthday and Christmas cards filled with his cartoons, caricatures of the Vic I sometimes took too seriously, sweating on a bike or standing on a mountain. I was a lighter, funnier version of myself when seen through his eyes.

In our twenties, as I travelled the world to train, he settled into work and life closer to home. We still spoke often, chatting over our landlines about anything and nothing. It wasn't that we took one another for granted, but, looking back, I know I could never have valued those calls as much as I long for them now. It is a strange feature of grief that the things that you yearn for, moments that in bereavement would be your one genie's wish, are things that, when you had them, you barely noticed.

At the age of thirty-two, he began teaching himself to play golf, a sport that he had only briefly played as a child with our grandad, Alf. He found that he was a fast learner, but more importantly, able to find joy in teaching himself. The learner's mindset reinvigorated him so much that he decided to leave his job and dedicate himself to it. He started working in the pro shop at a local course and used every free moment to practise. It was a change, it was an unknown and it had no guarantees of success beyond the joy he found in it every day, and that was exactly why he did it. What many of us call fear of change, failure or the unknown, he called the opportunity.

A few years later, his wife called my mum to say that he had come downstairs and his speech was slurred. She wanted to inform our family because she had called an ambulance. The day before he had been out in the garden, happily and healthily building decking, so we hoped these frightening signs proved to be nothing.

It was not nothing, and after a few days of tests we were told that he had a tumour in his brain, a terminal stage-four cancer with a prognosis of 12–18 months. In a short, present moment, his future contracted. A life that we had assumed would stretch out, and the partnership that we took for granted, would be ended without so much as a week's notice. I cancelled almost every plan I had for the following year, and said no to work, trips and social events. His immune system would be compromised, so I would have to be well, which meant staying at home to avoid picking up any germs that could hurt him. I did so without a moment's hesitation.

I cannot really speak to my sense of how that time passed. In some ways he died more quickly than I could imagine possible, and in others more slowly than I can bear to remember – a year felt like too little time to say goodbye and too long to keep him suffering. I was tied up in contradicting emotions, until I was not, and we finally parted ways on 22 June 2023, forty-two years after we became a team.

In the months after he passed, I fixated on the silence that fell upon him in his final days and regretted trying to control the noise of my own loud, messy human existence. Life, I had not yet realized, was in the noise. I grew guilty that it had been him and not me, fixating on the fact that my life was the one full of risks and bad choices, extra glasses of wine and post-tournament flus. I had pushed myself to the brink and yet I remained, and my brother, the one who had been healthy and conscientious, was lost to the world.

His loss was too great not to provide a lesson, and my pain was too pronounced to be left to its own devices, so I put aside my own fear of death to read and think more about the subject. I discovered the work of psychologists and bereavement counsellors who helped people like me understand the difference between guilt and regret. I saw that my thoughts were irrational, that I had no role in the loss and there was never any way that I could have swapped places with him or changed his outcomes with my behaviour. I began to think more about what he taught me in life and what he and others could help us confront through accounts of their own deaths.

That is the core message of this chapter, and in many ways this book. It is a testament to life, and the value that we must place upon living it joyfully if we fear losing it so deeply. Our fear of death is a call to action, to appreciate what we have and see life itself as an opportunity. We have discussed the good that comes when we take fears and see them as challenges, and the fear of death challenges us to see the wonder of being alive. Anything else is not fear but anxiety. It is a desire to control something that cannot be controlled, a worry over something that is inevitable and that waits for us all. Out of respect for those who have taken this path before us, it should be a lesson; to value the life that we continue to enjoy, and see our fear of death as a reminder of that.

In time I began to see that my sadness at his loss had to be equivalent to my appreciation of the time we shared. To feel grief at losing him without some sense of how incredible it was to have him would be disproportionate, and cruel. I had to learn gratitude and I had to give myself over to awe. Our life together as twins, the strange fact that a quirk of evolution led to our consciousness and shared experience of forty-two years, could not always be understood, but it could generate awe through its unlikeliness.

The ways in which I learned to value life in all its unlikely glory, the acceptance I found and the presence I committed to, reflected the teachings of the many dying authors I read. The first whose work I came upon was Jarem Sawatsky, who wrote the wonderful *Dancing with Elephants*[1] about his experiences of Huntingdon's disease and his steady physical and mental decline. I drew a great deal of meaning from the way he framed his growing appreciation of life through the approach of death, and I have used his conceptual categories about a life well lived as a starting point for my description of what we can learn from death as a teacher. These categories are:

1. The Importance of **Presence** in life

2. The necessity of **Acceptance** of death

3. The value of **Awe** in existence

4. **Gratitude** for life over fear of death

5. Humour, joy and dancing or **Lightness** in life rather than a fixation on the darkness of death

6. **Curiosity** about all that we can learn in life and in death

7. **Communication About Death**

8. **Human Connection** as life

9. **Nature Connectedness** and the sense of death as a continuation of this

What I found was that although Sawatsky introduced me to these ideas, they appear consistently in the works of people who understood life by confronting their own death. Many of these thinkers implore us not to fixate on what is lost, but to appreciate what we have. Consciousness, connection and a world to explore, a present moment that is guaranteed and a future that is not. I learned that the dying see living with a clarity that we should not ignore, and if we engage with the reality that life and death exist in a constant cycle, we can appreciate them both and feel anxiety about neither.

Life is fleeting. It is short. It matters too much to be worried about and more than enough to be appreciated. Our fear about death is not an alarm telling us that we're running out of oxygen, but a reminder to enjoy breathing. So let's start with an activity and then discuss the wisdom of a number of great thinkers who have documented their experiences of facing death and all the fears we project on to it.

EXERCISE: THE MEMENTO MORI PERSPECTIVE SHIFT

Confronting our fear of death provides an opportunity to see our everyday anxieties and worries in a new context, encouraging greater perspective, gratitude and courage in daily living.

Step 1: List Some Common Anxieties

Take five minutes to write down a list of everyday anxieties or worries. These could include things like:

- Anxiety about saying the wrong thing in a meeting
- Worry about being late
- Concern about how you look today

Step 2: Imagine Your Ninety-Year-Old Self

Close your eyes and imagine yourself at the end of your life, perhaps at age ninety or older. Picture yourself looking back over your life with wisdom and compassion.

Step 3: Revisit Each Anxiety

One by one, read each anxiety aloud (or silently). For each, ask yourself:

- 'From the perspective of my ninety-year-old self, how important does this anxiety seem?'
- 'Will I remember this worry at the end of my life?'
- 'What advice would my older self give me about this anxiety?'

Write down any insights or advice that come to you.

Step 4: Reflect and Reframe

After reviewing your list, reflect on:

- Which anxieties seem less significant when viewed through the lens of mortality?
- Are there daily experiences or opportunities you might embrace more fully if you let go of these worries?

O What would you do differently today if you remembered that life is short, and every day is precious?

Step 5: Daily Reminder

Write a short 'memento mori' statement or mantra inspired by your reflection (e.g., 'In the end, these small anxieties won't matter – so live boldly today!'). Keep it somewhere visible as a daily prompt.

I. Presence

Our anxiety (not fear) about death often fixates on absence, darkness, stillness or silence, but many authors implore us instead to notice how presence and light are the currencies of life. The neurosurgeon Paul Kalanithi wrote the book *When Breath Becomes Air* about his experience of life after a terminal lung-cancer diagnosis. The realization that death could arrive so quickly, and so unexpectedly, gave him a deeper appreciation of the present, and a realization that our futures are never really guaranteed. While many of us spend our present moments thinking about those things in the future that could make us happy or sad, he saw in his diagnosis that these matters are beyond us. The future is not certain, but through effort we can certainly grow happy and appreciative of our present.

Our life is a series of present moments, our past once was and our future will be too, for the present is all there really is. While we cannot change our past or guarantee our future, we can focus on what there is now. For Kalanithi, this means embracing each present moment, and making an effort to find meaning in it, whichever shape it's taking. What we see from many of these authors is that gratitude, awe, joy and mindfulness can always be practised, anchoring us both in the present and providing us with certain ways to appreciate it.

This emphasis on living in the present moment is at the heart of many spiritual practices and the essence of mindfulness itself. The philosopher and professor of medicine Jon Kabat-Zinn, founder of the Mindfulness-Based Stress Reduction programme at the University of Massachusetts Medical School, suggests that mindful awareness not only enhances our lived experience, but gives us a specific appreciation of our mortality. He advocates for 'present moment, non-reactive, non-judgemental, open-hearted presence'[2] as a means to reclaim the joy of the moment we are in from the fear of a future in which we might not be.

Mindful awareness is valuable in both living and dying. Jarem Sawatsky describes how he anchored himself in the present moment by tuning into his bodily sensations, both signifiers of life and the very forces of life itself. He practised mindful breathing and body scans to help him connect to both the pleasure of his existence and the pain of illness, as he grew aware that both were expressions of his being alive. If we feel such anxiety about the absence of life, then any sign of its presence, even pain, can be appreciated.

The political strategist Philip Gould, who wrote a book titled *Lessons from the Death Zone*[3] while facing terminal cancer, found that the intensity of his lived experience escalated when he knew he was dying and called it 'the most extraordinary time of my life'. He saw quite how amazing life was as he prepared to depart it, and grew in appreciation rather than anxiety. He found that life felt purposeful and meaningful now that he reflected on the fact that it had an end point (at least in this form). I think this speaks to the fact that life only seems like a chore because we take it for granted, and act like it will last for ever, when it will not. It is for this reason that phrases like 'memento mori' (remember you will die) are not so much a depressing emphasis on an onrushing absence but a call to appreciation of our presence. We do not miss a good thing until it's gone, but we may also not know how good something really is unless we remind ourselves that it will disappear. The impermanence of life is a key part of what makes it so special.

Gould also found himself investing in his relationships with a new sense of presence. He experienced a greater intensity of feeling and increased closeness when he approached his loved ones in light of the understanding that their relationship could not last for ever. This is true for all of us, not only those facing terminal diagnoses, and it is a wonderful lesson to learn. We should love in the way we would if we knew we were about to lose a loved one, because, in truth, we all are.

He also found himself accessing what he called states of 'ecstasy', where he felt intense enjoyment of life itself, of art and everyday experiences. This feels close to the experience of awe that comes when we remember that life is finite and gain a sense of how absurd and beautiful it is to even exist. In a universe of billions of planets and a span of billions of years, here we are on one where life emerged, in the very short period of time where we get to experience it. We only ever know living, and as a result assume it is much more commonplace than it really is. Those who remember they are about to die see quite how lucky we are.

2. Acceptance

Gould, like many of the others I have turned to in grief and appreciation of life, realized that he could not control his outcome. They had to accept their death and in time found it liberating. When we think deeply about living, most of us come to the conclusion that we would not want to live for ever, and as such we have to accept dying. Our anxiety often stems from a tension around this. Death is the ultimate uncontrollable, but it is also close to the only certainty in life. We have spoken many times about how the pursuit of control in situations where we cannot have it leads to anxiety or pain, and this is also true of living and dying. In some sense, we cannot really control all aspects of our life or death, but both can be enjoyed. For Sawatsky, we are better off focusing on learning to enjoy life, as 'the dying usually takes care of itself'.

For him, we should learn to let go of the need to control or fix everything and instead embrace situations for what they are. When we do so, we free our mind from the relentless effort of trying to make things right and open up space for enjoying how things are. It is in this space that our attention can move towards experiences like awe, gratitude and laughter.

This is not only a philosophical stance, but a clinically supported one. In 2017, the Australian psychologist Esther L. Davis, PhD conducted a survey involving seventy-three patients in end-of-life care.[4] Her team of doctors and palliative care practitioners assessed levels of acceptance, anticipatory grief, anxiety and depression in the group. Their analysis revealed that acceptance was the strongest predictor of reduced anticipatory grief (the grief that dying people feel in advance of their own death), even when accounting for factors like anxiety and depression. The more someone was able to emotionally accept their approaching death, the more likely they were to experience psychological peace rather than distress. Acceptance, in this light, is not resignation, but release – an active shift in posture that allows the individual to step into life's final chapter with clarity and grace.

3. Awe

Dacher Keltner, a professor of psychology at UC Berkeley known for his research on emotion and human connection, and Jonathan Haidt, a renowned social psychologist and expert in moral psychology, propose that experiences of awe have two key components:[5]

1. Perceived vastness: Which refers to anything experienced as being much larger than the self or one's ordinary level of experience, whether physically, socially or conceptually; and

2. The need for accommodation: The process of adjusting mental structures that cannot assimilate this new experience, requiring a shift or expansion in our understanding of the world.

This readily describes a feeling we discussed earlier. How the scope of space and time (perceived vastness) requires us to adjust our view of ourselves and our lives (need for accommodation) in light of it. I think that we often take living for granted, and normalize the experience of being alive, conscious and able to live on this planet. Somehow, the reality of death, when confronted, reminds us that our experience is a small part of a much greater whole. Death brings the scale of the universe into focus; it helps us to perceive vastness, and in accommodating that vastness into our worldview we expand our appreciation of our world.

Death is not a requirement for awe; you have probably felt it in grand natural spaces, at moments of peak connection such as births, the life milestones of loved ones, or in spiritual or religious experiences. However, we should pay heed when people who are dying remind us how powerful awe can be. Dr Keltner proposes that awe is the key aspect that makes numerous different sorts of experiences positive for our wellbeing. From nature connection to the enjoyment of music or spiritual contemplation, for him it is the awe that these experiences generate that impacts our wellbeing, increases our life satisfaction and reduces our anxiety. He later went on to argue that awe doesn't only impact our lives in grand ways (even if grandeur is a part of the package), but also reduces our day-to-day experiences of stress.[6]

While the mechanisms by which awe has such profound impacts

on our lives are still being investigated, the following neuro-physiological and psychological changes have been studied in people who introduce a greater sense of awe into their experience:

- **Reduced self-focus.** An emphasis on *vastness* seems to counteract the negative forms of self-focus which can underpin anxiety.

- **Increased prosociality and social connections.** This may be a result of reduced self-focus, but it may also stem from an increased sense of the shared smallness, and vulnerability, of all humans. We are more likely to care for one another when we realize that no one is too big or too small to merit our attention.

- **Elevated sense of meaning.** By connecting our experiences to the grandeur of the universe, we imbue every act with *awesomeness*. Our small acts are meaningful because they are part of something that we have begun to see as truly great.

- **Decreased rumination.** The temptation to look inward negatively seems to decrease when we are looking outward and upward positively.

- **Increased resilience.** *Enduring* feels more like *exploring* when we are reminded that existence alone is, quite simply, amazing.

In my eyes, awe and fear are often two parts of the same experience. When I recall the most frightening and satisfying experiences of my life, from skydives to mountain climbs or rogue waves, my senses of awe and fear are entwined. Awe makes us feel small, and part of something large – the sky above, the mountain we climb or the waves that crash with such force. Fear is what bridges that gap between us and them; it's the thing that says 'I can't believe I'm here, that I'm (probably?) capable of this, it's frightening and incredible'. The awe is a sense of scale, and of opportunity.

I think that the phrase 'Isn't it incredible?' does much of the heavy lifting in terms of introducing a sense of awe into our lives and accessing its myriad benefits. Whether we are facing down a ten-foot wave or heading out on our daily commute, repeating the words 'Isn't it incredible that . . .' opens up a space in which a sense of awe can grow. We are always small and there is always something large to be in awe of – we just have to prime our perspective to notice its scale.

And while it's true that people who face death are particularly well placed to see how amazing life and existence really is, the living are uniquely well placed to put that appreciation to use going forwards.

4. Gratitude

Appreciation, or gratitude, is a result of awe, but it can also be understood as a singular practice in life and death, with trans-formative impacts on our wellbeing. I was brought towards gratitude by my realization that I couldn't solely fixate on my sadness at Alex's loss without feeling an equivalent gratitude for his presence. You cannot have grief without love. In my experience, the vulnerability and sadness that came with our human connection was a necessary part of the package. So I am grateful that I have learned to value the forty-two years we had as much as I grieve over the years we will not.

The appreciation of life is the necessary response to any fear of death. Gratitude for love shared is the most powerful counter-point to the experience of love lost. In a finite existence, where we would never truly want to be immortal, we should try as much as possible to see life as a gift, rather than death as some theft. This is pivotal in all of the ways we can better approach living and dying. If we take living for granted, as a given (and why would we not, since it is all any of us have ever known?), we tend to see it as neutral, when in fact it is the most incredible, awesome thing in the cosmos.

Sawatsky describes diving into an 'Ocean of Gratitude'. This requires us to submerge ourselves in appreciation of the awesomeness of life, the beauty of the small things within it and the wonder of the relationships we have. That ocean is not so far away – many of us simply forget that we are swimming in it.

EXERCISE: GRATITUDE PRACTICE

Part I: Everyday Gratitude

Objective: To bring attention to the immediate, tangible aspects of life that often go unnoticed.

Take a few moments to settle into a quiet space. Breathe deeply and bring your attention to the present moment. Then, write down five things you are grateful for today. These can be big or small – ranging from a conversation you had, the taste of your breakfast, or the fact that you woke up this morning.

Tip:
Try to be specific. Rather than writing 'my family', you might write, 'the way my sister made me laugh over coffee'.

Part 2: Pre-Life Perspective

Objective: To expand your sense of gratitude by imagining life as a profound opportunity rather than a given.

Now, shift your perspective. Imagine that you have not yet been born. You are on the edge of existence – aware, but without having yet experienced the world. You have never walked, spoken, or seen a sunset. From this viewpoint, write a second list of five things you imagine you would feel deeply grateful for if you were about to begin your life for the first time.

Prompt questions to guide you:

O What would feel like an unimaginable gift?

O What simple experience would feel like a miracle?

O What small human moment would be worth cherishing?

Reflection (Optional):

Compare your two lists.

O What overlaps?

O What did you take for granted in the first list that feels sacred in the second?

O How might this exercise help you reframe your day-to-day life?

Gratitude is accessible when we remember that life, and all of the joy within it, is not a given but a gift. So try to see your life with new eyes.

5. Lightness

I recently described my relationship with Alex to a friend. In doing so I dwelt (gratefully and awe-fully, I hope) on the depth of our connection and how amazing it was to have someone who understood me so well and approached my life with conscientious compassion. They remarked that it reminded them of watching two truly connected dance partners. You may have seen such a pair; they know each other's moves before they make them, position themselves in anticipation and appreciation, and through that understanding seem to create a unit far greater than the sum of its parts. I thought that was accurate, but also spoke to an important perspective on life and death that has been shared by many wise people. We are more likely to appreciate life and less likely to be consumed by anxiety around death if we can treat it lightly; as a joy, a laugh or a dance.

I am not telling you to laugh at your grief. Only that laughing, dancing and *enjoying* life is as important a project as we will ever find. I think it's particularly important given that we tend to overestimate the importance of *seriousness*. We fear that we are not *serious* people, worry that our children don't take things *seriously*, and when we are afraid that we won't be heard we tell people that we are being *serious*. I think this is a mistake; what we value in that serious person might be their *commitment* or the *value* they place on some project at hand. When we ask the child to be serious, we more often want them to be *conscientious*. Our desire to be heard is not a matter of seriousness, a call for frowns, but a plea for connection. We say 'I'm serious', but we mean 'I'm hurt', 'I'm sure' or 'this matters to me'. The problem with using seriousness as a descriptor for all of these things is that we tend to see it as the opposite of joyfulness, playfulness or (and I mean this as a good thing) silliness. As a result, we treat our fears too seriously (to the point where they become blockers) and our joy as silly (to the point where some doubt is enough to stop us pursuing it).

But silliness is not silly (by which we sometimes mean frivolous or unimportant). Silliness contains self-awareness, love and an appreciation of other people's perspectives and joy. It's also a powerful form of care. The doctor Patch Adams (immortalized by that scion of silliness Robin Williams in an eponymous film) invested a great deal of attention to the importance of humour in medical care. He believed humour had a healing power that complemented (but never replaced) traditional medical interventions. In his eyes, patients deserved to be treated not only physically, but emotionally and socially too. While the illness of his patients was serious and medicine was a serious practice, that did not mean there was no room for joy. He encouraged his doctors and patients to try to enjoy their time together, and found that they connected more deeply for it. They were no longer limited to the sole focus of avoiding death, because they were given freedom to try to enjoy life.

Adams's approach has been borne out by research. Humour interventions are now well appreciated as a vital approach in palliative care.[7][8][9] These interventions take many forms; in some, patients are prompted to remember funny episodes from their past and recognize humorous aspects of the present, while in others they are visited by clowns, do magic tricks or play with instruments. There is yet to be a study where such interventions have not provided some benefit. In humour-based care, bad mood and stress are regularly reduced, with cheerfulness increased. The beauty of these studies is that they not only offer people in palliative care access to joy and prove the value of joy itself in a clinical setting, but they also go some way to undermining *seriousness* itself. We do not think of moods, laughter and cheerfulness as the sorts of things we study in *serious* settings like palliative care or *serious* medical journals, but when their usefulness is evaluated in these settings we see that they do belong, and a serious setting does not rule them out.

Incorporating playfulness and humour into daily life is a mindfulness strategy. Sawatsky speaks often about levity as a fundamental foundation of a life well lived, which we all know on some intuitive level. The more we can weigh positive emotions such as joy and humour, the more enjoyable our lives will be, and this is something we owe to those whose lives have ended. We often think of optimism and mindful joyfulness as unserious things and the preserve of unserious people. We pour scorn on optimism with terms like 'Panglossian' or a 'Pollyanna', but this is unfair and only leaves us frightened to choose joy. Put simply, life is worth appreciating, but it's not worth taking *seriously* (in that starched-suit, Victorian, company-man sort of way). And the very act of appreciating it means we have to avoid the cruelty of seriousness.

Many of us choose not to be silly, to appear too publicly joyful or optimistic because we fear it will make us look unserious, that we will look *stupid* or stand out. Death reminds us that life is too important to be lived beneath these fears, particularly so given that very little of what we do will be remembered. To deny ourselves joy in the name of being taken (but not remembered) seriously, is an act of self harm.

Here, think about someone you have loved and lost. Can you remember anything silly they did that was actually *worth* them being embarrassed about? I would imagine not, but you can remember something silly I'm sure. If you were asked to speak about that moment with them now, from beyond the grave, do you think *either of you* would describe it in the language of shame? Or would you laugh about it? Would you hug and would you cry with joy at the sheer beauty of having lived, in silliness, together?

EXERCISE: HOW THOSE WE HAVE LOST CAN TEACH US TO VALUE THOSE WE STILL HAVE

Try thinking about someone you have loved and lost. Picture a conversation with them that lasted for an hour. Picture all of the directions in which that conversation would go, the loved ones you would update them on, the funny stories you would recount, the long, lasting embraces you would hold.

Now ask yourself: how could you approach someone living with that same depth? That love, that joy, that profound appreciation of what it is to be alive?

We should hold the people we love as intensely as we would mourn them. Just as we should live with as much joy, awe and gratitude as the dying see on offer.

Alex was like a perfect dance partner, and as I get older I start to see life more like a dance than hard work. When we take life too seriously, we treat it like a job in which we must strive to be promoted to the next level, struggle to make it through the day and *work* for it to be of *worth*. It is not there to be lived like that; life is to be enjoyed, to be danced or played like a song. This view is well articulated by the Hindu concept of 'Lila', which can loosely be translated as 'divine play' as a way to describe life and creation. The idea of divine play is that creation was not made with purpose (although there is diverse scholarship within denominations and interpreters about what this should mean), there is no endpoint or goal, everything simply *is* and the God Brahman created reality *for fun*.

I think that this captures my sense of Alex as a dance partner, and life like a song or dance, far better than I ever could. The whole point of dancing is the dance; the point of music is in the playing and the listening. We do not need to think of life as some means to an end, a job with a purpose, but as joy itself. Our present moment should not exist in service of a goal; it should be enjoyed, and any temptation we have to let our fears stand between us and that joy should be treated as silly.

6. Curiosity

Which brings me to curiosity. You see, we can be curious in play, in a dance or a song; we can be interested, and that is something that generates great meaning. In *When Breath Becomes Air*,[10] Kalanithi suggests that we need to find meaning in life, if we're to find it in death, too. This is a view that has deep philosophical and historical roots. In the Daoist *Zhuangzi* (a 2,000-year-old text that forms the basis of the Chinese religion) it is said that 'what has made my life good will make my death good'. We see, time and again, that an emphasis on the value and enjoyment of life is the only focus worth having in the face of death. What we usually call the fear of death, as we have discussed, is more a sort of anxiety (fears can be connected to action, they can motivate us to respond and overcome their cause). Unlike fear, death anxiety does not generate a response or a proportionate reaction that helps us deal with the problem at hand, it simply makes us feel uneasy because there is really nothing we can do about it. We *can* be curious about life, use that curiosity to generate awe and in awe feel deep gratitude for the experience of living.

Todd Kashdan is a psychologist and professor who studies psychological flexibility and wellbeing. In his influential book *Curious? Discover the Missing Ingredient to a Fulfilling Life*,[11] he argues for curiosity as a vital pathway to wellbeing and meaning in life, and this philosophy is at the root of many of the fear-facing practices we have described. Curiosity is what drives us to seek new information and experiences; it is what allows us to embrace uncertainty, makes us interested and invested in understanding the thoughts and feelings of others and seek new and sometimes intense situations. He presents this through his '5D model of curiosity' which centres on:

- Joyous exploration;
- Deprivation sensitivity;
- Stress tolerance;
- Social curiosity; and
- Thrill-seeking.

He emphasizes how higher levels of joyous exploration and social curiosity are associated with greater psychological well-being, while deprivation sensitivity may be linked to stress and rumination, and how an understanding of our own curiosity provides us with access to motivation and growth. I see, only now, that much of what I have said about facing fear builds on developing curiosity, about ourselves, others and the world.

I believe we can benefit, too, from being a bit more curious about death and communicating more about it.

7. Communication About Death

Since Alex died I have tried to remain closer to death. By this I mean I do not hide from death or from the fact that people and animals I have loved died, and that others will too. They are everywhere on my walls and I am unafraid to speak to those I have lost when the feeling takes me. I also speak about death as much as I can. I think in many Western cultures, and in British culture in particular, we try to create distance from death and dying through secrecy and an unwillingness to communicate on the subject.

This secrecy sometimes even extends to 'information concealment', whereby patients are denied information about their own condition. This culture of concealment is so prevalent that researchers in numerous countries (from Spain[12] to China[13] and Turkey[14]) have tried to create context-specific scales to monitor the extent of information concealment in their own country. The hope is that by having a scale, they can determine the effectiveness of approaches that reduce it.

I reached out to Kate Woodthorpe, the director of the Centre for Death and Society at Bath University, to discuss how death fits into people's lived experience in the twenty-first century. Kate is lively and vivacious and our conversation spanned everything from the archaeological evidence of early-human mourning rituals to the wonderful Disney film *Coco*, which centres on the Mexican 'Day of the Dead' tradition. She told me that humans have always been aware of death and tried to make sense of it through religion, but that a decline in religiosity has contributed to a culture of privacy and isolation around death itself. This can make both the experience of dying and grieving more lonely and vulnerable than ever before.

When we add into this reality the increasing medicalization of death, we see that it becomes a hidden phenomenon, one which we are not reminded of regularly. In this way it is more like an unknown threat that we try to keep at bay, rather than a knowable productive thing that we might fear but can try to understand and react to.

Her hope, and mine, is that more discussions of death provide an opportunity to come to an increased appreciation of life and death as shared, and therefore less frightening, experiences. It really is the *one* thing *every* one of us will experience, and thus ties us to humans and animals past and present, establishing a powerful sense of community. These discussions need to be prioritized. She pointed me to a campaign by the National Association of Funeral Directors to have bereavement put on the national curriculum, and I think that it would be a great initiative.[15] It could be incredibly impactful for children and their families to open up those conversations, to counteract the loneliness that dying and bereaved people are forced to experience by a culture of secrecy.

Sadly, we do not pay great attention to the experiences of the bereaved. In Woodthorpe's eyes, this owes in part to the exhausting nature of bereavement itself. People who have been through the experience of loss and grief are often too tired to campaign for their own recognition or care. Instead they are pathologized, with conditions like 'Complicated Grief' marked out as a psychological condition. I'm sure there is some value to providing medical professionals with access to knowledge through diagnostic criteria, but in absence of an appreciation of the experiences of grieving people and the complexity of their experience (socially rather than medically), it feels like another step towards the 'culture of concealment' and medicalization of death.

Rather than death becoming more private, and grieving becoming a medical condition, we should start with more public conversations about death and greater recognition of the commonality and community of grief. Death may be frightening, but it should not feel like a secret. It should be something real in our day-to-day lives that informs how we live, rather than some hidden inevitability that we try to conceal in hospitals, care homes and the isolated experiences of the grieving.

8. Human Connection

Quite possibly, this can be placed back under Dr Rosalind Watts's banner of connectedness. The intimacy of mine and Alex's connection to one another was what made it so special, and I hope that in his death I can encourage greater connection between all of us. If this connection takes the form of better social ties or more intimate support for the dying and grieving, then I think we can render both experiences more meaningful.

So many of the thinkers that we have discussed focused on how powerfully they connected to others in light of their terminal diagnoses, and I believe it's a beautiful thing that human connectedness could be impactful both in the pursuit of a better life and a better death. If we can move dying and grieving from a world of private loss to a collective, shared experience, we will gain so much.

Molly Conisbee is a social historian who also conducts research at the Centre for Death and Society at Bath University. In her 2025 book, *No Ordinary Deaths*, she dives into how the history of ritual around death and dying in everyday life provided vital support for dying people, but also fostered a powerful sense of community between the living.[16] When I spoke with her, she mentioned the importance of historical traditions of sitting with the dying, particularly watchers who were charged with gathering families and friends around dying people and ensuring they were never left alone. She also mentioned how common it was until the last century to be around the bodies of the deceased, to prepare them for their funeral and be present with them in a 'wake'. She pointed towards the 'death positive movement', which is trying to bring these traditions back into public practice, as there is evidence that this not only helps people process grief (she is also a grief counsellor), but to create more engagement with death and dying in communities of the living.

For her, a more open relationship with dying and death could help to rebuild the sense of community that often feels lacking in modern developed societies. Grief, historically, was shared. We would know when anyone in our community was in the process of mourning a loved one and we would feel compelled to speak with them and support them through that difficult time. Death encouraged us to connect with others in our community.

The closer we are to those who are grieving, the more intimately we connect to those we love who are dying, and the more open we are about some of the challenges of that reality, the less we need to worry about our own experience of it. It need not be something completely alien, new and novel if we confront our fear and take time to experience it with others that we care about as they grieve or die.

Because in death or bereavement, none of us should be alone.

9. Nature Connectedness

Finally, and in relation to Dr Watts's connectedness again, we see that 'nature connectedness' underpins wellbeing both in life and in death. While we have discussed the power of this view in life, there are certain particular benefits to this form of connectedness when dying. Experiences of the natural world in life encourage us to confront the basic cyclicality of living and dying. Trees fall, mosses and fungi grow, and then new saplings and creatures rise from the life that the tree gifted back into the natural system. We grow more conscious of the reality that we too are part of that system.

Our desire for control as complex human animals often leads us to believe we exist above the natural world, where death is *necessary* for life and in a sense a gift to it. During research into psilocybin-assisted therapy for people in end-of-life care that has been conducted at NYU[17] and Johns Hopkins University[18] in the US, study participants remarked on improvements in their attitudes about life, self, mood, relationships and spirituality, but also spoke about how they developed an idea of death as a transition rather than an end. Some even grew in the belief that they could remain connected to the world after death. This is very hard to pin down academically (*seriously* even), but on an intuitive level I can understand it. The version of ourselves that moves through the world, that *sees* and *does*, may end in death, but every atom in our body and electron in our brain continues. We do not need to be religious or even very spiritual to see that consciousness arose from the matter of this universe and it will rise again.

I am unafraid to admit that there is a lot I do not understand about life and death, and I would be suspicious of anyone who claimed that they had all the answers about such grand themes before they have lived and died through them. All I know is that our lives *are* temporary and short, but it is only by really engaging with our fear of death that we can make it productive. That's the opportunity. Our fear that life will end reminds us to focus on the appreciation of what we have, rather than what we will lose.

That is perhaps the core message of this book. Do not worry about what *might* happen; do not avoid doubt or struggle to keep change at bay. Ask yourself what *is* happening now, tune in to what you appreciate and understand that change is part of our incredible shared journey. Life is not to be lived in *absence* of hardship, but in the mindful presence of itself.

That is the message from my time spent thinking about fear, and it is the message that lives on in the words of those who have bravely spoken about their experience of facing death.

KEY TAKEAWAYS

1. Focusing on the present moment is both an antidote to past rumination and future worries, but more importantly it is pivotal to appreciating life.

2. Accept what you cannot change in life; accept that death is an experience we will all share.

3. Try to experience awe, at the beauty, kindness and sheer magnitude of the universe.

4. Remember life is an incredible gift – we should be grateful for it.

5. Laughing, smiling and dancing are serious matters.

6. Be curious about the things that scare you and those that bring you joy.

7. Speak about death, reach out to the grieving and those who are soon to die.

8. Remember that we are not above the natural world, we are of it and will return into it when we die.

**Live life with the vitality of one who knows
it doesn't last for ever.**

10. The Opportunities in Our Fears

Every Myth We've Busted

When it comes to fear, very little is as it first seems. Every chapter in this book takes our fears and reframes them for the opportunity that they could be. I hope you've gained something by looking at the things that tend to scare us in this new light. You may not drastically change your life, your habits or your plans, but when it comes to what you fear, I hope I've helped you change your mind. Through researching this book – and examining my own motivations for going so regularly outside of my comfort zone – what has become clear to me is that just a small shift in perspective can turn fear from being a problem into being part of the solution. Because many things that we try to avoid offer benefits that we should pursue, and by pursuing them we could reduce our anxiety, build our confidence, and reconnect to who we really are.

People often talk about optimism in terms of our outlook, but I think it is also the driver of outcomes. None of the things that scare us have materially changed, but how we feel about them is transformed when approached from a different perspective. *We* are transformed with the benefit of that perspective. When we decide to approach fear as an ally, we step into the world with a sense of our own strength, rather than our weakness, with proactivity not avoidance, by looking up, not down. This *makes* us stronger, proactive and optimistic. We can then mould the events of our life into a shape that reflects what we might want rather than what we could lose.

Colombian author and recipient of the Nobel Prize for Literature, Gabriel García Márquez, told his biographer that 'What matters in life is not what happens to you, but what you remember and how you remember it.'[1] I think he's right, but I would argue we can go further. His point was that experiences we've undergone are transformed entirely depending on how we think about them afterwards – that's to say, depending on our chosen perspective. I think that this is as true for our present and future as he suggested it was of our past.

In this chapter we will revisit some of the myths around our fears and see how this new perspective can create a reality in which they are not so much problems as opportunities. Let's look again at the ways in which we have approached various fears from a new direction, and think about what this means for us all going forwards. What could your life look like now that you approach yourself and your challenges with a sense of appreciation?

> **Myth:** Children play fearlessly because they don't understand what risk and danger are. As adults, it's our job to stop them, so that they stay safe.

> **Reality:** Children play in ways that seem dangerous to us because they understand the power of fear in ways that adults have forgotten. We should encourage them (within reason!) and learn from the way they see the world.

We discussed how children are attracted to risky play, and how this often frightens us as adults. I learned how the underlying assumption, that children play this way because they do not understand risk, was entirely wrong. Children play in ways that seem dangerous to us, because they understand there is an opportunity to learn through fear. We saw that playtime is not the opposite of education, but one of its deepest foundations. If we adults can learn to play, we too may *play to learn* and we might raise future generations with a far better sense of risk and reward than our generation has. The impacts of this could be incredible. They would be more resilient, self-sufficient and capable of accessing all of the goods we have described from a fear-facing approach to life. If we are brave enough to let our children take risks, they will never need a book like this, because they will understand these messages intuitively, as it is adults who rob them of their appreciation of the guiding power of fear. Their risk assessment and their sense of reward is what will empower them to make principled decisions, stand up for themselves and rise again when they inevitably fail. For these reasons, a more happy and principled world could be a matter of child's play.

This might stress us out, but I hope we have come to understand that stress is not always a bad thing. In fact, our second chapter looked at the very opposite of that. **Stress is good for us** when it's tied to a goal. It's our body preparing itself to act on something. Perhaps the stress we sometimes feel at children's disinhibited play is just the motivator we need to share it with them and be as brave as they are.

THE FEAR OPPORTUNITY

Watch without rushing in

The next time a child climbs, balances or explores something that makes you nervous, pause. Observe their judgement, focus and confidence. Step in only when there is clear, imminent danger – not just discomfort. Let their curiosity guide you before your instinct to protect does.

Ask questions instead of giving warnings

Instead of saying, 'Be careful!', try: 'How do you know that's safe?' or 'What's your plan if it wobbles?' This invites reflection, builds risk awareness, and helps children internalize safety skills without fear overriding their initiative.

Do something playful that stretches your own comfort zone

Climb a tree, jump into cold water, try a cartwheel, or balance on a fallen log. Re-engaging in physical, slightly uncertain play reminds you what fear and excitement feel like when they're alive in the body – and helps you reconnect with the child's point of view.

Myth: Our stress responses, and fear responses (e.g., increased heart rate/sweating), are a sign of a problem.

Reality: They are *exactly* what our body must do to respond to a problem, and learning to appreciate that makes them do so even more effectively.

Regardless of how we put our stress response to use, understanding that it's doing something we actually need is empowering. And, as we learned from our experts in Chapter 2, the knowledge that our stress response is useful *makes* it even more so. It's not a wave of dread that washes over us, but a surge of adrenaline and energy that provides an opportunity to surf right to the edge of our comfort zone. It's at that edge that our view of ourselves, how strong we are, and everything we can achieve, starts to expand. The beauty of acting at the edge of what we believe possible is that it grows our self-image and encourages us to reach further and grow more.

This is because every practice where we gradually extend our comfort zone is subject to the principle of 'dopamine stacking', the process by which we can start by doing small satisfying things and use that satisfaction as motivation to do slightly harder, incrementally more satisfying ones. This stacking, when understood as part of our heroic journey, our progress, only grows more awesome and feels more grand because we see it as heroic.

THE FEAR OPPORTUNITY:

Reframe your physical reactions as allies, not enemies

The next time your heart races or your palms sweat, remind yourself these are your body's tools gearing up to help you face a challenge – not signals that something is wrong.

Practise mindful awareness during moments of stress

Instead of pushing away or judging these sensations, gently observe them with curiosity. Notice how they rise, peak and fall, and how your body feels once the response has passed. This awareness trains your nervous system to respond with more ease over time.

Engage in a physical activity that channels your stress response productively

Go for a brisk walk, dance, or do some light cardio when you feel stress building. Using your body this way helps your physiological response complete its cycle and resets your system, making you more resilient next time.

Myth: Our lives are ordinary, and feeling fear means we must lack the tools to flourish, even in the face of that ordinariness.

Reality: We can change our perspective and learn to see our lives as extraordinary stories, hero narratives, with ourselves at the centre. We feel fear because we're preparing to be heroic.

Where your heroic journey takes you is your choice, but if you can flip your idea of what an adventure is and see yourself as an adventurer, then you will see that what you once feared is an opportunity for growth and joy. Adventure is anything that takes you outside of your comfort zone. An action or activity that you decide to take on today is an adventure if you would have felt uncomfortable doing it yesterday. If you can do it in the natural world, it will only benefit you further. Physically, green and blue spaces have incredible health benefits. Psychologically, they make us calm. Experiences in nature provide an opportunity to connect with ourselves and others, and we've seen how this improves our wellbeing in life, and even when approaching death.

THE FEAR OPPORTUNITY:

Look at your life so far as a heroic journey

Every mistake you have made, time you have failed or chance you have missed led you to where you are today. It taught you something that empowers you to face your next trial.

Call new experiences *adventures*

You aren't going speed-dating; you're starting an adventure in love. It isn't a caravan holiday in Scotland; it's a mobile Highland adventure. When you adventure, you cannot fail, because the ups and downs are a necessary part of the experience.

See your next hurdle as another chapter in your heroic journey

A hero becomes worthy of their name by overcoming trials. By calling your journey through life heroic, you make those trials into opportunities for growth, progress and learning. See it for what it could teach you or how it will add to your heroic story.

Myth: Adventure is risky, it is traditionally masculine and it involves 'conquering' nature. It *should* be frightening.

Reality: Adventure can be as safe as we desire, can be described in terms of peace, self-knowledge and connection, and aligns with nature. Frightening or not, it *should* be about learning.

Some people may feel afraid of adventure because they've never seen people they consider 'adventurers' who look like they do. But when we examine more closely what an adventure and an adventurer really are, we see things quite differently. An adventure can be internal, a process of self-discovery. It can be social, going to a new place with new people and embracing the joy and uncertainty of those interactions. It *can* also be more like that traditional view of an adventure, an epic journey that takes us to new, unseen places, but it need not involve conquest or ego.

If you do not look like a so-called adventurer, then you have an opportunity to create a brand new image of one. You may not be a Victorian man (none of us are) or a frat-bro, but you are an adventurer as soon as you decide to go on an adventure. It isn't what we look like that makes us brave, but what we do, and what we set out to learn.

THE FEAR OPPORTUNITY:

Redefine adventure on your own terms

Choose activities that bring you peace and connection – like walking quietly in a forest, or simply observing wildlife – reminding yourself that this is adventure.

Reflect on what you learn from each experience

After any outdoor or adventurous activity, take a moment to journal or talk about what you discovered about yourself, the environment, or your limits. Viewing adventure as a learning journey transforms fear into curiosity.

Invite others to share in your adventure

Connect with friends or family to explore nature together, fostering shared experiences that build bonds and reinforce the idea that adventure is about connection, not competition or risk alone.

Myth: We fear failure because we will lose our value and people will judge us. Their judgement will reflect that we are worth less than we thought we were.

Reality: We fear the consequences of failure, but we can never say for sure what they will actually be. Our value is constant and it is not tied to our actions, so we should choose what we do based on what gives us meaning, strength and joy.

The fear many of us have around entering new spaces or doing new things is not really a fear that they will be dangerous, hard or frightening, but that we won't be accepted, will be judged, or look stupid. But in my experience people are much more accepting than our anxious minds imagine them to be. I have had to learn this gradually, across an introvert's lifetime, and in part I learned it by understanding my fear of failure. **We do not fear failure** (anything from going to a new group and failing to connect with people, to starting a business that is unsuccessful); **we fear the consequences**. In the first example, we fear that people in the group will be cruel, in the second that others will think less of us for failing in industry. Those experiences make us feel worth less – they compromise our idea of our own value. But in fact, we can separate those potential consequences from our own value, and when we do, we see that we have less to lose. It might be reasonable to prepare for the financial consequences of a business failure, but there is no use in dwelling on ideas of how our *own value* might be impacted. So you must remember:

You have value, simply for being you.

No failed attempt, disappointment or judgement from someone else makes you less valuable. We all hold internalized beliefs about external things that give us our worth: that we are smart or people like us, that we command respect or act as a peacemaker. But none of these are what *actually* give us our value, and no instance where we fail to achieve them reduces it. If we can spend time getting to know ourselves, we can identify these core beliefs and separate them from the reality of our true worth: that it is ours simply for being ourselves. We cannot always be right, or make people like us; there will be times when they may not respect us or the peace is too hard to maintain. If we can always remember that we have value regardless, then there is no failure worthy of our precious fear, only opportunities for progress.

THE FEAR OPPORTUNITY:

Name the fear – but question the story

When you're afraid to try something, ask yourself: What exactly am I afraid will happen? Then ask: How likely is that? What else might happen instead? This shift opens space between fear and action, and helps you see that imagined consequences often lose their grip when examined closely.

Reconnect with what gives you meaning

Make a list of three things that matter deeply to you – not because you're good at them, but because they make you feel alive. Let those be your compass, even when success isn't guaranteed. Value-driven action builds self-trust, regardless of outcome.

Practise failing on purpose

Try something you're not good at, in low-stakes ways: sing badly, speak a new language imperfectly, or cook without a recipe. Doing this with humour and intention helps rewire your association with failure – proving it's survivable, sometimes joyful, and never a measure of your worth.

Myth: Change is frightening because we have so much to lose; we cede control and we face challenges that we are not prepared for.

Reality: Change is beautiful because we have so much to gain; we have the chance to craft the lives that we want and learn just how capable we are.

Our sense of our inherent value is also an anchor through times of change. Life is a process of continuous flux, or movement and growth, death and rebirth. This is what makes it beautiful, and enjoyable, but we still often feel unmoored and afraid when change is thrust upon us. That fear is a vital form of energy if it can be matched with a sense of security about the parts of ourselves that do not change with it. Self-knowledge allows us to approach change as an opportunity to gain something new rather than worry about what we might lose. Our inherent sense of self-worth, and knowledge of our core values, is what makes us secure enough to look upon change as an opportunity rather than a threat. It reminds us that no change can break us and our core values will still be in place to help us make new choices in our changed circumstances.

Because change can be an end, or it can be a beginning. Endings often make us feel powerless because we define them by absence – something we liked has gone, and we can't do anything about it. A beginning, on the other hand, is bursting with potential energy, and the more we can see change in terms of beginnings rather than ends, the more we can see it as a moment of opportunity. The emotion I associate with the perspective that sees change as an ending is anxiety, while I link fearful, nervous excitement with seeing change as a beginning. Anxiety is a powerless state of being; there is little that we can do about it and little we can do *with* it. But fear is proactive. It marshals resources such as adrenaline and the anabolic hormones of growth, so when we see change as a beginning we tap into that energy. Our bodies follow our minds when we see it as an opportunity.

If we can frame life changes as beginnings, we can start to feel excited by them rather than bereft. Think of the moment in Nina Simone's 'Feeling Good' when she looks at her new life and the horn section comes in? Bam . . . babam . . . babam . . . babam, badada-dadDUM – that's what change as a beginning feels like. There's a reason why people, in the first flush of new love or an exciting new hobby, say things like 'I feel like a kid again'. Children are beginners; they're curious and they're always learning. An ending gives us plenty to learn from, but the absence that follows it is a vacuum for curiosity. Making a decision to stay curious, and develop a learner's or growth mindset, helps us see change as a beginning. Change is not something that we can control; it's an inevitable feature of the universe and it's only when we see it as such that we can harness it as progress rather than resist time's effort to take something away.

So think about change in terms of what you can and can't do. Your core values and many of your skills will remain relevant, but there will be chances to apply them in different ways and new settings. It's an opportunity for you to learn and apply entirely new skills, things that you can't do *yet*. This is a powerful reminder to look forwards, because a change may bring a loss, but it also makes space for gain. The more time we take to understand ourselves, what we want and what makes us happy, the more room we have to add skills, experiences and connections that reflect who we really are. Many of us simply fall into life, into careers or relationships, dependencies or habits. Most often a change takes the form of a shift in one of these. We should not fear that the experiences we have had are undone by the change – everything that we enjoyed and achieved stays with us – but see the opportunity to add new contours to our lives.

THE FEAR OPPORTUNITY:

List what you might gain, not just what you fear losing

When facing change, write down three things the change might bring you – even if they feel uncertain or distant. This simple act shifts your focus from threat to possibility, helping you open to growth.

Recall a time you handled change well

Think back to a moment in your life when something shifted unexpectedly, and you adapted. What did you learn? What strengths did you uncover? Let that memory remind you that you're likely more prepared than you think.

Take one small step towards the life you want

Change doesn't have to be sweeping. Send the message, make the plan, sign up for the class – any small action that aligns with a life you want to build. Each step reinforces your agency and helps transform fear into momentum.

Myth: The unknown is terrifying; it could be filled with horror, pain and disappointment. It makes me feel anxious because it's not only beyond my understanding but my control.

Reality: The unknown contains everything that is new and good; it could be filled with discovery, joy and satisfaction. If I'm calm and mindful then the outcome is far more likely to be positive, I will feel in control and the experience will be transformed.

Remind yourself that *all* good things start as unknowns. You could not have known what you would build before you started. The career, the family or the passion that is now changing was not something that you could have predicted when you began building it. It was unknown. It may also have been frightening, so as you approach any change try to remember how you felt the last time you began to do something new. There was probably some nervous excitement, trepidation or fear on your first day at that job which became your career, when you first said 'I love you' or even when you first went to a new exercise class.

So we must begin by reminding ourselves that uncertainty is not a bad thing, and that we should be mindful of treating uncertainty as a catastrophe waiting to happen. We have to work to develop the skill of reading our own mind when we face uncertainty, and identify when we are trying to protect ourselves from the negative assumptions we make about unknown or uncertain things. Once we have noticed our very normal tendency to think uncertainty is a bad thing, we should act to build uncertainty tolerance by practising approaches that calm our bodies and our minds. We will never be able to completely control the outcome of an uncertain situation, but if, through mindfulness or logical thinking, we can approach that situation with a calm body and mind, we will never *lose* control. Outcomes are uncontrollable, but our responses always are, and that is a powerful grounding force that gives us the strength to approach uncertainty confidently and fairly. That fairness means appreciating that outcomes may be good or they may be bad, but that we can act in ways which make better outcomes more likely and the experience more joyful. We can harness our fear of the unknown and feel excited; we can face that uncertainty and grow curious, because everything good or bad is at one point uncertain, so we have to get used to it. If we are to enjoy life itself, we must learn to enjoy stepping out into the unknown, because it's just another word for the future.

THE FEAR OPPORTUNITY:

Notice your first reaction – and pause before following it

When uncertainty arises, pay attention to your initial response. Do you tense up, catastrophize, or try to escape it? Take one deep breath, and ask: What else could this mean? That pause is where possibility begins.

Seek out a small unknown on purpose

Try something unfamiliar: take a new route home, speak to someone you don't know well, or explore a subject you know little about.

Embracing low-stakes uncertainty builds the muscle for navigating life's bigger unknowns with curiosity instead of fear.

Ground yourself with calming practices

Before entering an uncertain situation, use a technique that brings you into the present – slow breathing, body scanning or mindful walking. The more regulated your nervous system, the more likely your experience of the unknown will be one of openness, not overwhelm.

Myth: Standing out or being different is terrifying because it means I will be judged, left out or somehow unacceptable.

Reality: We do not fear difference, but isolation. We can be different from others and connected. That will allow us to be both satisfied in our authenticity and connected in ways that reflect who we really want to be.

The process that led me to my lowest point involved alienation from myself and my core values, disconnection from other people and a broken relationship with the natural world. With thought and effort, each three of these pillars of connection was rebuilt. I remembered that my inherent value was not compromised by my hardship, that a failure did not mean effort and reward were no longer related, that I could reconnect to other people and I could be happy again in the natural world which had always brought me such joy.

The opposite of anxiety is, for me, connection. Fear is fine; it's a deeply connected emotion that ties us to tasks, people and responses. Anxiety alienates us from ourselves, from others and from the world around us. You have the opportunity to connect with yourself, through a project of self-discovery, questioning or mindfulness. You can choose to seek the company of others, for connection's sake, rather than validation or conformity. Or you can spend time connecting with the natural world.

Any of these efforts will make you feel more connected in those other ways. As long as you are choosing to connect, in your own way, for your own reasons, you have the opportunity to be more authentically connected. This will save you from anxiety about standing out, and remind you of what that feeling really speaks to: your desire for connection.

THE FEAR OPPORTUNITY:

Notice when you're editing yourself – and ask why

Pay attention to the moments you hold back a thought, opinion or instinct to fit in. Ask yourself: Am I protecting myself from rejection, or am I giving up something essential? This awareness helps you choose authenticity with intention, not fear.

Seek connection through shared values, not surface sameness

Spend time with people who respect who you are, not just who you pretend to be. When you build relationships rooted in honesty and shared meaning, difference becomes a source of depth, not distance.

Express your uniqueness in a small, visible way

Wear something you love, speak up when it matters, or share a personal perspective – even if it feels different. Tiny acts of visible authenticity help you build the confidence that being yourself doesn't lead to isolation – it leads to the right kind of connection.

Myth: Death is frightening. I spend my life in fear of it.

Reality: Death can be anxiety-inducing if we try to hide from its inevitability and necessity. Any fear we feel should be a reminder to appreciate life and others within it.

We need to decide who we want to be, what makes us happy and how we want to touch the world around us. Because life is short; it is an incredible, rare thing and it is too important not to be enjoyed. Many of us, me included, spend years worrying about whether we are right or wrong, fitting in or standing out, doing as we *should*. There is no right way of living. Life is not a job, with key performance indicators. It is not a sport that we can score or a piece of work to be graded. It is something to be lived, and to be enjoyed. When we think about our worries, they usually centre on whether we are doing it all wrong and what we might lose. When we remember that there is no correct way, only happiness and kindness, we see that moral designations such as right or wrong are only worth applying to moral acts, but not living itself. When we see that **life is an incredible gift**, we can see our fear of losing it as an opportunity to remember how much we have to gain simply by doing it, and enjoying it.

THE FEAR OPPORTUNITY:

Let thoughts of death sharpen your focus on life

When the thought of death arises, don't push it away. Ask: What does this moment make me grateful for? Who do I need to appreciate today? Let the fear redirect your attention to what truly matters, rather than to what you can't control.

Engage in a ritual of appreciation

Each day, take a few minutes to notice and name three things – people, experiences, sensations – you're grateful to have while you're here. Regular gratitude helps transform abstract fear into tangible presence.

Have a gentle conversation about death

Speak to someone you trust about your thoughts or questions around dying. Naming what we fear out loud softens its power and invites connection. Often, these conversations open doors to deeper understanding – and to peace.

Life is more like a song, a dance or a game than a trial. We are *all* playing dress-up and dolls houses and worrying whether we are doing it right. Anyone who has played games with small children knows that there is no right way of doing it. The horses can have a tea party with the dolls and a dinosaur might be serving the biscuits. That sounds absurd, but life is too. It sounds silly. But so are we. What sounds more silly, and more absurd, is telling that child that they are doing it wrong, that they are not playing properly, because in trying to do it properly we lose all sense of play.

So go out and play. As soon as you start, you will find you are doing it right. Then you can learn what exhilarates you. When you feel that exhilaration, be grateful for it, because that is the energy, the fear, that makes you into a hero (or that dinosaur who is serving the biscuits).

Remember that you are creating an example of the sort of hero that you might have been denied. The sort of hero who fails, and knows just how useful that is. Who changes and shows someone else that change is the making of all of us. That change is the making of all things.

Be proud to say that you don't know, and be brave enough to enter the unknown, even in the smallest of ways. It's what heroes do and it's where we find opportunities to learn, adapt and grow stronger.

Do it your own way, proudly, and remember that you do not fear being different but want the joy of connection. Because connecting with ourselves, with others and with this world around us is the essence of life. And life is a precious gift. Temporary and short. If you fear losing it, then enjoy having it.

In our fears we find our greatest opportunities, for they direct us towards what matters; the leaps that make our hearts beat faster and the people and places that take our breath away. Unlike our worries, they ask us for solutions and present challenges that demand every last drop of our strength. It is only then that we learn how strong we really are, or push beyond to grow even stronger. It is only there that we become more confident; between the knowledge of our fear and the presence of our reaction.

So don't worry, be fearful. It's the bravest thing you can do.

Because your fears are your guide.

And they are telling you to *live*.

Yours fearfully,
Victoria Pendleton

Acknowledgements

I was in limbo for a couple of years: the passing of my darling twinnie, after a terminal brain tumour, had left me totally lost and struggling to find purpose in what felt like a cruel and unnecessary world. I felt less than half. The half Alex had provided gave me drive and determination, ambition and equality, which moulded my character immeasurably.

The patience and gentle encouragement of a few people helped me find purpose again with this unexpected book project. They saw potential in exploring the conundrum of my unusual lived experience. Long had I felt that there was something wrong with me and my choices to pursue the things that challenged and pushed me rather than shy away from them. They saw my life in ways I had not.

First of all thank you to Nora Millar, whose dedication and perseverance to find opportunity, combined with the constant support through my lows in self-esteem, made the difference. I would have been stuck without you.

To Carly Cook, my literary agent, for being supportive and steadfast, helping make decisions and navigate the project with experience and calm.

Pan Mac and particularly Jodie for being so enthusiastic about this idea from the very first conversation and giving me the confidence to pursue this book project.

To the many academics and experts who so willingly and generously gave up time and their wisdom about their research, their ideas and insights. I appreciate all the wonderful discussions we experienced.

My most humble gratitude goes to my co-writer Oscar Millar, thank you for the monumental amount of work you have put in writing this book with me, I genuinely could not have done it without you. I am in awe of your inquisitive and diverse thoughts and your nuanced and eloquent delivery. I thoroughly enjoyed working with you and hope we get to do it again soon. I don't think it is a coincidence your birthday is on the same day as Alex and I; I'm glad to share that day with you too.

Finally, to my family – Pauline, Max, Nicola and Alex – who gave me the opportunity and support I needed to do extraordinary things with my life.

References

Chapter 1

1 van Rooijen, M., Lensvelt-Mulders, G., Wyver, S., & Duyndam, J. (2020). Professional attitudes towards children's risk-taking in play: Insights into influencing factors in Dutch contexts. *Journal of Adventure Education and Outdoor Learning, 20(2)*, 138–154. https://doi.org/10.1080/14729679.2019.1568893

2 Zvolensky, M. J., Bernstein, A. & Vujanovic, A. A. (eds), *Distress Tolerance: Theory, Research, and Clinical Applications* (New York: Guilford Press, 2011).

3 Mohsenabadi, Z., Pirmoradi, S., Zahedi Tajrishi, K. & Gharraee, B., 'A transdiagnostic approach to investigate the relationships between anxiety sensitivity and health anxiety: the mediated roles of distress tolerance and emotion regulation', *Frontiers in Psychiatry* 16 (2025), 1478442.

4 Pilatti, A., Bravo, A. J., Michelini, Y., Aguirre, P. & Pautassi, R. M., 'Self-control and problematic use of social networking sites: Examining distress tolerance as a mediator among Argentinian college students', *Addictive Behaviors Reports* 14 (2021).

5 Årnes, A. P., Nielsen, C. S., Stubhaug, A., Engdahl, B. & Knudsen, A. K. S., 'Longitudinal relationships between habitual physical activity and pain tolerance in the general population', *PLOS ONE* 18:5 (2023), e0285041. doi: 10.1371/journal.pone.0285041

6 Brussoni, M., et al., 'What is the Relationship between Risky Outdoor Play and Health in Children?' *International Journal of Environmental Research and Public Health* 12:6 (2015), 6423–54.

7 O'Connor, J., 'Is it time for the risky classroom? Dealing with risk and uncertainty is essential for resilience and confidence in adulthood', 11th International Technology, Education and Development Conference (2014). doi: 10.21125/inted.2017.1490

8 Dodd, H. F., 'Risky play and mental health'. In: Tremblay, R. E., Boivin, M., Peters, R. De V. (eds), 'Outdoor play: According to experts', *Encyclopedia on Early Childhood Development* (2024). https://nifplay.org/play-note/adult-play/#emotional-and-mental-health-benefits

9 Guedes, A. I., et al., 'Educational strategies for tolerance to uncertainty in students and health professionals: systematic review', *RevEspEduMed* 3 (2023), 62–75. doi: 10.6018/edumed.576711

10 Dyment, J. E. & Bell, A. C., 'Grounds for Movement: Green School Grounds as Sites for Promoting Physical Activity', *Health Education Research* 23:6 (2008), 952–62. http://www.jstor.org/stable/45110512

11 https://www.mdpi.com/2076-2615/12/3/383

12 Tyne, W. P., Fletcher, D., Paine, N. J. & Stevinson, C., 'Effects of outdoor recreational physical challenges on general self-efficacy: A randomized controlled trial', *Psychology of Sport & Exercise*, 74, 102693 (2024). doi:10.1016/j.psychsport.2024.102693

13 Falon, S. L., Hoare, S., Kangas, M. & Crane, M. F., 'The coping insights evident through self-reflection on stressful military training events: Qualitative evidence from self-reflection journals', *Stress and Health*, 38(5) (2022), pp. 902–18. doi:10.1002/smi.3141

Chapter 2

1 Antonovsky, A., *Health, Stress, and Coping* (San Francisco, CA: Jossey-Bass, 1979).

2 Arnold, R., 'Thriving under pressure: Insights and recommendations for PMAs from a midwifery stress audit', National Professional Midwifery Advocate (PMA) Conference (2025).

3 Arnold, R. & Moore, L., 'Exploring the Mental Health, Well-Being,

and Burnout of Athlete Support Personnel in the UK High Performance Sport System' (2025).

4 Selye, H., 'The Stress Concept: Past, Present and Future'. In Cooper, C. L. (ed.), *Stress Research Issues for the Eighties* (New York, NY: John Wiley & Sons, 1983), pp. 1–20.

5 Crum, A. J., Salovey, P. & Achor, S., 'Rethinking stress: The role of mindsets in determining the stress response', *Journal of Personality and Social Psychology* 104:4 (2013), 716–33. https://doi.org/10.1037/a0031201

6 Crum, A. J., Langer, E. J., 'Mind-set Matters: Exercise and the Placebo Effect', *Psychological Science* (2007), 165–71. https://pubmed.ncbi.nlm.nih.gov/17425538/

7 Crum, A. J., Corbin, W. R., Brownell, K. D., Salovey, P., 'Mind over milkshakes: mindsets, not just nutrients, determine ghrelin response', *Health Psychology* 30:4 (July 2011), 424–9; discussion 430–1. doi: 10.1037/a0023467

8 Campbell, J., *The Hero with a Thousand Faces* (Novato, CA: New World Library, 2008; originally published 1949).

9 The Heroic Imagination Project. www.heroicimagination.org

10 Baumeister, R. F., Vohs, K. D., Aaker, J. L. & Garbinsky, E. N., 'Some key differences between a happy life and a meaningful life', *Journal of Positive Psychology* 8:6 (2013), 505–16. https://doi.org/10.1080/17439760.2013.830764

11 Waters, T. E., Fivush, R., 'Relations Between Narrative Coherence, Identity, and Psychological Well-Being in Emerging Adulthood', *Journal of Personality and Social Psychology* 83:4 (Aug 2015), 441–51. doi: 10.1111/jopy.12120

Chapter 3

1 Nelson, J. A., Global Development and Environment Institute Working Paper No. 12-05: 'Are Women Really More Risk-Averse than Men?' (Tufts University, September 2012).

2 Sekścińska, K., Jaworska, D., Rudzinska-Wojciechowska, J., Kusev, P., 'The Effects of Activating Gender-Related Social Roles on Financial Risk-Taking', *Experimental Psychology* 70:1 (Jan 2023), 40–50. doi: 10.1027/1618-3169/a000576

3 Weaver et al., 'Intrepid, Imprudent, or Impetuous?: The Effects of Gender Threats on Men's Financial Decisions', *Psychology of Men & Masculinity* 14:2 (2013), 184–91. doi: 10.1037/a0027087

4 Croson, R. & Gneezy, U., 'Gender Differences in Preferences', *Journal of Economic Literature* 47:2 (2009), 448–74. doi: 10.1257/jel.47.2.448

5 Beckmann, D. & Menkhoff, L., 'Will Women Be Women? Analyzing the Gender Difference among Financial Experts', *Kyklos* 61:3 (2008), 364–84. https://doi.org/10.1111/j.1467-6435. 2008.00406.x

6 Booth, A. L. & Nolen, P., 'Gender Differences in Risk Behaviour: Does Nurture Matter?' *The Economic Journal* 122:558 (2012), F56–F78. https://doi.org/10.1111/j.1468-0297.2011.02480.x

7 Borghans, L., et al., 'Gender Differences in Risk Aversion and Ambiguity Aversion', *Journal of the European Economic Association* 7:2–3 (2009), 649–58. https://doi.org/10.1162/ JEEA.2009.7.2-3.649

8 de Goede, M., 'Repoliticizing financial risk', *Economy and Society* 33:2 (2004), 197–217. https://doi.org/10.1080/030851404100 01677120

9 Eckel, C. C. & Grossman, P. J., 'Sex differences and statistical stereotyping in attitudes toward financial risk', *Evolution and Human Behavior* 23:4 (2002), 281–95. https://doi.org/10.1016/ S1090-5138(02)00097-1

10 Meier-Pesti, K. & Penz, E., 'Sex or Gender? Expanding the sex-based view by introducing masculinity and femininity as predictors of financial risk taking', *Journal of Economic Psychology* 29:2 (2008), 180–96. https://doi.org/10.1016/j. joep.2007.05.002

11 Leckelt, M., König, J., Richter, D., et al., 'The personality traits of self-made and inherited millionaires', *Humanities and Social Sciences Communications* 9:94 (2022). https://doi.org/10.1057/ s41599-022-01099-3

12 Finucane, M. L., Slovic, P., Mertz, C. K., Flynn, J. & Satterfield, T., 'Gender, race, and perceived risk: The "white male" effect', *Risk Analysis* 20:4 (2000), 1–12. https://doi. org/10.1080/713670162

13 Ibarra, H., 'Provisional selves: Experimenting with image and

identity in professional adaptation', *Administrative Science Quarterly* 44:4 (1999), 764–91. https://doi.org/10.2307/2667055

14 González-Pérez, S., Mateos de Cabo, R. & Sáinz, M., 'Girls in STEM: Is It a Female Role-Model Thing?' *Frontiers in Psychology* 11 (2020). doi: 10.3389/fpsyg.2020.02204

15 Harris, C., Michael, J. & Dale, G., 'Gender differences in risk assessment', *Judgment and Decision Making* 1:1 (2006), 48–63.

16 UNICEF Maternal Mortality Rates. https://data.unicef.org/topic/maternal-health/maternal-mortality/

17 Weaver, J. R., et al. 'Intrepid, Imprudent, or Impetuous?: The Effects of Gender Threats on Men's Financial Decisions', *Psychology of Men & Masculinity* 14:2 (2013), 184–91. doi: 10.1037/a0027087

18 Apollo, M., Mostowska, J., Legut, A., Maciuk, K. & Timothy, D. J., 'Gender differences in competitive adventure sports tourism', *Journal of Outdoor Recreation and Tourism* 42 (2023), 100604. https://doi.org/10.1016/j.jort.2022.100604

19 Reid, P. & Brymer, E. (eds), *Adventure Psychology: Going Knowingly into the Unknown* (1st ed., Routledge, 2022). https://doi.org/10.4324/9781003173601

20 Tyne, W. P., Fletcher, D., Paine, N. J. & Stevinson, C., 'A Prospective Evaluation of the Effects of Outdoor Adventure Training Programs on Work-Related Outcomes', *Journal of Experiential Education* 48:2 (2024), 310–31. https://doi.org/10.1177/10538259241268998 (Original work published 2025)

21 Boudreau, P., Mackenzie, S. H. & Hodge, K., 'Adventure-based mindsets helped maintain psychological well-being during COVID-19', *Psychology of Sport and Exercise* 62 (2022), 102245. doi: 10.1016/j.psychsport.2022.102245

Chapter 4

1 Müller-Pinzler, L., Czekalla, N., Mayer, A. V., et al., 'Negativity-bias in forming beliefs about own abilities', *Scientific Reports* 9 (2019), 14416. https://doi.org/10.1038/s41598-019-50821-w

2 How To Take Feedback Without Getting Defensive. https://nickwignall.com/how-to-take-feedback-without-getting-defensive/

3 Stefan, M., 'A CV of failures', *Nature* 468:467 (2010). https://doi.org/10.1038/nj7322-467a

Chapter 5

1 Schwartz, S. H., 'An Overview of the Schwartz Theory of Basic Values', *Online Readings in Psychology and Culture* 2:1 (2012). doi: 10.9707/2307-0919.1116

2 Hayes, S. C., Strosahl, K. D. & Wilson, K. G., *Acceptance and Commitment Therapy: An Experiential Approach to Behavior Change* (Guilford Press, 2006).

3 Steele, C. M., 'The psychology of self-affirmation: Sustaining the integrity of the self'. In L. Berkowitz (ed.), *Advances in experimental social psychology, Vol. 21. Social psychological studies of the self: Perspectives and programs* (Academic Press, 1988), 261–302.

4 Creswell, J. D., Dutcher, J. M., Klein, W. M. P., Harris, P. R., Levine, J. M., 'Self-Affirmation Improves Problem-Solving under Stress', *PLOS ONE* 8:5 (2013), e62593. https://doi.org/10.1371/journal.pone.0062593

5 Wang, S., Luo, X., Zang, X., Ma, Y. & Yang, J., 'Impact of social reward on stress circuit function and regulation: Path differences between value affirmation and emotional support', *International Journal of Clinical and Health Psychology* 24 (2024), 100499. 10.1016/j.ijchp.2024.100499

6 Sah, S., *Defy: The Power of No in a World that Demands Yes* (Penguin Random House, 2025)

7 Toubiana, M., Ruebottom, T. & Hakak, L. T., 'When a Major Life Change Upends Your Sense of Self', *Harvard Business Review* (2022). https://hbr.org/2022/01/when-a-major-life-change-upends-your-sense-of-self

8 Kübler-Ross, E. & Kessler, D., *On Grief and Grieving: Finding the Meaning of Grief Through the Five Stages of Loss* (Scribner, 2005).

9 Prochaska, J. O., Redding, C. A. & Evers, K. E., 'The transtheoretical model and stages of change'. In K. Glanz, B. K.

Rimer & K. Viswanath (eds), *Health behavior and health education: Theory, research, and practice* (4th ed., Jossey-Bass/Wiley, 2008), 97–121.

10 Ryan, R. M. & Deci, E. L., 'Self-determination theory and the facilitation of intrinsic motivation, social development, and well-being', *American Psychologist* 55:1 (2000), 68–78. https://doi.org/10.1037/0003-066X.55.1.68

11 Dweck, C. S., *Mindset: The New Psychology of Success* (Random House, 2006).

12 Duckworth, A., *Grit: The Power of Passion and Perseverance* (Scribner/Simon & Schuster, 2016).

13 Penn Resilience Program and PERMA™ Workshops, https://ppc.sas.upenn.edu/services/penn-resilience-training

Chapter 6

1 de Berker, A., Rutledge, R., Mathys, C., et al., 'Computations of uncertainty mediate acute stress responses in humans', *Nature Communications* 7 (2016), 10996. https://doi.org/10.1038/ncomms10996

2 Sexton, K. A. & Dugas, M. J., 'Defining distinct negative beliefs about uncertainty: validating the factor structure of the Intolerance of Uncertainty Scale', *Psychological Assessment* 21:2 (2009), 176–86. doi: 10.1037/a0015827

3 Fitzgerald, F. Scott, 'The Crack-Up', *Esquire* (1936).

4 Conniff, S. & Templar Lewis, K., *The Uncertainty Toolkit: Worry Less and Do More by Learning to Cope with the Unknown* (Bluebird, 2025).

5 Sugawara, A., Terasawa, Y., Katsunuma, R. & Sekiguchi, A., 'Effects of interoceptive training on decision making, anxiety, and somatic symptoms', *BioPsychoSocial Medicine* 17:14:7 (2020). doi: 10.1186/s13030-020-00179-7

6 Tsakiris, M. & De Preester, H. (eds), *The Interoceptive Mind: From Homeostasis to Awareness* (Oxford University Press, 2019).

7 Kandasamy, N., Garfinkel, S., Page, L., et al., 'Interoceptive Ability Predicts Survival on a London Trading Floor', *Scientific Reports* 6 (2016), 32986. https://doi.org/10.1038/srep32986

8 Damasio, A. R., *Descartes' Error: Emotion, Reason, and the Human Brain* (New York: G. P. Putnam, 1994).

9 Balban, M. Y., et al., 'Brief structured respiration practices enhance mood and reduce physiological arousal', *Cell Reports Medicine* 4:1 (2023), 100895. doi: 10.1016/j.xcrm.2022. 100895.

10 Brown, R. P. & Gerbarg, P. L., 'Sudarshan Kriya yogic breathing in the treatment of stress, anxiety, and depression', *Journal of Alternative and Complementary Medicine* 11:2 (2005), 189–201.

11 Jerath, R., Edry, J. W., Barnes, V. A. & Jerath, V., 'Physiology of long pranayamic breathing: Neural respiratory elements may provide a mechanism that explains how slow deep breathing shifts the autonomic nervous system', *Medical Hypotheses* 67:3 (2006), 566–71. https://doi.org/10.1016/j.mehy.2006.02.042

12 Ma, X., et al., 'The effect of diaphragmatic breathing on attention, negative affect and stress in healthy adults', *Frontiers in Psychology* 8 (2017), 874. https://doi.org/10.3389/fpsyg.2017.00874

13 Schultchen, D., et al., 'Effects of an 8-Week Body Scan Intervention on Individually Perceived Psychological Stress and Related Steroid Hormones in Hair', *Mindfulness* 10 (2019). doi: 10.1007/s12671-019-01222-7

14 Hofmann, S. G., *An Introduction to Modern CBT: Psychological Solutions to Mental Health Problems* (Wiley-Blackwell, 2012).

15 Kross, E., et al., 'Self-talk as a regulatory mechanism: how you do it matters', *Journal of Personality and Social Psychology* 106:2 (2014), 304–24. doi: 10.1037/a0035173

16 McGonigal, J., *Imaginable: How to See the Future Coming and Feel Ready for Anything – Even Things that Seem Impossible Today* (Spiegel & Grau, 2022).

Chapter 7

1 Hatzigeorgiadis, A., et al., 'Mechanisms underlying the self-talk–performance relationship: The effects of motivational self-talk on self-confidence and anxiety', *Psychology of Sport and Exercise* 10:1 (2009), 186–92. doi: 10.1016/j.psychsport.2008.07.009

2 Hatzigeorgiadis, A., et al., 'Self-Talk and Sports Performance: A

Meta-Analysis', *Perspectives on Psychological Science* 6:4 (2011). doi: 10.1177/1745691611413136

3 Blanchfield, A., et al., 'Talking Yourself Out of Exhaustion: The Effects of Self-Talk on Endurance Performance', *Medicine and Science in Sports and Exercise* 46:5 (2013), 998–1007. doi: 10.1249/MSS.0000000000000184

4 Gross, J. J. (ed.), *Handbook of Emotion Regulation* (The Guilford Press, 2014, 2nd ed.).

Chapter 8

1 Van Vugt, M. & Schaller, M., 'Evolutionary approaches to group dynamics: An introduction'. In: *Group Dynamics, Theory, Research, and Practice*, Vol. 12, Issue 4 (American Psychological Association, 2008), pp. 353–62.

2 Chopik, W., et al., 'Changes in need for uniqueness from 2000 until 2020', *Collabra: Psychology* 10:1 (2024). https://doi.org/10.1525/collabra.121937

3 Abofol, T., Erev, I. & Sulitzeanu-Kenan, R., 'Conformity and Group Performance', *Human Nature* 34:3 (2023), 381–99. https://doi.org/10.1007/s12110-023-09454-2

4 Google People Analytics Team, *Project Aristotle: Understanding team effectiveness*. (Google, 2016). https://rework.withgoogle.com/intl/en/guides/understanding-team-effectiveness

5 Cacioppo, J. T. & Cacioppo, S., 'The growing problem of loneliness', *Lancet* 391:10119 (2018), 426. doi: 10.1016/S0140-6736(18)30142-9

6 Alexander, B. K., 'The dislocation theory of addiction'. In: *The Globalization of Addiction: A Study in Poverty of the Spirit* (Oxford University Press, 2010), 153–72. https://doi.org/10.1093/med/9780199588718.003.0008

7 Ceatha, N., Mayock, P., Campbell, J., Noone, C. & Browne, K., 'The Power of Recognition: A Qualitative Study of Social Connectedness and Wellbeing through LGBT Sporting, Creative and Social Groups in Ireland', *International Journal of Environmental Research and Public Health* 16:19 (2019), 3636. doi: 10.3390/ijerph16193636

8 Deitz, R. L., Hellerstein, L. H., St George, S. M., Palazuelos, D. &

Schimek, T. E., 'A qualitative study of social connectedness and its relationship to community health programs in rural Chiapas, Mexico', *BMC Public Health* 20:1 (2020), 852. doi: 10.1186/s12889-020-09008-6

9 Millar, O. & Warwick, I., 'Music and refugees' wellbeing in contexts of protracted displacement', *Health Education Journal* 78:1 (2018), 67–80. https://doi.org/10.1177/0017896918785991

10 Roseman, L., Demetriou, L., Wall, M. B., Nutt, D. J. & Carhart-Harris, R. L., 'Increased amygdala responses to emotional faces after psilocybin for treatment-resistant depression', *Neuropharmacology* 142 (2018), 263–9. https://doi.org/10.1016/j.neuropharm.2017.12.041

11 Hofmann, S. G., Grossman, P., Hinton, D. E., 'Loving-kindness and compassion meditation: potential for psychological interventions', *Clinical Psychology Review* 31:7 (2011), 1126–32. doi: 10.1016/j.cpr.2011.07.003

12 Rahe, M. & Jansen, P., 'A closer look at the relationships between aspects of connectedness and flourishing'. *Frontiers in Psychology* 30:14 (2023), 1137752. doi: 10.3389/fpsyg.2023.1137752

13 Capaldi, C., Passmore, H-A. & Vowinckel, J., *A Beautiful Connection: Nature Connectedness Mediates the Relationship Between Engagement with Natural Beauty and Well-Being* (2016). doi: 10.13140/RG.2.2.36654.54085.

Chapter 9

1 Sawatsky, J., *Dancing with Elephants: Mindfulness Training for Those Living with Dementia, Chronic Illness or an Aging Brain* (Red Canoe Press, 2017).

2 Kabat-Zinn, J., *Wherever You Go, There You Are: Mindfulness Meditation in Everyday Life* (Hyperion, 1994).

3 Gould, P., *When I Die: Lessons From the Death Zone* (Little, Brown, 2012).

4 Davis, E. L., Deane, F. P., Lyons, G. C. B. & Barclay, G. D., 'Is Higher Acceptance Associated With Less Anticipatory Grief Among Patients in Palliative Care?' *Journal of Pain and Symptom Management* 54:1 (2017), 120–25. doi: 10.1016/j.jpainsymman.2017.03.012

5 Keltner, D. & Haidt, J., 'Approaching awe, a moral, spiritual, and aesthetic emotion', *Cognition and Emotion* 17:2 (2003), 297–314. https://doi.org/10.1080/02699930302297

6 Monroy M. & Keltner, D., 'Awe as a Pathway to Mental and Physical Health', *Perspectives on Psychological Science* 18:2 (2023), 309–20. doi: 10.1177/17456916221094856

7 Linge-Dahl, L., Kreuz, R., Stoffelen, M., Heintz, S., Ruch, W., von Hirschhausen, E. & Radbruch, L., 'Humour interventions for patients in palliative care – a randomized controlled trial', *Support Care Cancer* 31:3 (2023), 160. doi: 10.1007/s00520-023-07606-9

8 Linge-Dahl, L. M., Heintz, S., Ruch, W. & Radbruch, L., 'Humor Assessment and Interventions in Palliative Care: A Systematic Review', *Frontiers in Psychology* 9 (2018), 890. doi: 10.3389/fpsyg.2018.00890

9 Kessler, A. G., et al., 'Humor therapy as a new concept in palliative care', *Journal of Clinical Oncology* 28 (2010), e19583–e19583. doi: 10.1200/jco.2010.28.15_suppl.e19583

10 Kalanithi, P. & Verghese, A., *When Breath Becomes Air* (Random House, 2016).

11 Kashdan, T. B., *Curious?: Discover the Missing Ingredient to a Fulfilling Life* (New York: HarperCollins, 2009).

12 de la Piedra-Torres, A. J., López-Martínez, A. E. & Ramírez-Maestre, C., 'Information concealment in palliative patients: Development and pilot study of a new scale for caregivers', *Health and Social Care in the Community* 30:6 (2022), e4504–e4512. doi: 10.1111/hsc.13854

13 Zhang, Y., Zhu, K., Li, S., Wang, X., Xu, R., Cao, Y., Ye, H. & Duan, P., 'Latent profile analysis of spousal information concealment in patients with cancer: A cross-sectional study', *Asia-Pacific Journal of Oncology Nursing* 12 (2024), 100626. doi: 10.1016/j.apjon.2024.100626

14 Çamcı, G., Oğuz, S. & Ziya Özdemir, M., 'Validity and reliability of the Turkish version of the Information Concealment Scale for Caregivers of palliative care patients', *Palliative and Supportive Care* 1–6 (2024). doi: 10.1017/S1478951524000853

15 National Association of Funeral Directors, 'Petition: Add content on death, dying and bereavement to the national curriculum',

https://www.nafd.org.uk/2023/01/01/petition-add-bereavement-
to-the-national-curriculum/#:~:text=NAFD%20President%20
John%20Adams%20has,part%20of%20compulsory%20
Relationships%20education.

16 Conisbee, M., *No Ordinary Deaths: A People's History of Mortality*
(London: Profile Books, 2025).

17 Ross, S., et al., 'Single dose of hallucinogenic drug psilocybin
relieves anxiety and depression in patients with advanced cancer',
Journal of Psychopharmacology (published online, NYU Langone
Medical Center, 1 December 2023).

18 Griffiths, R. R., et al., 'Psilocybin produces substantial and
sustained decreases in depression and anxiety in patients with
life-threatening cancer: A randomized double-blind trial', *Journal
of Psychopharmacology* 30:12 (2016), 1181–97. doi: 10.1177/
0269881116675513

Chapter 10

1 García Márquez, G., *Love in the Time of Cholera* (translated by
Edith Grossman; Vintage International, 2003).